Google Sites Made Simple

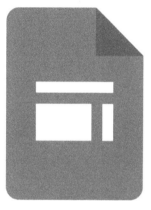

Create and Manage Your Website with Ease

Kiet Huynh

Table of Contents

CHAPTER I
Introduction to Google Sites

1.1 What is Google Sites?

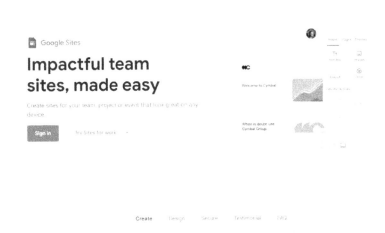

Introduction

In the modern digital age, having an online presence is essential for individuals, businesses, educators, and organizations. Websites serve as a platform for sharing information, engaging with audiences, and collaborating effectively. However, creating a website has traditionally been a technical task requiring knowledge of coding, web hosting, and design principles. Google Sites changes this by offering a simple, user-friendly solution for building and managing websites without any programming experience.

This section will introduce you to Google Sites, its purpose, and how it fits into the broader ecosystem of website creation. By the end of this chapter, you will have a clear understanding of what Google Sites is, who can benefit from it, and how it simplifies website creation.

Definition of Google Sites

Google Sites is a free website-building tool developed by Google that allows users to create and manage websites easily using a drag-and-drop interface. It is part of the Google Workspace (formerly G Suite) suite of applications and integrates seamlessly with other Google tools, such as Google Drive, Docs, Sheets, and Forms.

Unlike traditional website-building platforms that require extensive knowledge of HTML, CSS, or JavaScript, Google Sites offers a no-code experience, making it accessible to anyone, regardless of technical expertise. With its intuitive interface, users can quickly design and publish websites for various purposes, including business, education, personal portfolios, and team collaboration.

Key Characteristics of Google Sites

Google Sites stands out from other website builders due to its unique characteristics:

1. **No Coding Required** – Google Sites eliminates the need for programming skills, making website creation as simple as editing a document.

2. **Drag-and-Drop Interface** – Users can add text, images, videos, and embedded content effortlessly by dragging elements onto the page.

3. **Integration with Google Workspace** – Google Sites allows seamless embedding of Google Docs, Sheets, Slides, Forms, and Drive files, making it a great tool for teams and educators.

4. **Cloud-Based and Auto-Saving** – Since Google Sites is entirely cloud-based, users don't need to worry about saving their work manually or losing progress.

5. **Responsive Design** – Websites created with Google Sites automatically adjust to different screen sizes, ensuring a good user experience on desktops, tablets, and smartphones.

6. **Collaboration Features** – Like Google Docs and Sheets, Google Sites enables real-time collaboration, allowing multiple users to edit and manage content simultaneously.

History and Evolution of Google Sites

Google Sites was initially launched in 2008 as a successor to Google Page Creator. Over the years, it has undergone multiple transformations to enhance its functionality, usability, and integration with Google's ecosystem.

- **2008** – Google Sites was introduced as part of Google Apps for businesses and organizations.

- **2016** – A major redesign introduced a modern, simplified interface, moving away from the classic version to what is now known as "New Google Sites."

- **2017-Present** – Google has continued to refine the platform, adding better customization options, integration capabilities, and responsive design features.

The transition from "Classic Google Sites" to "New Google Sites" marked a significant shift toward a more streamlined and user-friendly experience, with improved compatibility across devices.

Who Can Use Google Sites?

One of the biggest strengths of Google Sites is its versatility. It caters to a broad range of users, including:

1. **Educators and Students** – Teachers can create class websites, organize resources, and publish assignments, while students can use it for project presentations and portfolios.

2. **Businesses and Entrepreneurs** – Companies can use Google Sites for internal documentation, team collaboration, intranet portals, and public-facing websites.

3. **Nonprofits and Organizations** – Nonprofit groups can create websites to share information, raise awareness, and engage with donors or volunteers.

4. **Personal Users** – Individuals can create personal blogs, portfolios, or event websites without needing web development expertise.

5. **Teams and Project Managers** – Teams working on projects can use Google Sites to centralize documentation, updates, and resources in one accessible location.

Common Use Cases for Google Sites

Google Sites can be used for a variety of purposes, such as:

1. **Internal Team Websites** – Companies can build private intranet sites for sharing policies, training materials, and collaboration tools.

2. **Project Management Hubs** – Teams working on projects can create dedicated sites to track progress, share files, and document milestones.

3. **Educational Websites** – Schools and universities can use Google Sites for class pages, study resources, and student portfolios.

4. **Event Websites** – Event organizers can build simple websites for conferences, weddings, or corporate events with schedules, maps, and registration details.

5. **Personal Portfolios** – Creatives, freelancers, and job seekers can showcase their work in a visually appealing and professional manner.

6. **Community and Nonprofit Sites** – Organizations can use Google Sites to promote their mission, publish updates, and engage with supporters.

Google Sites vs. Other Website Builders

While Google Sites is a great tool, it is important to compare it with other popular website builders to understand its advantages and limitations.

Feature	Google Sites	WordPress	Wix	Squarespace
Ease of Use	Very easy (drag-and-drop)	Moderate (requires setup)	Easy	Moderate
Coding Required	No	Some customization may require coding	No	No
Cost	Free	Free/Paid	Paid	Paid
Customization	Limited	Extensive	Extensive	High
Best For	Internal sites, simple websites	Blogs, business websites	Creative websites	Professional portfolios
Hosting	Google-hosted	Self-hosted or WordPress.com	Wix-hosted	Squarespace-hosted

As shown in the comparison, Google Sites is best suited for simple websites that do not require extensive customization. However, for users who need more advanced design flexibility, platforms like WordPress, Wix, or Squarespace may be better options.

Limitations of Google Sites

While Google Sites is a powerful tool for beginners, it does have some limitations:

1. **Limited Design Customization** – Users cannot fully customize themes or add custom CSS.

2. **No E-Commerce Functionality** – Unlike platforms like Shopify or Wix, Google Sites does not support online stores.

3. **No Blog Features** – Google Sites lacks built-in blogging capabilities, making it less suitable for content-heavy websites.

4. **URL and Domain Limitations** – Users must use a Google-provided domain unless they set up a custom domain separately.

5. **Limited Third-Party Plugins** – Unlike WordPress, Google Sites does not support third-party plugins or extensive integrations.

Conclusion

Google Sites is an excellent tool for users who want to create simple, functional websites quickly and without coding knowledge. Its deep integration with Google Workspace makes it particularly useful for businesses, educators, and teams looking for a collaborative and easy-to-manage web solution. While it has some limitations, its simplicity and accessibility make it an ideal choice for users who do not require advanced web development features.

Now that we have covered the basics of Google Sites, the next chapter will guide you through the process of getting started, including creating your first site and navigating its interface.

1.2 Why Use Google Sites?

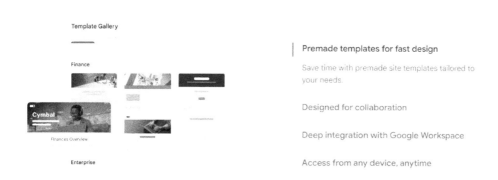

In today's digital age, having an online presence is essential for individuals, businesses, and organizations. Whether you need a personal portfolio, a team collaboration space, or a public-facing website, Google Sites provides a user-friendly and free platform for building websites with ease. Unlike traditional website builders that require technical knowledge in coding and design, Google Sites offers a drag-and-drop interface that simplifies the website creation process.

This section explores the key reasons why Google Sites is a valuable tool for different users, covering its ease of use, integration with Google Workspace, cost-effectiveness, collaboration features, and its suitability for various purposes.

Ease of Use and No Coding Required

One of the biggest advantages of Google Sites is its **simplicity**. Unlike other website-building platforms that require knowledge of HTML, CSS, or JavaScript, Google Sites allows users to create and manage websites **without any coding experience**.

- **Drag-and-Drop Functionality**: Users can easily add text, images, videos, and documents to their site using simple drag-and-drop features. This eliminates the need to write any code or manually adjust layouts.

- **Pre-Designed Templates**: Google Sites provides **structured templates** that help users get started quickly. These templates come with predefined sections and layouts, making it easy to customize them according to specific needs.

- **Minimal Learning Curve**: Even first-time users can create a functional website in minutes. The intuitive design and straightforward editing tools make it accessible to all skill levels.

This ease of use makes Google Sites an excellent choice for individuals who need a quick and efficient way to establish an online presence without investing time in learning web development.

Seamless Integration with Google Workspace

Google Sites is part of the Google Workspace ecosystem, which means it integrates smoothly with Google Drive, Google Docs, Google Sheets, Google Slides, Google Calendar, Google Forms, and Google Maps. This integration makes it particularly useful for businesses, educators, and teams that already rely on Google's tools for their daily operations.

How Google Sites Works with Google Workspace:

- **Embedding Google Docs, Sheets, and Slides**: Users can directly embed documents, spreadsheets, and presentations into their Google Site. Any updates made to the original file in Google Drive will automatically reflect on the website.

- **Adding Google Forms**: Surveys, registrations, and feedback forms can be easily embedded into a site, allowing visitors to submit responses directly from the webpage.

- **Displaying Google Calendars**: Businesses and organizations can share event schedules, meeting calendars, or project deadlines by embedding a Google Calendar on their site.

- **Using Google Maps**: If a business or event location needs to be displayed, Google Maps can be integrated seamlessly into the website.

This level of integration eliminates the need for manual uploads or third-party plugins, streamlining content management for businesses, educators, and personal users alike.

Free and Cost-Effective Solution

One of the most compelling reasons to use Google Sites is that it is **completely free**. Unlike many website builders that require monthly subscriptions or premium plans for additional features, Google Sites offers full functionality at no cost.

Why is Google Sites a Budget-Friendly Option?

- **No Hosting Fees**: Google hosts the website for free, eliminating the need to purchase hosting services.

- **No Domain Fees**: Users can publish their site using a **Google-provided URL** (e.g., sites.google.com/view/yourwebsite). However, if they prefer a custom domain, they can link it through Google Domains or another provider.

- **No Paid Plugins or Add-ons**: Unlike other website builders that require premium plans for extended features, Google Sites includes **all essential features without additional costs**.

This makes Google Sites a perfect solution for **small businesses, non-profits, educators, students, and individuals** who need an online presence but have a limited budget.

Collaboration and Teamwork Capabilities

Google Sites is **designed for collaboration**, making it an excellent tool for teams, businesses, and educational institutions. Just like Google Docs and Google Sheets, multiple people can work on a Google Site simultaneously, which is ideal for **projects, knowledge sharing, and internal documentation**.

Key Collaboration Features:

- **Real-time Editing**: Multiple users can edit a Google Site at the same time, seeing updates instantly.

- **Role-Based Access Control**: Users can be assigned different permission levels:

  - **Viewers** can only see the published site.

o **Editors** can edit and update content.

o **Owners** have full control, including managing permissions and site settings.

- **Seamless Communication**: Because Google Sites is part of the Google Workspace suite, teams can easily discuss changes via **Google Chat, Google Meet, or email** while working on the site.

This makes Google Sites a powerful tool for **internal documentation, wikis, project management, and company intranets**.

Mobile-Friendly and Responsive Design

Websites created with Google Sites are **automatically responsive**, meaning they adjust to different screen sizes on **desktop, tablet, and mobile devices** without requiring manual adjustments.

Why Is Mobile Responsiveness Important?

- **Better User Experience**: A website that adapts to different screen sizes ensures that visitors have a smooth browsing experience on any device.

- **No Need for Separate Mobile Design**: Many website builders require users to create separate mobile versions, but Google Sites handles this automatically.

- **Improved SEO Performance**: Although Google Sites is not the best platform for advanced SEO (Search Engine Optimization), having a mobile-friendly website is a ranking factor in Google Search.

This makes Google Sites a great option for users who want a **hassle-free, mobile-optimized website** without additional effort.

Best Use Cases for Google Sites

Google Sites is a versatile tool that can be used for various purposes. Here are some common use cases:

1. Personal Websites and Portfolios

- Ideal for students, freelancers, and job seekers to showcase their work, resume, and achievements.

2. Business and Corporate Websites

- Companies can create informational websites, client portals, and internal knowledge bases without needing a professional web developer.

3. Educational Websites

- Teachers can create class pages, share learning resources, and organize assignments for students.

- Schools and universities can use Google Sites for announcements and faculty collaboration.

4. Project Management and Team Collaboration

- Teams can create **internal wikis, project dashboards, and knowledge-sharing platforms**.

5. Event Websites

- Google Sites can be used for weddings, conferences, community events, and fundraisers to share event details, schedules, and RSVP forms.

Conclusion

Google Sites is a powerful, free, and easy-to-use tool for creating websites with zero coding knowledge required. Its seamless integration with Google Workspace, collaborative features, mobile responsiveness, and cost-effectiveness make it an excellent choice for personal, professional, and educational use.

Whether you need a personal portfolio, a team collaboration site, or a business webpage, Google Sites provides a simple yet effective solution.

In the next chapter, we'll explore how to get started with Google Sites, including creating a site, choosing templates, and setting up a blank site.

1.3 Key Features of Google Sites

1.3.1 Drag-and-Drop Interface

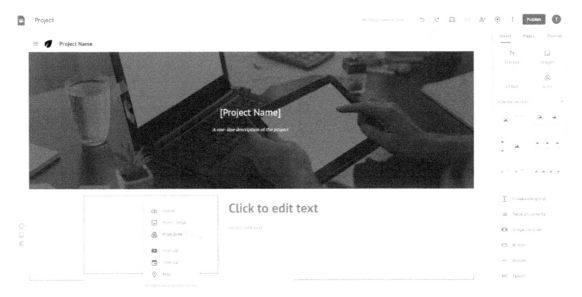

Click to edit text

Google Sites is designed to be an intuitive and user-friendly platform, and one of its standout features is the **drag-and-drop interface**. This functionality allows users to build and customize websites without needing any coding or web development skills. By simply dragging elements and placing them where needed, users can create visually appealing and highly functional websites in minutes.

In this section, we will explore the **drag-and-drop interface** in detail, covering:

- The benefits of using a drag-and-drop website builder

- How to use the drag-and-drop interface in Google Sites

- Common elements that can be added via drag-and-drop

- Best practices for designing a structured and professional-looking website

Benefits of Using a Drag-and-Drop Website Builder

Traditional website creation typically requires knowledge of **HTML, CSS, and JavaScript**, which can be overwhelming for non-technical users. Drag-and-drop website builders, such as Google Sites, eliminate this barrier by providing an easy-to-use interface where users can simply move elements into place. Here are some key benefits of this approach:

1. No Coding Required

One of the biggest advantages of the drag-and-drop interface is that it eliminates the need for manual coding. Users can build professional-looking websites using a graphical user interface (GUI), making website creation accessible to **students, teachers, small business owners, and professionals** who lack programming experience.

2. Fast and Efficient Website Building

With the drag-and-drop functionality, creating a website is significantly faster than traditional web development. Instead of manually writing code for each page layout, users can **instantly arrange text, images, videos, and other elements** by dragging them into position. This speed is particularly useful for those who need to create and launch a website quickly.

3. Full Visual Control

Google Sites allows users to **see changes in real time** while they edit, eliminating the need for previewing pages separately. Users can visually structure their websites exactly how they want, ensuring **proper alignment, spacing, and design consistency** without needing extensive trial and error.

4. Seamless Integration with Other Google Services

The drag-and-drop system supports **Google Drive, Google Docs, Sheets, Slides, Forms, Maps, and YouTube**. Instead of copying and pasting code or links, users can simply **drag files from their Google Drive or embed content directly from other Google apps** into their site.

5. Responsive Design for Mobile and Desktop

Since Google Sites automatically adjusts content for different screen sizes, users don't need to worry about mobile responsiveness. The drag-and-drop interface ensures that elements are correctly aligned on both **desktop and mobile devices** without additional customization.

How to Use the Drag-and-Drop Interface in Google Sites

Using the drag-and-drop functionality in Google Sites is straightforward. Below is a step-by-step guide on how to leverage this feature effectively.

Step 1: Open Google Sites

1. Go to Google Sites.

2. Click the **blank template** or choose an existing template.

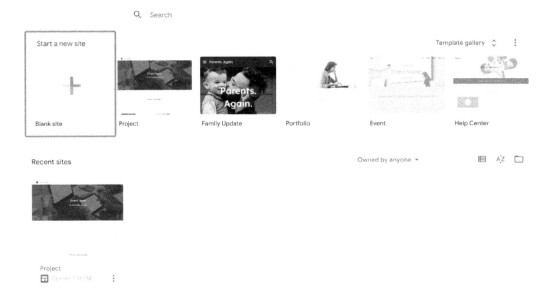

Step 2: Access the Editing Interface

Once inside, you'll see the **Google Sites Editor**, which consists of:

- The **toolbar** (at the top)

- The **sidebar menu** (on the right)

- The **canvas (main editing area)** where elements are placed

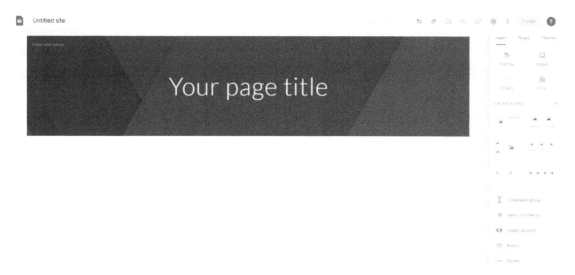

Step 3: Adding Elements Using Drag-and-Drop

1. **Text Box:** Drag a text box from the sidebar onto the page to add headings, paragraphs, or lists.

2. **Images:** Drag images from your computer or Google Drive directly onto the page.

3. **Google Docs, Sheets, and Slides:** Click on **"Insert"**, find the file you want, and drag it onto the site.

4. **Videos:** Drag and embed YouTube videos into your site effortlessly.

5. **Buttons:** Drag and drop buttons to link to other pages or external websites.

Step 4: Adjusting Elements

- **Repositioning:** Click and hold an element, then drag it to a new location.

- **Resizing:** Use the corner handles of elements to **adjust their size**.

- **Aligning:** Google Sites automatically suggests alignment guides when moving objects, ensuring **consistent spacing**.

Common Elements You Can Add via Drag-and-Drop

Google Sites allows users to add various **content blocks, multimedia, and widgets** through the drag-and-drop interface. Below are some of the most commonly used elements:

1. Text and Titles

- Drag a **text box** to add **headings, paragraphs, or bulleted lists**.
- Use **different font styles and formatting** to create emphasis.

2. Images and Galleries

- Drag images from **Google Drive, local storage, or online sources**.
- Resize images by dragging the corner handles.
- Use the **gallery feature** to create an image slideshow.

3. Embedded Videos

- Drag and drop **YouTube videos** directly into the page.
- Adjust the **video size and placement**.

4. Google Drive Files

- Drag and drop Google **Docs, Sheets, and Slides** for **live document embedding**.
- Viewers can interact with these embedded files **without leaving the website**.

5. Google Maps and Location Pins

- Drag Google Maps onto the site and **pin locations**.

- Use this feature for **contact pages, event locations, or travel guides**.

6. Buttons and Hyperlinks

- Drag a **button** onto the page and customize the text and URL.

- Use hyperlinks to **connect pages within your website or link to external sources**.

7. Layout Sections

- Drag **pre-designed layouts** to create a professional structure.

- Adjust the section order using the drag-and-drop tool.

Best Practices for Using the Drag-and-Drop Interface

To make the most of Google Sites' drag-and-drop feature, consider the following **best practices**:

1. Maintain a Clean Layout

- Use **consistent spacing and alignment**.

- Avoid **cluttered designs**—keep the page **organized and readable**.

2. Use High-Quality Media

- Upload **high-resolution images** to avoid pixelation.

- Ensure embedded videos **enhance the user experience** rather than distract.

3. Optimize for Mobile Devices

- Preview your site on **mobile screens** to check formatting.

- Ensure buttons and interactive elements are **easily clickable**.

4. Keep Navigation Simple

- Use **logical page structures** and categories.

- Ensure that visitors can find information **quickly and efficiently**.

5. Use Templates for a Head Start

- Google Sites provides **ready-made templates** that can be modified using drag-and-drop.

- Save time by selecting a **pre-built layout** and customizing it to fit your needs.

Conclusion

The **drag-and-drop interface** in Google Sites makes website creation accessible to everyone, regardless of technical expertise. By leveraging this feature, users can **effortlessly add, arrange, and customize** content, resulting in **professional and functional websites**. Whether you're building a **business website, educational resource, or personal portfolio**, the drag-and-drop system streamlines the process and enhances productivity.

By mastering this feature, you'll be able to **quickly design, edit, and publish** a visually appealing website with minimal effort. In the next section, we will explore **Google Sites' integration with Google Workspace**, which allows for seamless collaboration and advanced functionalities.

1.3.2 Integration with Google Workspace

Google Sites is a powerful website-building tool that seamlessly integrates with Google Workspace (formerly known as G Suite). This integration makes it easy for individuals, teams, businesses, and educational institutions to create collaborative websites that incorporate content from various Google apps. Whether you need to display live spreadsheets, embed presentations, or share documents securely, Google Sites' deep connection with Google Workspace enhances productivity and simplifies content management.

In this section, we will explore the key benefits of integrating Google Sites with Google Workspace, the specific apps that work well with Google Sites, and practical use cases for leveraging this integration.

Benefits of Google Workspace Integration

Biểu mẫu	Chrome	Chrome Enterprise	Chromebook
Chromecast	Chuyến bay	Danh bạ	Dịch
Drive	Earth	Expeditions	Family Link
Files	Gboard	Gemini	Gmail
Google Alerts	Google Arts & Culture	Google Cast	Google Chat
Google Fit	Google Fonts	Google Lớp học	Google Meet
Google One	Google Pay	Google Play	Google Play Phim & TV
Google Play Sách	Google Play Trò chơi	Google Shopping	Google Store
Google TV	Google Wallet	Google Wifi	Groups
Keep	Lens	Lịch	Messages
Nest	News	Ô tô có tích hợp	Pixel

Integrating Google Sites with Google Workspace offers several advantages:

1. Unified Content Management

Google Workspace enables seamless content sharing across Google apps. When you integrate Google Docs, Sheets, Slides, and other tools into Google Sites, your website becomes a dynamic hub for updated content. Instead of manually uploading and updating documents, you can embed files that automatically reflect the latest changes.

2. Enhanced Collaboration

Since Google Workspace is designed for collaboration, Google Sites benefits from the same real-time editing and sharing capabilities. Multiple users can work on embedded documents, spreadsheets, or presentations directly from the site, making it ideal for team projects, internal company portals, and educational resources.

3. Improved Accessibility and Permissions Management

With Google Workspace, you can control access to content embedded in Google Sites. Users can configure sharing settings for individual documents or site-wide permissions, ensuring that sensitive information remains secure.

4. Seamless Updates and Real-Time Data

Google Sites automatically reflects updates from Google Workspace apps, eliminating the need to manually update website content. This is particularly useful for dashboards, reports, schedules, and event calendars.

Key Google Workspace Apps Integrated with Google Sites

Google Sites supports direct embedding and interaction with multiple Google Workspace applications. Below are some of the most commonly used apps:

1. Google Docs: Embed and Collaborate on Documents

Google Docs can be embedded into a Google Site to share reports, policies, meeting notes, or any other text-based content. When users update a Google Doc, the changes are instantly reflected on the website without requiring re-uploads.

Use Case: A company can embed a shared employee handbook in Google Sites, ensuring everyone always has access to the most recent version.

2. Google Sheets: Display Live Data and Reports

Google Sheets integration allows users to display live data, charts, and reports. Visitors can interact with spreadsheets, filter data, and view real-time updates.

Use Case: A sales team can publish their latest performance dashboard with real-time sales figures, pulling data directly from a Google Sheet.

3. Google Slides: Embed Presentations Seamlessly

Presentations from Google Slides can be inserted into a site for training, educational courses, or corporate updates. The slides remain interactive, allowing visitors to navigate through them without leaving the website.

Use Case: A university department can embed course presentations on their website so students can review lecture slides anytime.

4. Google Forms: Collect Data and Feedback

Google Forms can be added to a site for surveys, event registrations, or feedback collection. Submissions are automatically stored in Google Sheets for easy analysis.

Use Case: An event organizer can create an RSVP form embedded in a Google Site to track attendance.

5. Google Calendar: Keep Schedules Updated

Google Calendar integration allows users to display event schedules, deadlines, and important dates. Any updates made to the calendar will instantly reflect on the website.

Use Case: A school can embed a calendar with class schedules and assignment deadlines for students and parents to view.

6. Google Drive: Store and Share Files

Google Drive folders and files can be embedded in Google Sites, providing easy access to documents, images, and videos stored in the cloud.

Use Case: A project team can use a Google Site as a centralized hub for documents, making it easier to organize resources.

7. Google Maps: Provide Location Information

Google Maps integration allows businesses, event organizers, and schools to embed interactive maps that show locations, directions, or service areas.

Use Case: A local business can embed a map on their Google Site to help customers find their store locations.

How to Integrate Google Workspace Apps into Google Sites

Adding Google Workspace content to Google Sites is a straightforward process. Follow these steps to integrate different Google apps into your site.

1. Embedding Google Docs, Sheets, and Slides

1. Open your Google Site and navigate to the page where you want to insert a document.

2. Click the **"Insert"** tab in the right-hand menu.

3. Scroll down and select **"Docs"**, **"Sheets"**, or **"Slides"** (depending on the content you want to add).

4. Choose the file from your Google Drive.

5. Click **"Insert"** and adjust the display size as needed.

6. Publish the site to make the content visible.

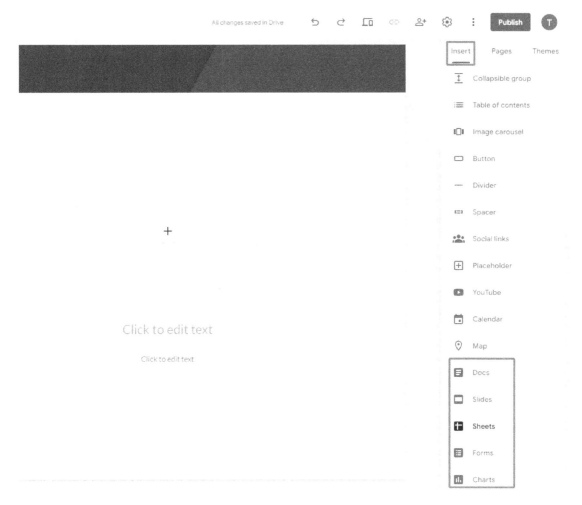

2. Adding Google Forms to Your Site

1. Create a form in Google Forms and copy its URL.

2. In Google Sites, click **"Insert"** > **"Forms"**.

3. Select the form you want to embed.

4. Adjust the size and layout.

3. Displaying Google Calendar Events

1. Click **"Insert"** in Google Sites and select **"Calendar"**.

2. Choose a calendar from your Google account.

3. Customize visibility and event display settings.

4. Click **"Insert"** to add it to your site.

4. Embedding Google Maps for Location Display

1. Click **"Insert"** > **"Maps"** in Google Sites.

2. Enter an address or location.

3. Adjust the map view and size.

4. Click **"Insert"** to add it to your page.

Best Practices for Using Google Workspace with Google Sites

To maximize the effectiveness of Google Workspace integration, consider the following best practices:

✓ **Keep Permissions Consistent** – Ensure that embedded documents, spreadsheets, and calendars have the right sharing settings to avoid "access denied" errors.

✓ **Use Google Drive for Centralized File Management** – Store all important files in a shared Google Drive folder and link it to your Google Site for easy access.

✓ **Organize Content for Easy Navigation** – Structure your Google Site in a way that makes it easy for users to find and interact with embedded content.

✓ **Optimize for Mobile Users** – Google Sites automatically adjusts for mobile viewing, but test embedded elements to ensure they display correctly.

✓ **Update Content Regularly** – Since Google Sites reflects live data from Google Workspace, make sure documents and spreadsheets are updated with accurate information.

Conclusion

Google Sites' deep integration with Google Workspace makes it a powerful tool for creating interactive, collaborative, and dynamic websites. Whether you're building an internal company portal, an educational resource, or a personal project site, leveraging Google Docs, Sheets, Slides, Forms, and other apps can enhance usability and efficiency.

By understanding the various ways to embed and manage Google Workspace content, users can create feature-rich websites without any coding knowledge. With its seamless updates, accessibility controls, and ease of use, Google Sites stands out as an essential platform for teams and individuals looking to share information in a structured and professional manner.

1.3.3 Responsive Design and Accessibility

Introduction

One of the standout features of Google Sites is its **responsive design and accessibility**. A well-designed website should be able to **adapt seamlessly** to different screen sizes and devices while ensuring that all users, including those with disabilities, can navigate and interact with the content effectively.

Google Sites provides **built-in responsiveness**, meaning that websites automatically adjust to different screen sizes—whether viewed on a desktop, tablet, or smartphone. Additionally, it offers **accessibility features** to comply with best practices, allowing users with disabilities to access content through screen readers and keyboard navigation.

In this section, we will explore:

- The importance of responsive design

- How Google Sites ensures mobile-friendliness

- Key accessibility features and best practices

- How to test and improve accessibility on Google Sites

Understanding Responsive Design in Google Sites

What is Responsive Design?

Responsive design is a **web development approach** that allows a website to adapt and function properly on **different devices and screen sizes**. Instead of creating separate versions of a site for desktops and mobile devices, **a single design dynamically adjusts** to fit the screen resolution.

With responsive design, elements like **text, images, buttons, and layouts** adjust automatically, ensuring that users have an **optimal viewing experience** without the need for manual resizing or scrolling.

Why Responsive Design Matters?

A responsive website is essential for several reasons:

- **Improved User Experience:** Visitors can easily navigate the site without zooming or excessive scrolling.

- **Mobile Optimization:** With a growing number of users accessing websites on mobile devices, a responsive design ensures the site remains readable and functional.

- **SEO Benefits:** Google prioritizes **mobile-friendly websites** in search rankings, meaning that a responsive site improves search engine optimization (SEO).

- **Future-Proofing:** As new devices emerge, a responsive site ensures continued usability across different screen sizes.

How Google Sites Implements Responsive Design

Google Sites simplifies the process by making all websites **automatically responsive** without requiring coding or additional plugins. When you build a site with Google Sites:

- **Layouts and sections adjust dynamically** based on screen size.

- **Images and text scale proportionally** to prevent content from becoming too small or too large.

- **Navigation menus adapt** to mobile screens, transforming into a mobile-friendly menu format (hamburger menu).

- **Google Sites uses flexible grids** and smart resizing to ensure all elements remain visually balanced.

Ensuring Mobile-Friendliness on Google Sites

Previewing Your Site on Different Devices

Google Sites allows users to preview their site across multiple screen sizes before publishing. You can check how your site looks on:

1. **Desktop screens** (large monitors, laptops)

2. **Tablets** (medium-sized screens)

3. **Mobile phones** (small screens)

To preview a site in different formats:

1. Click on the **Preview** button (eye icon) in the Google Sites editor.

2. Use the **device preview toolbar** to switch between **desktop, tablet, and mobile views**.

3. Identify any layout issues and adjust content accordingly.

Best Practices for Mobile Optimization

To ensure a smooth mobile experience:

- **Use simple layouts:** Avoid overly complex designs that may not translate well on smaller screens.

- **Keep text readable:** Use large, legible fonts that don't require zooming.

- **Ensure clickable elements are spaced out:** Buttons, links, and menus should be large enough for easy tapping.

- **Optimize images:** Use high-quality but compressed images to ensure fast loading.

- **Avoid excessive scrolling:** Keep pages concise and well-structured for quick navigation.

Google Sites' Automatic Mobile Navigation

Google Sites **automatically converts menus into a mobile-friendly "hamburger" menu** when viewed on small screens. This collapsible menu allows visitors to access navigation links without cluttering the screen.

You can **customize navigation settings** by:

1. Clicking on **Site Settings** in the editor.

2. Selecting **Navigation Mode** and choosing between:

    o **Top Navigation** (better for desktop)

    o **Side Navigation** (better for mobile)

Accessibility Features in Google Sites

What is Web Accessibility?

Web accessibility ensures that people with disabilities can perceive, understand, navigate, and interact with a website. This includes users who have visual, auditory, motor, or cognitive impairments.

Accessible websites follow guidelines such as:

- WCAG (Web Content Accessibility Guidelines)

- ADA (Americans with Disabilities Act) compliance

Google Sites' Built-in Accessibility Features

Google Sites incorporates several accessibility-friendly features, including:

1. Screen Reader Compatibility

- Google Sites is compatible with screen readers like NVDA, JAWS, VoiceOver, and ChromeVox.

- Users can navigate the site using keyboard shortcuts and listen to content through text-to-speech software.

2. Keyboard Navigation Support

Users who cannot use a mouse can navigate Google Sites using only the keyboard. Common shortcuts include:

- **Tab key:** Move between links and buttons.

- **Enter key:** Select an item.

- **Arrow keys:** Scroll through content.

3. Alternative Text for Images (Alt Text)

- Users can add **alternative text (alt text)** to images to help visually impaired visitors understand the content.

- To add alt text:

    1. Click on an image in the editor.

    2. Select **Alt Text** and enter a brief description.

4. High-Contrast Mode for Better Visibility

Google Sites allows for **high-contrast themes** to improve visibility for users with low vision.

- Dark text on a light background enhances readability.

- Avoid using color alone to convey important information.

5. Closed Captions for Videos

- When embedding YouTube videos, enable **automatic closed captions** to provide subtitles for hearing-impaired users.

- Users can also manually upload transcripts for better accuracy.

Testing and Improving Accessibility in Google Sites

Using Accessibility Testing Tools

To ensure your Google Site meets accessibility standards, consider using:

- **Google Lighthouse** (a built-in Chrome tool for accessibility audits)

- **WAVE (Web Accessibility Evaluation Tool)**

- **Axe Accessibility Checker**

Best Practices for an Accessible Google Site

1. **Use clear headings** (H1, H2, H3) to structure content logically.

2. **Provide descriptive link text** instead of vague "Click here" links.

3. **Avoid autoplay media** that may distract or disorient users.

4. **Ensure sufficient color contrast** for text readability.

5. **Enable keyboard navigation** and screen reader compatibility.

Conclusion

Google Sites excels in responsive design and accessibility, making it an excellent choice for users who want a mobile-friendly, inclusive website. With automatic responsiveness, mobile previews, and built-in accessibility features, you can create a site that is user-friendly for all visitors—regardless of device or ability.

By following best practices for mobile optimization and accessibility, you ensure that your website is easy to navigate, visually appealing, and accessible to a diverse audience. Whether you're building a personal portfolio, educational site, or business webpage, Google Sites provides the tools needed for an optimal user experience.

1.3.4 Collaboration and Sharing Features

One of the most powerful aspects of **Google Sites** is its seamless collaboration and sharing features, making it an excellent tool for teams, businesses, educators, and individuals working on projects together. With Google Sites, multiple users can **simultaneously edit, review, and contribute** to a website without needing technical expertise. This section will explore the various collaboration tools available, how to control access permissions, and best practices for managing team-based projects effectively.

1. Real-Time Collaboration

1.1 Multiple Users Editing Simultaneously

Google Sites supports **real-time co-editing**, allowing multiple people to work on the same site at the same time. Just like **Google Docs, Sheets, and Slides**, any changes made by one user appear instantly for others. This feature eliminates the need for **constant file uploads and version control issues**, making website management more efficient.

For example, in an organization:

- The **content team** can write and update text sections.

- The **design team** can adjust images and layout elements.

- The **marketing team** can integrate SEO and promotional content.

1.2 Live Updates and Auto-Saving

Every edit made in Google Sites is **automatically saved** in real-time, ensuring that no work is lost. This is particularly useful in collaborative environments where multiple users are modifying content simultaneously. If someone makes an error, **version history** allows users to restore previous versions of the site.

1.3 Commenting and Feedback Mechanism

While Google Sites doesn't have a built-in commenting system like Google Docs, team members can use other Google Workspace tools for feedback:

- Use **Google Docs or Google Keep** to maintain notes and discussions about site improvements.

- Use **Google Chat or Gmail** to discuss changes in real-time.

- Use **Google Drive's comments feature** on embedded files (Docs, Sheets, Slides) for direct collaboration within the website.

2. Sharing and Access Control

2.1 Managing Permissions and Access Levels

Google Sites offers robust sharing settings to control **who can view, edit, or manage** the site. The sharing options are:

- **Owner** – Has full control, can edit and manage permissions.

- **Editor** – Can edit content but cannot change site permissions.

- **Viewer** – Can only view the site but cannot make any changes.

These permissions allow website owners to customize access depending on the project requirements.

2.2 How to Share a Google Site

To share a Google Site with others:

1. Click the **"Share"** button in the upper-right corner of the Google Sites editor.

2. Enter the email addresses of the people you want to invite.

3. Select their role (**Viewer, Editor, or Owner**).

4. Click **"Send"** to notify them via email.

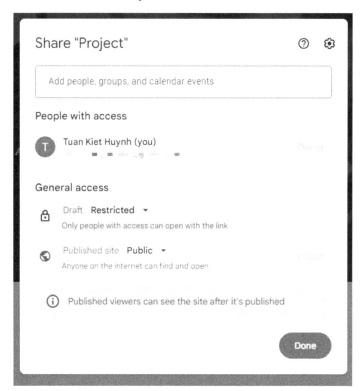

Alternatively, you can **generate a shareable link** and choose:

- **Restricted (default):** Only invited people can access.

- **Anyone with the link (Viewer or Editor mode):** Open sharing for broader access.

- **Public on the web:** Anyone on the internet can view the site.

2.3 Controlling Public vs. Private Access

- **For internal projects:** Keep the site private and restrict access to team members.

- **For educational use:** Schools can grant access to students while limiting external users.

- **For company websites:** Organizations can publish their Google Site publicly for marketing or client engagement.

Tip: Regularly review access settings to ensure the right people have appropriate permissions.

3. Version History and Backup

3.1 Reviewing and Restoring Previous Versions

Google Sites maintains a **version history**, allowing users to see past edits and restore previous versions if necessary. This is useful when:

- Someone accidentally deletes important content.

- A team wants to compare different designs before finalizing.

- A mistake is made, and an earlier version is needed.

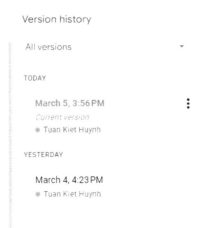

How to Access Version History:

1. Click **"More options"** (three dots) in the editor.

2. Select **"Version history"** to view past versions.

3. Click on a version and restore it if needed.

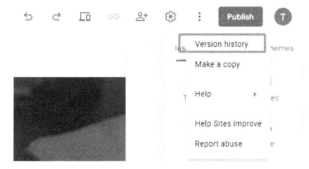

3.2 Duplicating a Site for Backup

Although Google Sites doesn't offer a direct backup feature, users can:

- **Make a copy of the site** for backup before making major changes.

- **Download individual pages** as PDFs for offline reference.

- **Use Google Drive storage** to maintain additional content backups.

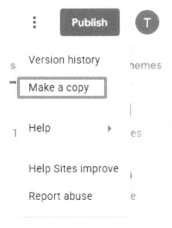

4. Embedding and Integrating Collaboration Tools

Embedding Google Workspace Apps for Collaboration

Google Sites allows users to **embed interactive Google tools** to enhance teamwork, such as:

- **Google Docs:** Share collaborative documents directly on the site.
- **Google Sheets:** Display real-time data for financial reports, schedules, or analytics.
- **Google Slides:** Include presentations for training or business reports.
- **Google Forms:** Gather feedback, registrations, or surveys from visitors.
- **Google Calendar:** Share important dates and events with team members.

Using Google Drive for Shared Resources

Organizations often use Google Drive to store and share resources. By embedding **Google Drive folders** in Google Sites, team members can:

- Upload and access files without navigating away from the website.
- Ensure content is always up to date.
- Organize files into categories for easier access.

How to Embed Google Drive Content:

1. Click **"Insert"** in Google Sites.
2. Select **"Drive"** and choose the file or folder to embed.
3. Adjust the display settings for better visibility.

5. Best Practices for Collaboration in Google Sites

Establish Clear Editing Guidelines

To avoid conflicts and messy edits, teams should:

- Assign roles (e.g., "John updates images," "Sarah manages layout").
- Create a shared document outlining content and design rules.
- Use **consistent formatting** for a professional look.

Use Google Groups for Easier Management

Instead of adding people one by one, organizations can:

- Create a **Google Group** (e.g., "Marketing Team").

- Share the site with the entire group at once.

- Manage permissions for the whole team easily.

Regularly Review and Update Content

To keep the site relevant:

- Schedule regular updates (weekly or monthly).

- Assign team members to **review outdated sections**.

- Encourage feedback and contributions from all members.

Ensure Mobile and Accessibility Compatibility

Since Google Sites is mobile-friendly, always:

- Preview the site on **different devices** before publishing.

- Use **alt text** for images to improve accessibility.

- Test embedded files to ensure they work properly on mobile.

Conclusion

Collaboration is at the core of Google Sites, allowing teams, businesses, and educators to **work together efficiently** in a no-code environment. By using real-time editing, access controls, version history, and integration with Google Workspace, users can **create, manage, and share** websites effortlessly.

Whether you're building an **internal team hub, a project site, or a public website**, Google Sites ensures that **collaboration remains simple, effective, and secure**. By following best practices, leveraging Google Drive and Workspace tools, and maintaining clear guidelines, teams can **maximize productivity** while ensuring their websites remain **organized and up to date**.

1.4 Understanding the Limitations of Google Sites

Google Sites is a powerful and user-friendly tool for creating websites without the need for coding or advanced technical skills. It offers an intuitive interface, seamless integration with Google Workspace, and excellent collaboration features. However, despite its advantages, Google Sites also has certain limitations that users should be aware of before committing to it as their primary website-building platform.

In this section, we will explore the key limitations of Google Sites in terms of design and customization, third-party integrations, SEO and analytics, e-commerce capabilities, and advanced functionalities. By understanding these constraints, users can make informed decisions and determine whether Google Sites is the right tool for their specific needs.

Limited Design and Customization Options

One of the most common criticisms of Google Sites is its limited customization capabilities compared to other website builders like WordPress, Wix, or Squarespace. While the platform provides a variety of built-in themes and layout options, users cannot extensively modify the visual design beyond what is offered in the interface.

1. Lack of Full CSS and HTML Editing

Unlike traditional website builders, Google Sites does not allow users to directly edit HTML, CSS, or JavaScript. This makes it difficult for users who want to implement custom styles, animations, or advanced formatting options. Other platforms offer the ability to modify CSS files to change colors, fonts, spacing, and more, but Google Sites restricts users to the default styling settings.

2. Limited Font and Color Choices

Google Sites provides a few preset themes with predefined fonts and color schemes, but users cannot freely choose their own fonts or create entirely custom color palettes. This can be a drawback for businesses or individuals who want to maintain a strong brand identity with unique typography and color combinations.

3. Inflexible Layout Customization

While Google Sites offers a drag-and-drop interface, it does not provide pixel-perfect design control. Users cannot freely move elements around the page or create complex layouts with overlapping images, text, or floating sections. Instead, they are restricted to the predefined layout structures provided by the platform.

Limited Third-Party Integrations

Google Sites integrates well with Google Workspace applications, but it lacks support for many third-party services that are essential for businesses and advanced users.

1. No Native Support for Plugins and Extensions

Unlike platforms such as WordPress, which has an extensive library of plugins, Google Sites does not support third-party extensions to add functionalities like social media feeds, advanced contact forms, or e-commerce features. This makes it harder to expand the capabilities of the website beyond the core functions provided by Google.

2. Limited API and Developer Access

Google Sites does not offer API access, meaning developers cannot programmatically extend or modify the platform to meet unique business needs. For organizations that require deeper integrations with CRM systems, databases, or external software, this can be a major limitation.

3. Challenges with Embedding External Content

Although Google Sites allows users to embed external content like YouTube videos and Google Forms, it does not support many advanced widgets, interactive maps, or custom JavaScript-based applications. Some embedded elements may not function properly due to security restrictions.

Limited SEO and Analytics Capabilities

Search engine optimization (SEO) is crucial for increasing a website's visibility on platforms like Google. However, Google Sites has several SEO limitations that make it difficult for users to fully optimize their content for search engines.

1. Lack of Advanced SEO Settings

Google Sites does not allow users to modify key SEO elements such as:

- Meta descriptions and title tags (limited customization available)

- Custom URLs for subpages (automatically generated)

- Canonical tags to prevent duplicate content issues

2. No Direct Integration with Google Search Console

Google Sites does not offer built-in integration with Google Search Console, making it harder to track search performance and indexation issues. Users need to manually verify their site using alternative methods.

3. Basic Google Analytics Support

While Google Sites allows users to integrate Google Analytics, the platform does not support advanced tracking features like custom event tracking, enhanced e-commerce analytics, or tag management with Google Tag Manager.

Lack of E-Commerce Functionality

If you plan to create an online store, Google Sites is not the best choice because it lacks built-in e-commerce features.

1. No Shopping Cart or Payment Integration

Google Sites does not have built-in support for payment gateways such as PayPal, Stripe, or Shopify. While users can add buttons that link to external payment processors, there is no way to manage inventory, shopping carts, or customer orders within Google Sites.

2. No Product Listing Features

Unlike dedicated e-commerce platforms like Shopify or WooCommerce, Google Sites does not offer:

- Product pages with filtering and sorting options

- Checkout and order processing systems

- Automated invoicing or tax calculations

For businesses looking to sell products online, alternative platforms like Shopify or WooCommerce would be a better fit.

Limited User Roles and Permission Controls

Google Sites does provide collaboration features, but it lacks granular permission controls for managing different levels of access.

1. Basic Editing and Viewing Permissions

Users can assign roles as either:

- Editor (can modify content)
- Viewer (can only see published content)

However, there is no intermediate role such as a "content contributor" who can add content without publishing changes.

2. No Version Control for Individual Elements

Google Sites allows restoring previous versions, but users cannot track changes to individual elements or pages like in Google Docs or WordPress.

Challenges with Mobile Optimization

While Google Sites is responsive, it does not provide mobile-specific customization options like other website builders.

1. No Mobile-Specific Design Adjustments

Users cannot create separate mobile layouts or adjust content positioning specifically for mobile devices. This can sometimes result in poor readability or formatting issues on smaller screens.

2. Limited Touchscreen Interactivity

Unlike modern web builders that allow fine-tuned mobile interactions, Google Sites does not support touch gestures like swiping carousels or interactive mobile menus.

Conclusion: Is Google Sites the Right Choice for You?

Despite its limitations, **Google Sites remains an excellent tool** for users looking for a **simple, free, and collaborative website builder**. It is particularly well-suited for:

✓ Internal company websites
✓ Educational websites and class projects

✅ Personal portfolios or information-based sites

✅ Team collaboration pages

However, if you need advanced design, SEO optimization, third-party integrations, or e-commerce functionalities, you may want to explore alternatives like WordPress, Wix, or Shopify.

By understanding these limitations, users can determine whether Google Sites aligns with their website goals and explore workarounds where necessary.

CHAPTER II
Getting Started with Google Sites

2.1 Creating a Google Site

2.1.1 Accessing Google Sites

Google Sites is a free and user-friendly website-building tool offered by Google. It allows individuals and teams to create and manage websites without needing coding or technical expertise. Before you can start designing your website, the first step is to access Google Sites. This section will guide you through the process of accessing Google Sites, logging into your account, and setting up the platform for your first website.

1. Accessing Google Sites on a Web Browser

Google Sites is a web-based application, meaning there is no need to download or install any software. To access it, all you need is a modern web browser such as **Google Chrome, Mozilla Firefox, Microsoft Edge, or Safari**. Follow these steps to open Google Sites:

Step 1: Open Your Web Browser

- Ensure that you are using an updated version of your browser for the best experience.

- Open a new tab or window in your preferred web browser.

Step 2: Visit the Google Sites Homepage

- In the address bar, type sites.google.com and press **Enter**.

- You will be directed to the **Google Sites dashboard**, where you can create and manage your websites.

Step 3: Sign in to Your Google Account

- If you are not already signed in, Google will prompt you to log in.

- Enter your **Google account email and password** to proceed.

- If you don't have a Google account, click **"Create Account"** and follow the instructions to set up a new account.

2. Accessing Google Sites from Google Workspace Apps

If you frequently use Google Workspace (formerly G Suite), you can access Google Sites directly from other Google apps such as **Gmail, Google Drive, or Google Docs**. Here's how:

Method 1: Accessing Google Sites from Google Drive

1. Open **Google Drive** by visiting drive.google.com.

2. Click on the **"+ New"** button on the left-hand menu.

3. Scroll down to **"More"** and click on **Google Sites**.

4. This will open a new blank Google Sites project, allowing you to start creating your website immediately.

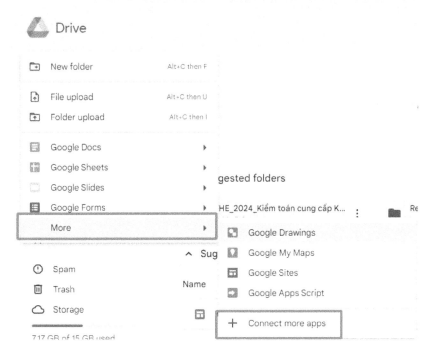

Method 2: Accessing Google Sites from the Google Apps Menu

1. Open **Google Chrome** or any browser where you are signed into your Google account.

2. Click on the **Google Apps icon** (a grid of nine dots) in the top right corner.

3. Scroll down and click on **Sites**.

4. This will take you to the Google Sites homepage.

3. Google Sites Interface Overview

Once you have successfully accessed Google Sites, you will see the **Google Sites dashboard**. This interface consists of the following main sections:

The Dashboard

The Google Sites dashboard is where you can manage all your previously created sites and start new ones. Here, you will find:

- **Recent Sites**: Displays a list of sites you have recently worked on.

- **Templates**: Pre-made designs that you can use to create a website quickly.

- **Blank Site Option**: Allows you to start from scratch with a completely new design.

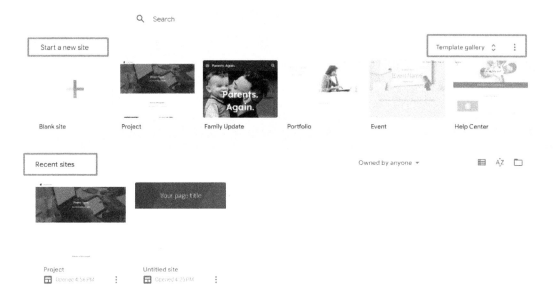

Creating a New Site from the Dashboard

To start a new website, you have two options:

1. **Use a Template**: Click on **"Template gallery"**, browse the available templates, and select one that fits your needs.

2. **Create a Blank Site**: Click on the **"+"** sign to open a blank Google Site.

After selecting an option, you will be directed to the **Google Sites Editor**, where you can start customizing your website.

4. Understanding Google Sites Account Types

Depending on your Google account type, you may have different features available when accessing Google Sites.

Personal Google Account

- If you are using a free **@gmail.com** account, you can create and share Google Sites for personal use.

- Your website will have a Google-assigned URL such as **sites.google.com/view/yoursite**.

- Some advanced features like custom domain mapping might not be available.

Google Workspace (Business or Education Account)

- If you are using a Google Workspace account from your company, school, or organization, you may have access to additional features.

- Your website may be restricted to internal users or made public depending on your administrator's settings.

- Google Workspace accounts allow **custom domain mapping**, meaning you can assign a domain like www.yourbusiness.com.

To check your account type:

1. Click on your profile icon in the top right corner of Google Sites.

2. Look for the email domain (e.g., **@company.com** indicates a business account, while **@gmail.com** indicates a personal account).

5. Troubleshooting Access Issues

If you encounter issues while trying to access Google Sites, here are some common problems and their solutions:

Issue 1: Cannot Sign in to Google Sites

- *Solution:* Ensure you are entering the correct Google account credentials. If you forgot your password, use the **"Forgot password?"** link to reset it.

Issue 2: Google Sites is Blocked on Your Network

- *Solution:* If you are using a school or workplace network, Google Sites may be restricted. Contact your IT administrator to request access.

Issue 3: Google Sites is Not Loading Properly

- *Solution:*

  - o Clear your browser cache and cookies.

  - o Try accessing Google Sites from a different browser or device.

  - o Check your internet connection to ensure you are online.

Issue 4: No Option to Create a New Site

- *Solution:*

  - o If you are using a Google Workspace account, your administrator may have disabled site creation. Check with your IT team.

  - o Try logging in with a different Google account that has full access.

Conclusion

Accessing Google Sites is a simple process, whether through a web browser, Google Drive, or the Google Apps menu. Once logged in, you can explore the dashboard, select a template, and begin designing your website. If you face any issues, troubleshooting steps can help you resolve them quickly.

Now that you have successfully accessed Google Sites, the next section (**2.1.2 Choosing a Template**) will guide you through selecting the best layout for your website.

2.1.2 Choosing a Template

When creating a website with Google Sites, choosing the right template is an essential first step. Google Sites provides users with a selection of pre-designed templates, each tailored for specific use cases. Whether you are building a portfolio, a business site, a project hub, or an educational platform, selecting the appropriate template can save time and ensure a well-structured and visually appealing website.

This section will guide you through the process of choosing a template, understanding the differences between various templates, and customizing them to fit your needs.

1. What Are Google Sites Templates?

Google Sites templates are pre-built website structures designed to simplify the website creation process. These templates include predefined page layouts, navigation menus, and basic design elements, allowing users to start with a ready-made framework instead of building everything from scratch.

Templates are particularly useful for beginners who may not be familiar with web design principles. By selecting a template, users can avoid the complexities of structuring a site manually and instead focus on adding content and making minor visual adjustments.

Key Benefits of Using a Template:

- **Saves Time:** Instead of creating a site from scratch, you can start with a pre-designed structure.

- **Consistent Layouts:** Templates ensure a professional look with well-organized sections.

- **Ease of Use:** Even users with no design experience can build an attractive website.

- **Customization Flexibility:** Templates can be adjusted to match your branding and content needs.

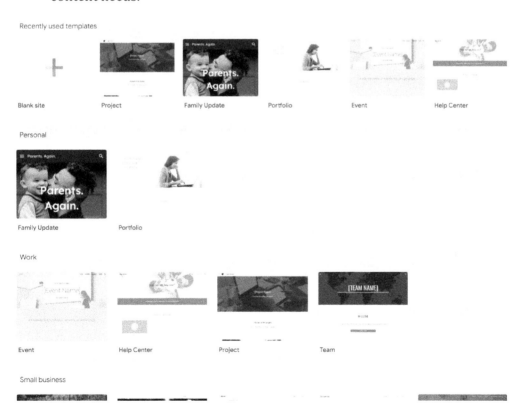

2. Types of Google Sites Templates

Google Sites provides a variety of templates suited for different purposes. Below are some common categories of templates available:

2.1 Business and Professional Templates

These templates are designed for businesses, organizations, and professional services. They include structured layouts for presenting company information, services, client testimonials, and contact details.

Examples:

- **Small Business Website** – Includes sections for services, about us, and contact information.

- **Company Intranet** – Useful for internal documentation and communication within a company.

- **Project Tracking Site** – Helps teams track progress, deadlines, and responsibilities.

2.2 Education and Classroom Templates

Educators and students can use these templates to create interactive learning resources, share study materials, or manage class activities.

Examples:

- **Class Website** – A site where teachers can post assignments, schedules, and announcements.

- **Student Portfolio** – Allows students to showcase their projects and academic achievements.

- **School Event Page** – Designed for promoting school functions and events.

2.3 Portfolio and Personal Branding Templates

If you are an artist, freelancer, or job seeker, portfolio templates help showcase your skills, experience, and achievements.

Examples:

- **Personal Portfolio** – Ideal for designers, photographers, and writers.

- **Resume Site** – A digital version of your resume to share with potential employers.

- **Consultant Page** – Useful for professionals offering individual services.

2.4 Nonprofit and Community Templates

These templates help nonprofits and community groups create awareness, share updates, and manage events.

Examples:

- **Nonprofit Organization Site** – Provides information about the cause, donation options, and upcoming events.

- **Volunteer Coordination Page** – Helps manage volunteers and schedule activities.

- **Community Hub** – Acts as a central place for sharing local news and initiatives.

3. How to Choose the Right Template for Your Website

Selecting the right template depends on your specific goals and the type of content you plan to display. Below are some factors to consider when making your choice:

3.1 Identify Your Website's Purpose

Before selecting a template, clearly define what you want to achieve with your website. Ask yourself:

- Is this a business site, personal portfolio, educational resource, or project management hub?

- Who is my target audience?

- What key features will my website need (e.g., forms, embedded documents, multimedia content)?

For instance, if you are a teacher creating a site for students, an education-focused template with built-in lesson sections and assignment pages would be ideal. On the other hand, if you are a freelancer, a portfolio template with image galleries and contact sections might be a better choice.

3.2 Consider the Layout and Design

Look at the structure of each template and determine if it suits your needs. Consider:

- Does the homepage provide enough space for important information?

- Is the navigation menu clear and easy to use?

- Does the template allow for future content expansion?

Some templates emphasize large hero images, while others focus on text-based content. Choose one that aligns with the type of content you will frequently update.

3.3 Check for Google Workspace Integration

If you plan to embed Google Docs, Sheets, or Forms, ensure that the template's layout accommodates these features. Templates that include dedicated sections for collaboration tools can enhance functionality.

3.4 Evaluate Mobile Responsiveness

Since many users access websites from mobile devices, check how the template appears on different screen sizes. Google Sites automatically optimizes for mobile viewing, but some templates may have better readability and design adaptability than others.

3.5 Test Before Committing

Before finalizing your choice, preview different templates and experiment with how content appears. You can always change the template later, but selecting the right one from the start reduces the need for major adjustments.

4. How to Select a Template in Google Sites

Once you have decided on the best template for your site, follow these steps to apply it:

Step 1: Access Google Sites Template Gallery

1. Go to Google Sites.

2. Click on the **Template Gallery** at the top of the page.

3. Browse through the available templates categorized by business, education, personal, and other uses.

Step 2: Preview and Select a Template

1. Click on a template to preview its layout and structure.

2. Review the built-in pages and sections.

3. If the template fits your needs, click **Use this template** to start editing.

Step 3: Customize the Template

1. Replace placeholder text with your own content.

2. Adjust colors, fonts, and images to match your branding.

3. Modify the navigation menu to add or remove pages as needed.

Step 4: Save and Continue Building

After selecting and customizing your template, save your changes and proceed with adding more content and interactive elements.

5. Customizing a Template to Fit Your Needs

While templates provide a great starting point, you may need to personalize them further. Here are some ways to make the template truly your own:

- **Modify the Color Scheme:** Adjust the theme colors to match your brand or organization.

- **Change Fonts and Typography:** Select fonts that improve readability and suit your website's tone.

- **Replace Default Images:** Upload custom images or use Google Sites' built-in options.

- **Rearrange Sections:** Drag and drop elements to create a unique layout.

- **Add Additional Pages:** Expand your website with new sections as needed.

Conclusion

Choosing a template is a crucial step in the Google Sites website-building process. With a variety of templates available, selecting one that aligns with your goals and content needs can significantly enhance the efficiency and appearance of your website. By carefully evaluating layout, functionality, and customization options, you can create a site that is not only visually appealing but also easy to navigate and update over time.

In the next section, we will explore how to set up a blank site from scratch for those who prefer a completely custom approach.

2.1.3 Setting Up a Blank Site

Creating a Google Site from scratch allows you to have full control over the design, structure, and content of your website. Unlike pre-designed templates, a blank site gives you the flexibility to tailor every aspect to fit your needs. Whether you're building a business site, an internal company portal, an educational resource, or a personal blog, starting with a blank slate ensures that your site is uniquely yours.

In this section, we will walk you through the entire process of setting up a blank site, from creating the site to adjusting basic settings before adding content.

Step 1: Creating a New Blank Google Site

To begin, follow these steps:

1. **Go to Google Sites:**

   o   Open your web browser and go to Google Sites.

   o   Make sure you're signed into your Google account. If you're using a business or school account, ensure that Google Sites is enabled by your administrator.

2. **Start a New Site:**

   o   Click on the **blank (+)** option to create a new empty site.

   o   A new site editor will open with an untitled page.

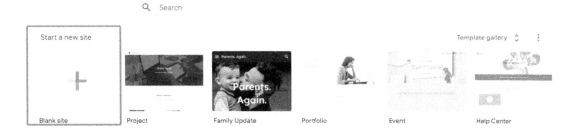

At this point, your blank site has been created, but it needs customization and setup to become a fully functional website.

Step 2: Understanding the Blank Site Interface

After creating your blank site, you'll be taken to the **Google Sites Editor**. This is where you'll design your pages, add content, and manage settings. The editor consists of several key sections:

1. The Top Toolbar

This toolbar contains essential options such as:

- **Undo/Redo**: Revert or redo changes.

- **Preview**: See how your site looks before publishing.

- **Publish**: Make your site live.

- **Settings Menu**: Access site-wide settings like navigation options and custom domain setup.

2. The Sidebar Menu

On the **right side of the editor**, you'll find three main tabs:

- **Insert**: Allows you to add text, images, videos, Google Drive files, calendars, and more.

- **Pages**: Manages the structure of your website by adding, removing, or organizing pages.

- **Themes**: Lets you choose a site-wide design, including fonts, colors, and layouts.

3. The Main Workspace

This is where you'll build your site. Clicking anywhere in the blank workspace allows you to add elements such as text boxes, images, and sections.

Step 3: Naming Your Site and Page Title

By default, your new Google Site is unnamed, so it's important to give it a meaningful title.

1. Naming Your Website

- Click the **"Untitled Site"** text in the upper-left corner of the editor.

- Type the name of your site. This name will be visible in the Google Sites dashboard but will not appear publicly.

2. Adding a Title to the Home Page

- Click on the default "Your Page Title" text in the center of the screen.

- Type in your preferred **homepage title** (e.g., "Welcome to My Website" or "Company Intranet").

3. Changing the Site Logo (Optional)

- Click the **Add Logo** button (found in the upper-left area of the editor).

- Upload your logo or select one from Google Drive.

- If you don't have a logo, you can skip this step.

Step 4: Configuring Basic Site Settings

Before adding content, it's a good idea to adjust a few basic settings:

1. Site Navigation Settings

- Click on the **Settings (⚙☐) icon** in the top-right corner.

- Select **Navigation** and choose between **Top Navigation** (menu appears at the top) or **Side Navigation** (menu expands from the left).

- If your site has multiple pages, Google Sites will automatically generate a navigation bar for visitors.

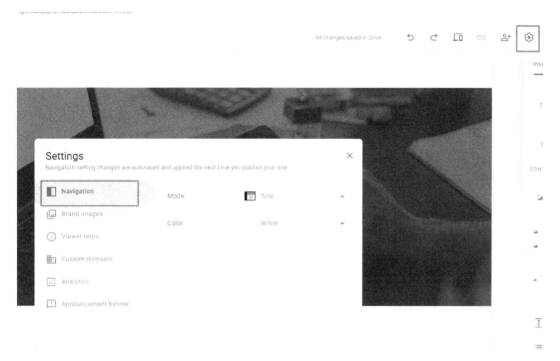

2. Choosing a Theme

- Click on the **Themes** tab on the right panel.

- Select a pre-designed theme or customize fonts and colors to match your style.

- Themes ensure that your site maintains a **consistent visual identity** across all pages.

3. Adjusting Page Width and Layout

- By default, Google Sites has a **responsive layout**, meaning it adjusts automatically based on the visitor's screen size.

- If you want a full-width layout, click **Settings > Appearance** and enable "Full Width."

Step 5: Adding Basic Content Elements

Now that your blank site is named and configured, it's time to add basic elements. Google Sites allows you to **drag and drop** elements easily.

1. Adding a Text Box

- Click on **Insert > Text Box** (or simply double-click in the blank area).

- Type your content (e.g., "Welcome to our website").

- Use the **text formatting options** (bold, italic, alignment, font size) to style your text.

2. Adding an Image

- Click on **Insert > Images** and choose one of the following:

  - Upload an image from your computer.

  - Select an image from Google Drive.

  - Use Google Search to find royalty-free images.

- Resize or reposition the image by dragging its corners.

3. Embedding a Google Drive File

- Click **Insert > Google Drive** and select a document, spreadsheet, or presentation.

- The embedded file will appear on your page, allowing visitors to view it without downloading.

4. Creating a Section Layout

- Google Sites provides **pre-designed section layouts** to organize content effectively.

- Click **Insert > Layouts** and select a multi-column format.

- Add text, images, or embedded content into each section.

Step 6: Previewing and Saving Your Work

After setting up your blank site, preview it to see how it looks on different devices.

1. Click the **Preview (□)** button in the top toolbar.

2. Toggle between different device views (desktop, tablet, and mobile).

3. If everything looks good, exit preview mode.

Google Sites automatically saves changes in real-time, so there's no need to click a "Save" button.

Step 7: Next Steps After Setting Up a Blank Site

Once your blank site is ready, the next steps include:

✅ **Adding more pages** (e.g., "About Us," "Contact," "Services").

✅ **Customizing the homepage** with branding elements.

✅ **Optimizing site navigation** for a better user experience.

✅ **Configuring site permissions** (public vs. private access).

✅ **Publishing the site** to make it accessible to others.

These steps will be covered in the upcoming chapters of this book!

Conclusion

Setting up a blank Google Site provides the ultimate flexibility in website creation. While templates can be useful for quick projects, starting with a blank site gives you complete control over layout, design, and content. By following this guide, you've successfully created a foundation for your website.

As you move forward, you'll explore advanced customization, embedding features, and publishing your site to the web. Keep experimenting with the available tools to make your Google Site both visually appealing and functionally effective. Happy site-building!

2.2 Navigating the Google Sites Interface

2.2.1 The Site Editor Layout

Introduction to the Site Editor

The Google Sites Editor is the core workspace where users create, design, and manage their websites. This intuitive, drag-and-drop interface simplifies website creation, even for those with no coding experience. Whether you're building a personal portfolio, a business landing page, or an internal site for your team, understanding the Site Editor layout is crucial for efficient and effective site management.

This section will explore the different components of the Google Sites Editor, helping you navigate its tools and maximize its features.

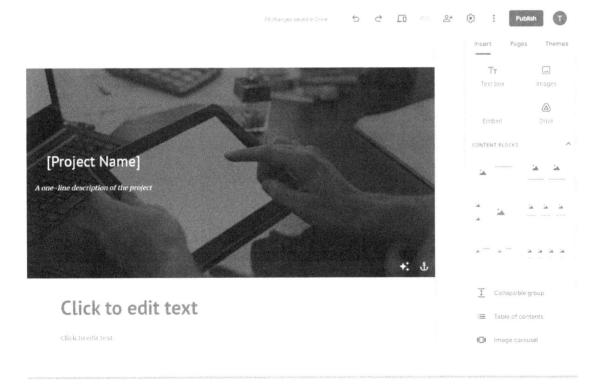

1. Overview of the Google Sites Editor

When you open a Google Site for editing, you are presented with a clean and user-friendly interface. The layout is divided into several key sections:

- **The Top Toolbar** – Provides options for site settings, previewing, publishing, and undo/redo functions.

- **The Left Sidebar (Navigation Panel)** – Displays the site structure, allowing you to organize and switch between pages.

- **The Right Sidebar (Insert, Pages, and Themes Panel)** – Offers tools for adding content, managing pages, and customizing site design.

- **The Main Canvas (Editing Area)** – The central workspace where you design your site by adding and arranging elements.

Each of these sections plays a critical role in building a well-structured and visually appealing website.

---

2. The Top Toolbar: Essential Site Controls

At the top of the Google Sites Editor, you will find the **Top Toolbar**, which includes several key functions:

2.1 Site Name & Document Title

- Located in the upper left corner, the site name helps you identify your website.

- The document title (visible only to you) is used for managing the site within Google Drive.

2.2 Undo and Redo

- These buttons allow you to revert or reapply changes, making it easy to experiment with design and layout.

2.3 Preview Button

- Clicking the **Preview** button (represented by an eye icon) lets you see how your site will appear on desktops, tablets, and mobile devices.

- This feature is useful for ensuring responsive design and layout consistency across different screen sizes.

2.4 Publish Button

- The **Publish** button makes your site live and accessible to viewers.

- Before publishing, you can configure site visibility settings to control who can access it.

2.5 Settings Menu

- The gear icon provides access to additional settings, such as site analytics, custom URLs, and navigation options.

3. The Left Sidebar: Site Navigation Panel

The **Left Sidebar**, also known as the **Navigation Panel**, is where you manage the structure of your site.

3.1 Managing Site Pages

- Clicking the **Pages** tab allows you to create, rename, or delete pages.

- You can organize pages hierarchically to create subpages and dropdown menus.

3.2 Rearranging Pages

- Drag and drop pages within the sidebar to reorder them.

- Nesting pages under parent pages creates a structured navigation system.

3.3 Page Settings

- Clicking on a page's three-dot menu provides options such as:

    o **Set as Homepage** – Makes the page the default landing page.

    o **Duplicate Page** – Creates a copy for easy replication.

    o **Hide from Navigation** – Removes the page from the site's main menu without deleting it.

4. The Right Sidebar: Content & Customization Tools

The **Right Sidebar** is divided into three tabs:

1. **Insert Tab** – Allows you to add content elements (text, images, buttons, etc.).

2. **Pages Tab** – Helps you manage and organize pages.

3. **Themes Tab** – Lets you customize the design and appearance of your site.

4.1 Insert Tab: Adding Content to Your Site

The **Insert** tab provides various elements that you can add to your site:

- **Text Box** – Add and format text.

- **Images** – Upload or embed images from Google Drive or the web.

- **Embed URL** – Insert external content by embedding links.

- **Google Drive Files** – Add Docs, Sheets, Slides, or PDFs directly from Google Drive.

4.2 Layout Options

- Google Sites offers pre-designed **layouts** to structure content efficiently.

- Drag and drop sections into the editing area to create visually balanced pages.

4.3 Special Elements

- **Buttons** – Create call-to-action buttons linking to other pages or external sites.

- **Dividers** – Insert horizontal lines to separate sections.

- **Collapsible Groups** – Create expandable sections for organizing content.

5. The Main Canvas: Editing and Designing Your Site

The **Main Canvas** is the workspace where you build and design your website.

5.1 Drag-and-Drop Editing

- Click on any section to modify content.

- Drag elements around to rearrange them easily.

5.2 Resizing and Alignment

- Resize images, text boxes, and other elements using the blue alignment guides.

- Google Sites automatically aligns elements to maintain a clean layout.

5.3 Section Backgrounds

- Customize section backgrounds with colors or images.
- Choose **Emphasis Levels** (default, light, or dark) for visual distinction.

6. Additional Features and Customization Options

Beyond the basic layout, Google Sites provides several additional features to enhance your website.

6.1 Using Headers and Footers

- The **Header** section allows you to add a logo, site title, and background image.
- The **Footer** section (at the bottom of each page) can include copyright notices or contact information.

6.2 Collaborating on Your Site

- Click the **Share** button to invite others to edit your site.
- Set permissions (Editor, Viewer, or Owner) for different collaborators.

6.3 Mobile Optimization

- Google Sites automatically adjusts for mobile viewing.
- Use the **Preview** tool to ensure a smooth experience on smaller screens.

7. Summary and Best Practices

Understanding the **Google Sites Editor Layout** is essential for efficiently designing and managing a website. Here are some best practices:

✅ **Familiarize yourself with the interface** – Spend time exploring the editor to understand its functionality.

✅ **Plan your site structure** – Use the **Pages** tab to organize content logically.

✅ **Utilize layout tools effectively** – Drag-and-drop elements to create visually appealing pages.

✅ **Test your site frequently** – Use the **Preview** button to check responsiveness.

✅ **Collaborate efficiently** – Share your site with team members to streamline content creation.

With this knowledge, you're now ready to start designing your Google Site confidently! 🚀

2.2.2 The Sidebar Menu

Google Sites is designed to be an intuitive and user-friendly platform, allowing users to create and manage websites without requiring any coding knowledge. One of the most important components of the Google Sites interface is the Sidebar Menu, which provides easy access to essential tools for building and customizing a website.

In this section, we will explore the functions, features, and best practices of using the Sidebar Menu effectively to enhance your Google Sites experience.

Understanding the Sidebar Menu

The Sidebar Menu in Google Sites serves as the primary control panel for managing your site's structure, pages, navigation, and settings. It is located on the right-hand side of the screen when you are in the editing mode of your website.

The **Sidebar Menu** consists of three main sections:

1. **Insert** – Allows you to add content elements to your page, such as text, images, videos, buttons, and more.

2. **Pages** – Helps you manage your website's structure by adding, renaming, reordering, and deleting pages.

3. **Themes** – Provides design customization options, including color schemes, fonts, and layout styles.

Each of these sections plays a crucial role in how you design and manage your Google Site. Let's take a closer look at each one.

1. The "Insert" Tab

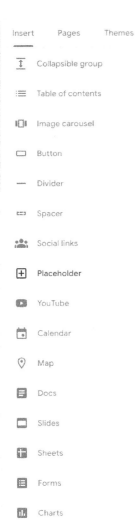

The **Insert tab** is the first option in the Sidebar Menu and serves as your **toolbox** for adding various content elements to your website. It contains **pre-built components** that you can drag and drop onto your pages to structure your content effectively.

1.1 Adding Basic Content Elements

Google Sites provides several fundamental elements that help you build an engaging website:

- **Text Box** – Adds a section where you can input and format text. This is essential for providing information, instructions, or descriptions on your website.

- **Images** – Allows you to upload images from your computer, insert them from Google Drive, or use web URLs. You can resize and position them easily.

- **Embed** – Lets you embed content from external websites using a URL or HTML code. This is useful for adding interactive elements like social media feeds, widgets, or third-party forms.

- **Drive** – Allows direct integration of files from Google Drive, such as PDFs, Docs, Sheets, Slides, and videos. This is particularly useful for businesses and educators who want to share documents with their audience.

1.2 Adding Layout Sections

Google Sites offers **predefined layout blocks** that make it easy to structure content. You can choose from a variety of layout styles, such as:

- **Single column** – Ideal for displaying full-width content, such as a blog post or a long piece of text.

- **Two or three columns** – Great for organizing content neatly, such as placing an image next to a text block.

- **Grid layouts** – Useful for creating galleries, service showcases, or team member introductions.

1.3 Advanced Components

For more interactive and dynamic sites, Google Sites includes additional elements:

- **Buttons** – Helps users navigate your site by linking to other pages or external websites.

- **Dividers** – Adds visual breaks between sections for better readability.

- **YouTube Videos** – Easily embed YouTube videos by searching within Google Sites or pasting a video URL.

- **Maps** – Insert Google Maps to show locations, useful for businesses or event pages.

- **Calendars** – Display Google Calendar to share events, schedules, or meetings with your visitors.

Using the **Insert tab** effectively allows you to build a **structured, visually appealing, and user-friendly website** without technical expertise.

2. The "Pages" Tab

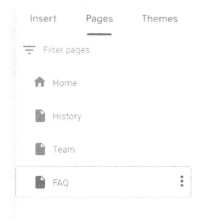

The **Pages tab** in the Sidebar Menu is where you **manage the structure and navigation** of your website. It allows you to create, modify, and organize the hierarchy of pages.

2.1 Creating and Managing Pages

To create a new page, follow these steps:

1. Click on the **"Pages" tab** in the Sidebar Menu.

2. Click the **"+" button** at the bottom to add a new page.

3. Enter a name for the page (e.g., "About Us," "Services," "Contact").

4. Click **"Done"**, and the page will be added to your site's navigation.

You can create multiple pages and arrange them into **subpages** to organize content effectively. To make a page a subpage:

- Drag and drop it under another page.

- Right-click the page and select **"Make subpage."**

2.2 Reordering and Deleting Pages

- To **rearrange pages**, click and drag them into the desired order.

- To **delete a page**, right-click on the page and select **"Remove"**.

Organizing pages properly ensures a **clean, intuitive navigation experience** for your site visitors.

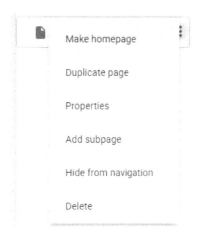

Aristotle

Vision

Level

3. The "Themes" Tab

The **Themes tab** allows you to **customize the overall look and feel** of your website. It provides **predefined themes** with different colors, fonts, and styles.

3.1 Choosing a Theme

To select a theme:

1. Click on the **"Themes" tab** in the Sidebar Menu.

2. Browse through the available themes.

3. Click on a theme to apply it to your website.

Themes control **background colors, font styles, and section formatting**, ensuring consistency across all pages.

3.2 Customizing Theme Elements

Each theme has additional customization options, such as:

• **Color schemes** – Adjust primary and secondary colors to match your brand.

• **Font styles** – Choose from a selection of font families for headings and body text.

• **Header type** – Select different header styles (default, large banner, or title-only).

Choosing the right **theme and customizations** helps create a **professional and visually appealing** website.

Best Practices for Using the Sidebar Menu Effectively

Now that you understand how to navigate the Sidebar Menu, here are **some best practices** to enhance your experience with Google Sites:

✅ **Plan Your Site Structure Beforehand** – Outline the pages and layout before building to avoid unnecessary rework.
✅ **Use Consistent Design Elements** – Stick to a uniform color scheme, font style, and layout for better readability.
✅ **Leverage Google Workspace Integrations** – Embed Docs, Sheets, Forms, and Calendars for seamless content sharing.
✅ **Optimize for Mobile View** – Regularly preview your site on mobile devices to ensure a responsive experience.
✅ **Keep Navigation Simple** – Avoid overloading the navigation menu with too many pages or subpages.

By mastering the Sidebar Menu, you can **efficiently build, customize, and manage** a Google Site that looks professional and functions smoothly.

Conclusion

The **Sidebar Menu** is the **control center** of Google Sites, offering essential tools for **inserting content, managing pages, and customizing design themes**. Understanding how to navigate and utilize these features effectively will enable you to **create a well-structured, visually appealing, and user-friendly website**.

In the next section, we will dive deeper into **site settings and customization**, where we'll explore how to adjust **site names, navigation settings, and permissions** to optimize your Google Site further.

2.2.3 The Toolbar and Formatting Options

Google Sites provides a simple and intuitive toolbar that allows users to format and style their content efficiently. Whether you are adding text, images, or embedded elements, the toolbar offers essential tools to enhance the appearance and readability of your site. This section will guide you through the various formatting options available in Google Sites, helping you create a professional and visually appealing website.

Understanding the Toolbar in Google Sites

The toolbar in Google Sites appears when you select or edit a text box, image, or embedded content. It provides a range of formatting options similar to those found in word processors like Google Docs or Microsoft Word. The toolbar helps you:

- Adjust text styles (headings, subheadings, and body text)

- Change font styles, colors, and sizes

- Align text and add bullet points

- Insert hyperlinks

- Manage media elements, such as images and videos

To access the toolbar, simply click on a text box, image, or embedded content within your site. A floating toolbar will appear with various formatting options.

Text Formatting Options

1. Text Styles and Headings

Google Sites provides several predefined text styles to ensure consistency across your site. These include:

- **Title** – The largest text style, typically used for the main page heading.

- **Heading** – A slightly smaller font, ideal for section headings.

- **Subheading** – A smaller font than headings, used for sub-sections.

- **Normal Text** – The standard body text style.

To change a text style:

1. Click on a text box.

2. Select the text you want to format.

3. Click on the "Text Style" dropdown in the toolbar.

4. Choose the appropriate style (Title, Heading, Subheading, or Normal Text).

Using headings and subheadings correctly helps structure your content, making it easier for visitors to navigate and understand.

2. Font Customization

Although Google Sites does not allow custom fonts, it provides basic font customization options:

- **Bold (B)** – Makes text bold for emphasis.

- **Italic (I)** – Slants text for emphasis or stylistic purposes.

- **Underline (U)** – Adds a line under text to highlight it.

- **Font Color** – Changes the color of the text.

To apply these styles:

1. Select the text.

2. Click on the respective formatting button in the toolbar.

3. Choose a color (for font color) if needed.

Using bold and italic text strategically can improve readability and draw attention to key points.

3. Text Alignment and Spacing

Google Sites allows you to align text to create a more structured layout:

- **Left Align** – Aligns text to the left (default setting).

- **Center Align** – Centers text on the page.

- **Right Align** – Aligns text to the right.

To change text alignment:

1. Select the text or text box.

2. Click on the "Alignment" button in the toolbar.

3. Choose the desired alignment option.

Proper alignment ensures a clean and professional look. Centered text works well for titles, while left-aligned text is best for body content.

4. Lists: Bullet Points and Numbering

Lists help organize content effectively. Google Sites supports:

- **Bullet Lists** – Great for unordered lists.

- **Numbered Lists** – Ideal for step-by-step instructions.

To create a list:

1. Click inside a text box.

2. Click on the "Bullet List" or "Numbered List" button in the toolbar.

3. Type your list items.

Lists improve readability, making complex information easier to digest.

Adding Hyperlinks

Hyperlinks allow users to navigate between different sections of your site or external sources. Google Sites supports linking to:

- Other pages on your site

- External websites

- Email addresses

How to Add a Hyperlink

1. Select the text you want to hyperlink.

2. Click on the "Insert Link" button (🔗) in the toolbar.

3. Enter the URL or choose an internal page.

4. Click "Apply."

Embed from the web

By URL   Embed code

|
Enter URL

Cancel   Insert

Hyperlinks are essential for site navigation and improving user engagement.

Image and Multimedia Formatting

Google Sites allows you to add and format images, videos, and embedded content.

1. Adjusting Image Size and Position

Once an image is inserted, you can:

- Resize it by dragging the corners.

- Align it left, center, or right.

- Wrap text around the image.

2. Adding Captions to Images

Although Google Sites does not have a built-in caption feature, you can:

1. Insert a text box below an image.

2. Type the caption inside the text box.

3. Align the text to match the image placement.

3. Embedding Videos and Other Media

To embed a YouTube video:

1. Click the "Embed" button in the toolbar.

2. Enter the video URL or search for a YouTube video.

3. Click "Insert" and adjust its placement.

Embedding multimedia enhances the user experience by providing interactive content.

Using Columns for Better Layout

Google Sites allows you to organize content into multiple columns for a structured layout.

How to Create Columns

1. Click on an empty section of your site.

2. Hover over the left side of the section until the "Column Layout" icon appears.

3. Click on the icon and select a column format.

Columns are useful for creating professional-looking pages with well-structured content.

Using Buttons for Call-to-Action (CTA)

Buttons help guide users toward important actions, such as:

- Visiting another page.
- Submitting a form.
- Downloading a file.

How to Add a Button

1. Click on "Insert" in the sidebar.

2. Select "Button."

3. Enter a name and link.

4. Click "Insert" and adjust its size and position.

Buttons improve user engagement and site navigation.

Final Tips for Formatting in Google Sites

- **Keep formatting consistent** – Use the same font styles and colors across your site.

- **Use whitespace effectively** – Avoid clutter by leaving spaces between sections.

- **Use contrast wisely** – Dark text on a light background improves readability.

- **Test on different devices** – Ensure your formatting looks good on mobile and desktop.

By mastering the toolbar and formatting options in Google Sites, you can create a visually appealing and easy-to-navigate website that meets your needs.

2.3 Site Settings and Customization

2.3.1 Changing the Site Name and Logo

When creating a Google Site, personalizing your website by changing the site name and logo is one of the first steps in making it unique and professional. A well-named site with a recognizable logo helps visitors identify your website easily and enhances its credibility. In this section, we will walk through the steps to update your site name and logo, discuss best practices, and provide troubleshooting tips for common issues.

1. Understanding the Site Name and Logo

The **site name** appears in the top left corner of your Google Site and serves as the main identifier of your website. It is visible to all visitors and is an essential branding element. The **logo** is an optional visual element that can replace the text-based site name, giving your site a more polished and professional appearance.

Where Do the Site Name and Logo Appear?

- **The Site Name** appears in the header area and the navigation bar of your site.

- **The Logo** is displayed in the top left corner and is also visible on mobile devices.

- If a logo is added, the site name may still appear in search results and page titles.

Why Customizing Your Site Name and Logo is Important

- **Brand Identity:** A clear site name and logo establish your brand and make your site recognizable.

- **Professional Appearance:** A customized logo makes your website look polished and trustworthy.

- **Easy Navigation:** A meaningful site name helps visitors quickly understand the purpose of your website.

2. Changing the Site Name

Step-by-Step Guide to Updating the Site Name

1. **Open Your Google Site**

   o   Go to Google Sites.

   o   Open the site you want to edit.

2. **Locate the Site Name Field**

   o   In the top left corner, you will see the current site name.

   o   Click on the **text field** where the site name is displayed.

3. **Enter a New Site Name**

   o   Type in the new name for your website.

   o   Press **Enter** or click outside the text box to save the changes.

4. **Check the Site Name Display**

   o   Your new site name will appear in the header and navigation bar.

   o   If you have a custom logo, the site name might not be visible depending on the logo settings.

Best Practices for Choosing a Site Name

- **Keep It Simple and Clear:** The site name should be easy to read and remember.

- **Make It Relevant:** Use a name that reflects the content or purpose of your site.

- **Avoid Special Characters:** Stick to letters and numbers for better compatibility.

- **Use Branding Elements:** If your site represents a business or organization, include the brand name.

3. Adding or Changing the Site Logo

Step-by-Step Guide to Updating the Site Logo

1. **Open Your Google Site**

   o   Navigate to Google Sites and open your site.

2. **Go to Site Settings**

   o In the top right corner, click on the **Settings (⚙️□) icon**.

   o Select **Brand images** from the menu.

   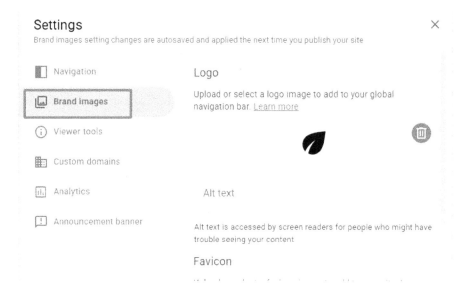

3. **Upload Your Logo**

   o Click on **Upload** to choose an image from your computer.

   o You can also drag and drop an image into the upload area.

4. **Adjust Logo Settings**

   o Once uploaded, Google Sites may provide options to adjust the size and positioning.

   o Make sure the logo fits well within the header area.

5. **Save Your Changes**

   o Click **Done** or exit the settings menu.

     ○   The new logo will now be displayed on your site.

Best Practices for Choosing a Logo

- **Use a Transparent Background:** A PNG file with a transparent background works best.

- **Keep It Simple:** Avoid complex designs that may not display well in small sizes.

- **Ensure High Quality:** A resolution of at least 200x200 pixels is recommended.

- **Make It Recognizable:** Use an image or icon that represents your brand or website theme.

4. Troubleshooting Common Issues

1. Site Name Not Updating

- **Try Refreshing the Page:** Sometimes, changes may take a few seconds to appear.

- **Check for Conflicting Extensions:** Browser extensions may interfere with Google Sites. Try disabling them.

- **Clear Cache and Cookies:** In your browser settings, clear cached data and reload the site.

2. Logo Not Displaying Correctly

- **Check the Image Format:** Use PNG or JPG files for better compatibility.

- **Resize the Image:** If the logo looks distorted, try resizing it to match Google Sites' recommended dimensions.

- **Re-upload the Logo:** If the upload failed, try again with a different file or internet connection.

3. Logo Overlapping Site Name

- **Adjust the Logo Size:** Make sure the logo is not too large.

- **Enable or Disable the Site Name Display:** If needed, turn off the site name to prevent overlap.

5. Enhancing Your Branding with a Custom Favicon

A **favicon** is a small icon displayed in the browser tab next to your site title. Adding a favicon helps your website stand out in bookmarks and tabs.

Steps to Add a Favicon in Google Sites

1. Go to Settings (⚙☐) in Google Sites.

2. Click on "Brand Images" and find the "Favicon" section.

Favicon

Upload or select a favicon image to add to your site. Learn more

Upload   Select

3. Upload a 16x16 or 32x32 PNG file.

4. Save your changes and refresh the site.

Best Practices for Favicons

- **Use a Simple, Recognizable Icon:** Keep it minimal to ensure clarity in small sizes.

- **Maintain Branding Consistency:** Use colors and symbols that align with your site's identity.

- **Optimize for Different Devices:** Test how it looks on desktop and mobile browsers.

6. Summary and Next Steps

In this section, we covered the importance of customizing your Google Site's name and logo, along with a step-by-step guide on how to update them. Here's a quick recap:
✓ Changing the **site name** helps in branding and recognition.

✓ Uploading a **logo** enhances professionalism and visual appeal.

✓ Using a **favicon** improves your site's identity in browser tabs.

✓ Following **best practices** ensures a clean and professional look.

2.3.2 Configuring Navigation Settings

Navigation is one of the most critical aspects of a website. A well-organized navigation system helps visitors find information quickly and efficiently. In Google Sites, configuring navigation settings allows you to control how users move through your site, ensuring a smooth and intuitive experience.

This section will cover:

- Understanding Google Sites' navigation system

- Setting up automatic vs. manual navigation

- Customizing the navigation appearance

- Creating drop-down menus for better organization

- Adding external links to your navigation

- Managing page visibility in navigation

Understanding Google Sites' Navigation System

Google Sites offers a simple but effective navigation system. Unlike traditional website builders that provide complex menu structures, Google Sites keeps navigation straightforward with a default **top navigation bar** (horizontal) or a **side navigation menu** (vertical).

By default, new pages added to your site automatically appear in the navigation menu. However, you can configure the settings to organize and customize the navigation based on your preferences.

Types of Navigation in Google Sites

Google Sites allows two main types of navigation:

1. **Top Navigation**

   o   Displays the menu as a horizontal bar at the top of your site.

   o   Best suited for simple websites with fewer pages.

   o   Provides a clean and modern look.

2. **Side Navigation (Drawer Menu)**

   o   Displays the menu in a collapsible sidebar on the left.

   o   Ideal for sites with many pages.

   o   Works well for mobile users, as it is more compact.

You can switch between these navigation styles based on your site's needs.

Setting Up Automatic vs. Manual Navigation

Automatic Navigation (Default)

By default, Google Sites automatically adds new pages to the navigation menu. This is convenient, but it may not always be ideal, especially if you want to create a custom menu structure.

Manual Navigation (Custom)

Manual navigation gives you full control over which pages appear in the menu and how they are organized. You can remove unnecessary pages, rearrange the order, or create a hierarchical menu structure.

How to Switch Between Automatic and Manual Navigation

1. Open your Google Site in **Edit Mode**.

2. Click on the **Settings (gear icon)** in the top right corner.

3. Select **Navigation** from the options.

4. Under the **Navigation Mode** section, choose between:

   o   **Automatic Navigation** (Google Sites manages the menu for you).

   o   **Manual Navigation** (You control which pages appear and their order).

If you select **Manual Navigation**, you will need to manually add, remove, and organize pages in the navigation bar.

Customizing Navigation Appearance

To ensure your site's navigation aligns with your design preferences, you can customize its appearance.

Changing the Navigation Style

1. Click the **Settings (gear icon)** in the top-right corner.

2. Select **Navigation**.

3. Under **Mode**, choose either:

   o **Top Navigation** (horizontal menu at the top).

   o **Side Navigation** (collapsible sidebar on the left).

Adjusting Navigation Colors and Theme

To make the navigation menu visually appealing, you can customize the colors:

1. Click the **Themes** tab in the right-hand sidebar.

2. Choose a theme that matches your site's branding.

3. Under **Theme Customization**, modify the **Header Background Color**, **Navigation Text Color**, and other style elements.

A well-designed navigation bar enhances readability and user experience.

Creating Drop-Down Menus for Better Organization

If your site has multiple related pages, using drop-down menus (nested menus) helps keep the navigation clean and organized.

Steps to Create a Drop-Down Menu

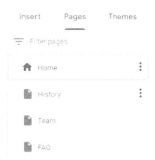

1. Open **Google Sites** in Edit Mode.

2. Click on the **Pages** tab in the right-hand panel.

3. Drag a subpage under a parent page.

4. Release the page when you see a slight indentation, indicating that it is nested under the main page.

For example:

- **About Us**
  - Our Team
  - Mission & Vision
  - Company History

Drop-down menus work best for:

✓ Large websites with multiple sections.

✓ Organizing content logically without overwhelming users.

✓ Reducing clutter in the navigation bar.

Adding External Links to the Navigation Menu

Sometimes, you may want to include links to external websites or resources in your navigation menu. Google Sites allows you to add custom links alongside regular site pages.

How to Add an External Link to Navigation

1. Click on the **Pages** tab in the right-hand panel.

2. Click the **+** (Add Page) button at the bottom.

3. Select **Add Link** instead of creating a new page.

4. Enter the URL and the **Link Title** (e.g., "Company Blog" or "Support Portal").

5. Click **Done** to add it to the navigation menu.

This feature is useful for linking to:

✓ Company or personal blogs.

✓ External documentation or support pages.

✓ Other Google Sites that complement your main site.

Managing Page Visibility in Navigation

In some cases, you may want certain pages to be accessible but not appear in the navigation menu. Google Sites allows you to hide pages from navigation while keeping them publicly accessible.

Steps to Hide a Page from Navigation

1. Open the **Pages** tab in the right panel.

2. Hover over the page you want to hide.

3. Click on the **three dots (⋮) menu**.

4. Select **Hide from navigation**.

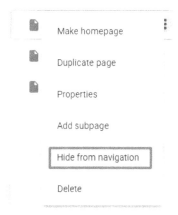

This is useful for:

✓ Pages that serve as landing pages for specific campaigns.

✓ Archived or less frequently used content.

✓ Hidden resources that users access through direct links only.

If you need to make the page visible again, repeat the steps and select **Show in navigation**.

Best Practices for Effective Navigation

To ensure a seamless user experience, follow these best practices:

✓ **Keep Navigation Simple** – Avoid overwhelming users with too many links. Stick to 5-7 primary menu items.

✓ **Use Descriptive Labels** – Menu items should clearly indicate their purpose (e.g., "Contact Us" instead of "Page 3").

✓ **Group Related Pages** – Use drop-down menus to categorize similar content for easier browsing.

✓ **Test Navigation on Different Devices** – Ensure menus work smoothly on desktops, tablets, and mobile phones.

✓ **Review and Update Regularly** – Adjust navigation as your site grows to keep it relevant and user-friendly.

Conclusion

Configuring navigation settings in Google Sites is essential for creating a well-structured and user-friendly website. By choosing the right navigation mode, customizing its appearance, organizing pages efficiently, and managing visibility settings, you can significantly enhance the browsing experience for your visitors.

In the next section, we will explore **Managing Site Permissions**, where you'll learn how to control who can view and edit your site, ensuring the right level of access for different users.

2.3.3 Managing Site Permissions

Google Sites provides a powerful and flexible way to control who can view or edit your website. Managing site permissions effectively ensures that your website remains secure while allowing the right individuals or teams to collaborate. This section will guide you through the various site permission settings, from basic sharing options to advanced access controls.

Understanding Site Permissions in Google Sites

Google Sites permissions are based on Google Workspace's sharing model, similar to Google Drive. There are three main roles you can assign to users:

- **Owner** – Full control over the site, including editing, sharing, and deleting the site.

- **Editor** – Can modify content, add new pages, and adjust settings but cannot delete the site or change ownership.

- **Viewer** – Can only view the site but cannot make any edits.

These roles help define how different users interact with your Google Site, ensuring that only authorized individuals can make changes.

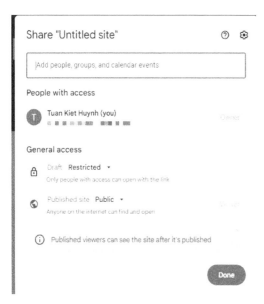

Accessing the Site Permissions Panel

To manage permissions for your Google Site:

1. **Open Your Site** – Navigate to Google Sites and select the site you want to manage.

2. **Click on the "Share" Button** – In the top-right corner, locate the "Share" button (which looks like a person icon with a plus sign).

3. **View the Sharing Settings** – A new window will appear, showing the list of users who currently have access to your site.

From this panel, you can add or remove users, adjust their permissions, and change the site's visibility settings.

Sharing Your Site with Specific People

Google Sites allows you to share your website with specific individuals or groups by entering their email addresses.

Steps to Share Your Site with Specific Users

1. **Open the Share Panel** – Click the "Share" button on the top-right of your Google Site.

2. **Enter Email Addresses** – In the "Add people and groups" field, type the email addresses of individuals you want to share the site with.

3. **Choose a Role** –

   o   Select **Editor** if they should have permission to modify the site.

   o   Select **Viewer** if they should only be able to see the published site.

4. **Notify Users (Optional)** – Check the box for "Notify people" if you want to send an email notification.

5. **Click Send** – The users will receive an email with a link to the site.

This option is useful when working on private company intranets, school projects, or team collaboration websites where access is restricted to a select group.

Making Your Site Public or Private

By default, Google Sites restricts access to only the site owner. However, you can modify the visibility settings based on your needs.

Adjusting Visibility Settings

1. **Go to the Share Panel** – Click "Share" in the top-right corner.

2. **Select the General Access Section** – At the bottom of the window, you will see options for site visibility.

3. **Choose an Access Level:**

   o   **Restricted** – Only people you have explicitly invited can access the site.

   o   **Anyone with the link** – Users with the link can access the site (depending on assigned roles).

   o   **Public** – Anyone on the web can access the published site.

Public vs. Private Sites: When to Use Each Option

Scenario	Best Visibility Option
Internal company site	Restricted (specific users only)
School project shared with classmates	Restricted or "Anyone with the link"
Portfolio or blog for public viewing	Public
Event website for limited guests	"Anyone with the link" (non-public)

If you choose to make your site **public**, be sure that all content is appropriate for a broad audience and that no sensitive information is included.

Managing Editors and Preventing Unauthorized Changes

If multiple users are editing a site, it is important to manage their access levels properly.

Preventing Editors from Changing Site Settings

By default, editors can modify site content and pages. However, to prevent them from changing site settings, follow these steps:

1. Open the **Share** settings.

2. Click on the dropdown next to an **Editor's** name.

3. Select **"Viewer"** or remove their access if needed.

To prevent unwanted edits, it's best to:
✓ Assign **Editor** access only to trusted collaborators.
✓ Keep **Owner** status limited to one or two administrators.

Revoking Access and Managing Permissions Over Time

If a user no longer needs access to your site, you can revoke their permissions.

How to Remove a User's Access

1. Click the **Share** button.

2. Locate the user you want to remove.

3. Click the **drop-down menu** next to their name.

4. Select **Remove Access** (trash icon).

5. Click **Done** to confirm.

Changing the Site Owner

If you need to transfer ownership of a site:

1. Open the **Share** panel.

2. Click the dropdown menu next to the user you want to make the owner.

3. Select **"Make Owner"**.

4. Confirm the ownership transfer.

Once ownership is transferred, you **lose full control** of the site unless the new owner grants you access again.

Collaborating with Teams and Google Groups

Google Sites supports collaboration with **Google Groups**, making it easier to manage permissions for large teams. Instead of adding individual users, you can:

1. Create a Google Group for your team.

2. Add the Google Group's email to the "Share" settings.

3. Assign permissions (Viewer, Editor, or Owner) to the entire group.

This method saves time when managing access for large organizations.

Using Google Sites in Schools and Businesses

For Schools

Teachers can restrict access to only students and faculty by using **Google Workspace for Education** settings.

- **Best Practice:** Set **"Restricted"** access to prevent external users from viewing school materials.

For Businesses

Companies often use Google Sites for internal documentation and project management.

- **Best Practice:** Set **"Anyone with the link"** with **Viewer** access for broad internal distribution while keeping editing rights restricted to select team members.

Best Practices for Managing Site Permissions

- ◆ Use the "Restricted" option for private or sensitive information.
- ◆ Grant Editor access only to those who need it.
- ◆ Use Google Groups for managing large teams.
- ◆ Regularly review and update permissions as needed.
- ◆ Avoid making your site public unless absolutely necessary.

By following these guidelines, you can ensure that your Google Site remains secure while allowing for efficient collaboration.

Conclusion

Managing site permissions in Google Sites is a crucial aspect of website management. Whether you're working on a personal project, a company website, or an educational resource, controlling who can view and edit your site ensures security and efficiency. By understanding permission settings, sharing options, and best practices, you can confidently manage your Google Site while keeping it accessible to the right audience.

CHAPTER III
Designing Your Google Site

3.1 Choosing a Theme and Layout

3.1.1 Built-in Themes and Customization Options

Google Sites offers a range of built-in themes that allow users to create visually appealing and well-structured websites without any coding or design expertise. These themes provide a foundation for site design, including color schemes, typography, and layout settings. By selecting and customizing a theme, you can ensure that your website looks professional and aligns with your personal or organizational brand.

In this section, we will explore the available themes in Google Sites, discuss their features, and guide you through customizing them to suit your needs.

Understanding Built-in Themes in Google Sites

When you create a new site in Google Sites, the platform provides several built-in themes to choose from. Each theme has a predefined style, including fonts, colors, and background settings, making it easy to create a cohesive look without spending too much time on design.

Key Features of Google Sites Themes

1. **Pre-Designed Aesthetics** – Each theme comes with a polished and professional look, reducing the need for extensive customization.

2. **Responsive Design** – Themes automatically adjust to different screen sizes, ensuring a seamless user experience across devices.

3. **Consistency Across Pages** – When you apply a theme, it maintains visual consistency across all pages of your site.

4. **Easy Customization** – While themes provide a starting point, you can modify colors, fonts, and other visual elements to match your preferences.

5. **Accessibility and Readability** – Themes are designed with readability in mind, ensuring text contrasts well with backgrounds.

Choosing the Right Theme for Your Site

The choice of theme depends on the purpose of your website. Google Sites provides a variety of themes suitable for different use cases, such as business websites, portfolios, personal blogs, or educational sites.

Popular Built-in Themes in Google Sites

Google Sites currently offers several themes, including:

- **Simple** – A clean and minimalistic theme with a modern look.

- **Aristotle** – Features bold typography and a structured design, suitable for professional presentations.

- **Diplomat** – Ideal for business and corporate websites, offering a professional and authoritative feel.

- **Vision** – A vibrant and colorful theme perfect for creative projects and portfolios.

- **Impression** – Offers a balance between professional and modern aesthetics, making it a good choice for various purposes.

- **Level** – A structured and professional theme, often used for corporate or educational websites.

Each of these themes has default fonts, colors, and styles, but you can tweak them to better align with your brand or personal preference.

Applying a Theme in Google Sites

To apply a theme in Google Sites, follow these steps:

1. **Open Your Google Site** – Navigate to Google Sites and open your existing site or create a new one.

2. **Go to the Themes Section** – On the right-hand menu, click on **"Themes"** to explore the available options.

3. **Select a Theme** – Click on a theme to apply it to your site. Your changes will be previewed instantly.

4. **Customize the Theme** – Modify colors, fonts, and other elements using the customization options available.

After selecting a theme, you can further personalize it to make your website unique.

Customizing Your Theme

Google Sites allows you to adjust various design elements of a theme to match your personal or business branding.

1. Changing Colors

Each theme comes with a set of default colors, but you can change them to align with your branding.

- Click on the **"Themes"** tab.

- Under the selected theme, look for the **"Color"** section.

- Choose a preset color or click on the **"Custom"** option to select your own.

- Ensure that the chosen colors maintain readability and accessibility.

Best Practices for Choosing Colors:

- Use **contrasting colors** for text and backgrounds to enhance readability.

- Stick to **two or three primary colors** for consistency.

- Consider using your **brand colors** if designing a business or organizational site.

2. Modifying Fonts

Google Sites themes come with preset fonts, but you can change them to match your style.

- Click on the **"Themes"** tab.

- Under the selected theme, navigate to the **"Font Style"** section.

- Choose from available font options (e.g., Classic, Elegant, Modern).

- Test different fonts to ensure they align with your site's tone and readability.

Font Selection Tips:

- Use **simple, easy-to-read fonts** for body text.

- Avoid using too many different fonts on the same site.
- Ensure the font size is large enough for comfortable reading.

3. Adjusting Header Styles

Headers play a crucial role in structuring content. You can customize header styles by:

- Clicking on the **"Themes"** tab.
- Selecting the **"Header Type"** (e.g., Large Banner, Title Only, Cover).
- Adjusting text alignment and size for better visibility.
- Adding a background image to make headers more visually appealing.

4. Adding Background Images

Google Sites allows you to enhance your theme with custom background images.

- Click on the **"Themes"** tab.
- Under the **"Background"** section, upload a new image or select one from Google's library.
- Choose whether the background should appear on all pages or only specific sections.

Tips for Choosing Background Images:

- Use **high-quality images** that don't distract from the content.
- Ensure the image complements the color scheme.
- Avoid overly complex images that make text hard to read.

Example: Customizing a Theme for a Business Website

Let's say you are creating a **corporate website** for a consulting firm. Here's how you might customize the **Diplomat** theme:

1. **Choose a Dark Blue Primary Color** – This conveys professionalism and trust.
2. **Use a Clean, Sans-Serif Font** – A font like Open Sans ensures readability.

3. **Adjust the Header to a Large Banner** – This allows the business logo to stand out.

4. **Add a Subtle Background Image** – A blurred office image creates a professional feel.

By making these changes, you can ensure that your Google Site reflects your company's identity while maintaining a polished appearance.

Final Thoughts

Built-in themes in Google Sites provide an excellent starting point for designing a professional-looking website. While they offer predefined styles, customization options allow users to tailor their sites to better fit their needs. By carefully selecting colors, fonts, and layout settings, you can create a unique and visually appealing website with ease.

In the next section, we will explore how to **adjust colors and fonts** in greater detail, helping you refine the look of your site even further.

3.1.2 Adjusting Colors and Fonts

Design plays a crucial role in creating an engaging and professional-looking website. Google Sites offers built-in customization options that allow you to adjust colors and fonts easily without requiring any coding or design expertise. This section will guide you through the process of customizing your website's colors and typography to enhance readability, aesthetics, and branding consistency.

1. Understanding the Importance of Colors and Fonts

Before diving into the customization process, it's essential to understand why colors and fonts matter in web design:

The Role of Colors in Web Design

- **Brand Identity:** Colors help reinforce your brand's identity. Consistent use of colors across your website creates a strong and recognizable presence.

- **Readability and Accessibility:** Poor color choices can make text difficult to read or cause eye strain. High contrast between text and background enhances readability.

- **User Experience:** Colors can evoke emotions and influence how visitors interact with your site. For example, blue conveys trust, while red signals urgency.

- **Navigation and Focus:** Using different colors for buttons, links, and call-to-actions (CTAs) helps guide users through your website effectively.

The Role of Fonts in Web Design

- **Legibility:** Choosing clear and readable fonts ensures that visitors can easily consume your content.

- **Consistency:** Using a consistent font style across headings, body text, and buttons provides a polished look.

- **Personality and Tone:** Fonts can set the tone of your website. Serif fonts (like Times New Roman) appear formal, while sans-serif fonts (like Arial) look modern and minimalistic.

2. Adjusting Colors in Google Sites

Changing the Theme Color

Google Sites offers predefined themes with color schemes that you can modify to match your brand or personal style.

Steps to Change the Theme Color:

1. Open your Google Site in **Edit Mode**.

2. Click on the **Themes** tab in the right-hand panel.

3. Select a theme that closely matches your preferred design.

4. Under **Theme Options**, you will see different **Color Schemes** available.

5. Choose a preset color or click the **+ Custom** button to pick a custom color.

6. Adjust the **primary color** to set the dominant hue for headers, buttons, and other key elements.

Tip: Choose a color scheme that aligns with your brand identity. If you're unsure, use an online color palette generator like Coolors or Adobe Color.

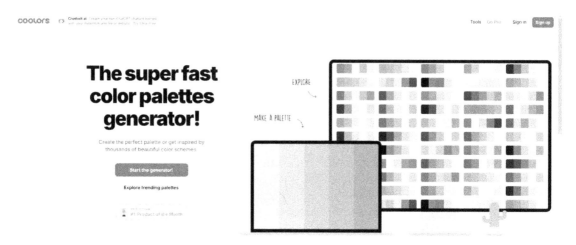

Customizing Background Colors

Google Sites allows you to change the background color of different sections to create contrast and visual hierarchy.

Steps to Change Background Colors:

1. Select the **section** you want to customize.

2. Click the **Palette Icon** on the left of the section.

3. Choose between:

   o **Default** (matches the theme)

   o **Emphasis 1 & 2** (slightly different shades)

   o **Image Background** (upload a custom background)

4. Click **Customize** to select a specific color.

Tip: Avoid using overly bright or dark colors for backgrounds, as they can make text difficult to read.

3. Adjusting Fonts in Google Sites

3.1 Changing the Default Font Style

Google Sites allows you to change fonts for **headings, subheadings, and body text**.

Steps to Change Fonts:

1. Open your Google Site in **Edit Mode**.

2. Click on the **Themes** tab on the right panel.

3. Scroll down to the **Font Style** section.

4. Choose from available font styles:

   o **Classic** (default fonts for a simple look)

   o **Modern** (sleek and contemporary)

   o **Decorative** (stylized fonts for artistic designs)

   o **Custom** (choose your preferred Google Fonts)

5. If using **Custom**, select your preferred fonts for:

   o **Title** (used in headers and page titles)

   o **Heading** (used for section titles)

   o **Body** (used for normal text)

Tip: Stick to a maximum of **two different fonts**—one for headings and one for body text—to maintain readability and consistency.

3.2 Adjusting Font Sizes

Google Sites automatically adjusts font sizes based on the selected style, but you can modify them manually:

Steps to Adjust Font Sizes:

1. Highlight the text you want to resize.

2. Use the formatting toolbar to select:

   o **Title** (largest size)

   o **Heading** (medium size)

   o **Subheading** (smaller heading)

   o **Normal text** (default size)

3. If you need finer adjustments, use the **More Fonts** option under Custom Themes.

Tip: Ensure your font sizes are large enough for mobile readability. Body text should be at least **16px** for optimal reading.

4. Best Practices for Using Colors and Fonts in Google Sites

Choosing a Professional Color Scheme

- Follow the 60-30-10 rule:

  o **60%** should be the primary color (background or dominant elements).

  o **30%** should be a secondary color (sections, highlights).

  o **10%** should be an accent color (buttons, links, CTAs).

- Use complementary colors that enhance readability.

- Check accessibility to ensure text has enough contrast against the background.

Selecting the Right Font Combination

- Pair a serif and sans-serif font for contrast (e.g., Playfair Display for headings and Roboto for body text).

- Avoid script or overly decorative fonts for body text as they reduce readability.

- Ensure font consistency across different sections of your site.

Maintaining Readability and Aesthetics

- Avoid using too many colors or fonts—keep your design clean and professional.

- Test your site on different devices to ensure fonts and colors look good on both desktops and mobile screens.

- Stick to web-safe fonts to avoid inconsistencies across different browsers.

Conclusion

Customizing colors and fonts in Google Sites is an essential step in making your website visually appealing, readable, and aligned with your brand identity. By using the built-in customization tools effectively, you can create a well-structured and aesthetically pleasing site without any design experience.

Key Takeaways:

✓ Use colors strategically to guide users and maintain consistency.
✓ Choose readable, web-safe fonts for headings and body text.
✓ Test your website on multiple devices to ensure good readability.
✓ Maintain a balance between aesthetics and accessibility.

By mastering these color and font customization techniques, you can design a polished, user-friendly Google Site that effectively communicates your message. In the next section, we will explore **how to add and format text effectively** to improve content presentation.

3.1.3 Using Section Layouts for Better Structure

Google Sites provides an intuitive way to organize content through **section layouts**. These layouts help structure your website visually, making it more engaging and user-friendly. Whether you're building a business site, an educational portal, or a personal blog, properly using section layouts can enhance readability, improve navigation, and create a professional appearance.

This section will cover:

- What section layouts are and why they matter

- How to insert and customize section layouts

- Best practices for using section layouts effectively

What Are Section Layouts?

Section layouts in Google Sites are pre-designed content blocks that help you organize text, images, and multimedia in a structured way. Instead of manually aligning elements on the page, you can use these built-in layouts to quickly format your content.

Google Sites offers several section layout options, including:

1. **Single-column layout** – A full-width section for content that requires focus, such as headlines or large images.

2. **Two-column layout** – A balanced section with content split into two equal parts, great for comparisons.

3. **Three-column layout** – Ideal for listing features, services, or displaying multiple content pieces in a row.

4. **Image-focused layout** – A section where images dominate, often paired with text descriptions.

5. **Text-and-image combinations** – Sections that allow images to be placed next to or above text for better content presentation.

Using these layouts strategically can help make your website **more visually appealing, easy to navigate, and engaging for visitors**.

How to Insert and Customize Section Layouts

Step 1: Inserting a Section Layout

To add a section layout in Google Sites, follow these steps:

1. Open your **Google Site** in editing mode.

2. Navigate to the page where you want to insert a layout.

3. Click on the **"Insert"** tab from the right-side menu.

4. Scroll down to the **"Content Blocks"** section.

5. Choose from one of the available layout options and click to add it to your page.

6. The selected layout will appear on the page as a placeholder with content areas ready for editing.

Step 2: Adding Content to the Layout

Once the section layout is inserted, you can begin adding content:

- Click on a **text placeholder** to start typing or paste text.

- Click on an **image placeholder** to upload an image, select one from Google Drive, or embed an external image.

- If your layout includes multiple columns, you can add different types of content in each column, such as videos, buttons, or embedded documents.

Step 3: Customizing the Layout

Google Sites allows some customization to improve the appearance and functionality of your sections:

- **Resize Columns:** Drag the divider between columns to adjust their width.

- **Background Customization:** Click the section and choose a background color, image, or Google Sites' built-in **"Emphasis"** options to highlight content.

- **Rearrange Sections:** Drag sections up or down the page to change the order of content.

- **Duplicate Sections:** If you want to reuse a layout, you can copy and paste the entire section.

By customizing layouts effectively, you can ensure that your site looks **professional, well-structured, and visually engaging**.

A brief description of the project's mission

Best Practices for Using Section Layouts Effectively

1. Keep Content Organized and Readable

- Use **single-column layouts** for headlines, introductions, or call-to-action sections.

- Use **multi-column layouts** to break up long paragraphs and make information more digestible.

2. Balance Text and Visual Elements

- Avoid text-heavy sections—mix in images, icons, or videos to keep visitors engaged.

- If using an **image-focused layout**, ensure that images are high quality and relevant.

3. Use White Space Wisely

- Don't overcrowd sections with too much content.

- Leave enough spacing between sections to create a clean and readable design.

4. Align Content with Your Website's Purpose

- If you're building a **business website**, use structured layouts to present services or team members clearly.

- For an **educational site**, organize sections logically to improve information flow.

- For a **portfolio site**, use image-based layouts to highlight work samples effectively.

Conclusion

Section layouts are one of the most powerful tools in Google Sites for structuring content in a visually appealing way. By using the right layout for each type of content, customizing sections effectively, and following best practices, you can create a website that is not only attractive but also **user-friendly and engaging**.

Now that you've learned how to use section layouts, the next step is to add and format text to enhance the clarity and readability of your content. In the next section, we'll dive into **how to use text boxes, apply styles, and organize information using bullet points and tables.**

3.2 Adding and Formatting Text

3.2.1 Using Text Boxes and Headings

One of the essential elements of any website is text. Text allows you to communicate your message, provide instructions, share information, and engage with visitors. In Google Sites, adding and formatting text is simple and intuitive, thanks to the drag-and-drop editor. This section will guide you through using text boxes, inserting headings, and optimizing your text for readability and visual appeal.

Understanding Text Boxes in Google Sites

What is a Text Box?

A text box is a flexible content container that allows you to insert, edit, and format text anywhere on your page. Unlike traditional website builders that require manual coding, Google Sites provides an easy-to-use text editor that supports rich text formatting, alignment, and customization.

Text boxes in Google Sites can be used for:

- Titles and headings

- Paragraphs and descriptions

- Lists and bullet points

- Quotes and call-to-action messages

Each text box can be positioned, resized, and styled independently, allowing you to create visually appealing and well-structured content.

Adding a Text Box to Your Google Site

Method 1: Using the Insert Menu

1. Open your Google Site in **Edit Mode**.

2. Navigate to the section where you want to add text.

3. Click on the **"Insert"** tab in the right-side panel.

4. Select **"Text box"** from the options.

5. A new text box will appear on your page. Click inside the box to start typing.

Method 2: Clicking on the Page

1. Hover your mouse over an empty space on your site.

2. Click directly on the page where you want to insert text.

3. A text box will appear automatically.

Once you have added a text box, you can move, resize, and customize it according to your needs.

Formatting Text in a Text Box

After adding a text box, you can format the text using the toolbar that appears above the text box. The toolbar includes options for:

- **Bold (B)**: Makes text stand out by thickening it.

- **Italic (I)**: Slants text to emphasize certain words.

- **Underline (U)**: Adds a line below text to highlight important sections.

- **Text alignment**: Aligns text to the left, center, or right.

- **Font size**: Adjusts the size of the text for better readability.

- **Lists**: Creates numbered or bulleted lists.

- **Links**: Inserts hyperlinks to other pages or external websites.

Step-by-Step Formatting Example

1. Select the text you want to format by clicking and dragging over it.

2. Use the toolbar to apply the desired formatting options.

3. Click outside the text box to save changes.

Using Headings in Google Sites

Why Use Headings?

Headings are an essential part of structuring your content. They help users quickly scan your page and improve the overall readability. Headings also assist in organizing information and making the content more engaging.

Google Sites provides three levels of text formatting:

- **Title** – The largest text style, used for main page titles.

- **Heading** – A slightly smaller style, suitable for section headings.

- **Subheading** – A medium-sized text style for subsections.

- **Normal text** – The default size for body content.

How to Insert a Heading

1. Click inside a text box.

2. Select the **text style dropdown menu** from the toolbar.

3. Choose **Title, Heading, or Subheading**, depending on your needs.

Example of Proper Heading Structure

If you're creating a page about "Healthy Eating Tips," you can structure it as follows:

Title: Healthy Eating Tips for a Better Life
Heading: 1. The Importance of a Balanced Diet
Subheading: 1.1 Nutrients Your Body Needs
Normal Text: Explanation and details go here.

Using headings effectively makes your content easier to navigate and improves user engagement.

Aligning and Positioning Text Boxes

Google Sites allows you to position text boxes anywhere on your page. To move a text box:

1. Click on the text box.

2. Hover over the **six dots** on the left side of the box.

3. Drag and drop the text box to a new position.

You can also resize the text box by dragging the edges. This feature helps in arranging text neatly and maintaining a professional layout.

Using Multiple Text Boxes for Better Layout

Instead of using one large text block, you can break content into multiple smaller text boxes. This technique helps in organizing content visually and improves readability.

Example:

✅ **Good Layout:**

- Separate text into small, readable sections.

- Use different text boxes for headings and content.

- Align text neatly using the grid layout.

✖ **Bad Layout:**

- Using one long paragraph without breaks.

- Mixing multiple ideas in a single text box.

- Not aligning text properly, making it hard to read.

Best Practices for Using Text in Google Sites

1. Keep Paragraphs Short and Concise

Avoid long walls of text. Break up content into short paragraphs for better readability.

2. Use Headings for Organization

Clearly define sections using headings and subheadings.

3. Use Bold and Italics to Emphasize Important Information

Highlight key points by making them bold or italicized.

4. Use Bullet Points for Lists

Make content easier to scan by using bullet points instead of long sentences.

5. Ensure Text Contrast for Readability

Choose a color scheme that provides good contrast between text and background.

6. Maintain Consistent Formatting

Use a uniform font style and size across your site for a professional look.

Conclusion

Using text boxes and headings effectively in Google Sites enhances the readability and visual appeal of your website. By following best practices and structuring content properly, you can create a website that is both informative and user-friendly.

In the next section, we will explore more advanced formatting techniques, including applying styles, organizing content with bullet points, and structuring text for better engagement.

3.2.2 Applying Styles and Formatting Options

When designing your Google Site, properly formatting your text is crucial for readability, organization, and user engagement. Google Sites offers a range of styling and formatting options that allow you to enhance the appearance of your content, making it more visually appealing and easier to navigate. In this section, we will explore different formatting tools available in Google Sites and best practices for applying them effectively.

1. Understanding Text Styles in Google Sites

Google Sites provides several pre-defined text styles that help maintain consistency across your website. These styles include:

- **Title** – The largest text size, used for the main heading of your page.

- **Heading** – A slightly smaller size, used for section headers.

- **Subheading** – A medium-sized text, used for sub-sections under a heading.

- **Normal Text** – The default paragraph text for body content.

- **Small Text** – A reduced-size font for captions, footnotes, or disclaimers.

Using these styles correctly helps ensure a structured and professional-looking page.

Setting Text Styles

To apply a text style in Google Sites:

1. Click on the text box containing your content.

2. Highlight the text you want to format.

3. Click on the dropdown menu labeled "Normal text" in the toolbar.

4. Select one of the predefined styles (Title, Heading, Subheading, etc.).

By applying text styles consistently, you create a hierarchy of information that enhances readability and usability.

---

2. Adjusting Font Sizes and Colors

In addition to predefined styles, Google Sites allows you to adjust text size and color to match your design preferences.

Changing Font Size

Although Google Sites does not offer complete font size customization (such as pixel-based sizing), it provides a few options for making text larger or smaller.

To adjust the text size:

1. Click inside a text box.

2. Select the text you want to modify.

3. Click on the formatting toolbar and choose between "Normal Text" or "Small Text" for paragraph content.

4. Use headings (Heading, Subheading) for a structured and visually distinct format.

Changing Text Color

You can change text color to emphasize certain words or improve contrast for readability.

To change the color of your text:

1. Select the text you want to modify.

2. Click the **Text Color** icon (represented by an "A" with a color underline) in the formatting toolbar.

3. Choose a color from the available options or click **Custom** to pick a specific shade.

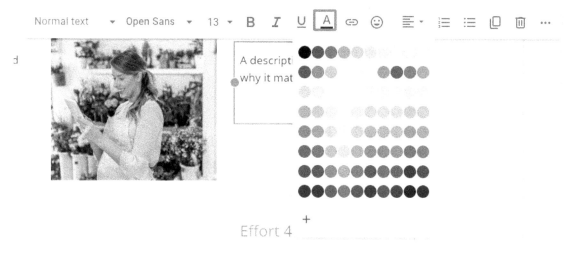

Best Practices for Using Colors:

- Use dark text on a light background and vice versa to ensure readability.

- Stick to a limited color palette for a professional look.

- Avoid using too many different colors, which can make your site appear unstructured or chaotic.

3. Applying Bold, Italics, and Underline

Text emphasis is an essential tool in web design, helping draw attention to key points and improve content scanning.

Making Text Bold

Bold text is useful for highlighting important words, section titles, or key points.

To bold text:

1. Select the text.

2. Click the Bold (B) icon in the formatting toolbar or press Ctrl + B (Cmd + B on Mac).

Using Italics for Emphasis

Italics are commonly used for quotes, foreign words, or subtle emphasis.

To italicize text:

1. Select the text.

2. Click the Italic (I) icon or press Ctrl + I (Cmd + I on Mac).

Underlining Important Text

Underlining is often used for headings, important notes, or links.

To underline text:

1. Select the text.

2. Click the Underline (U) icon or press Ctrl + U (Cmd + U on Mac).

🔲 Avoid overusing bold, italics, or underline, as excessive emphasis can make text harder to read rather than easier!

4. Aligning and Formatting Paragraphs

Google Sites allows you to align text in different ways for better content presentation.

Aligning Text

You can align your text to the left, center, or right.

To change text alignment:

1.   Select the text you want to align.

2.   Click on the **Alignment** icon in the toolbar.

3.   Choose from **Left, Center, or Right alignment**.

✦ **Tip:** Left-aligned text is the easiest to read for most users, while center-aligned text is best used for titles or call-to-action sections.

Adjusting Line Spacing

While Google Sites does not allow full control over line spacing, adding extra spacing manually can improve readability.

To create a line break without starting a new paragraph:

•   Press **Shift + Enter** instead of just Enter.

For bullet points or numbered lists, spacing is automatically optimized for clarity.

5. Using Lists for Organized Content

Lists help break down information in a structured and digestible way.

5.1 Creating Bullet Lists

To add a bulleted list:

1. Click inside a text box.

2. Select the **Bulleted List** icon in the toolbar.

3. Type each point and press **Enter** to create a new bullet.

Example:

- First point

- Second point

- Third point

5.2 Creating Numbered Lists

To add a numbered list:

1. Click inside a text box.

2. Select the **Numbered List** icon.

3. Type each point and press **Enter** to create the next item in the sequence.

Example:

1. First item

2. Second item

3. Third item

📌 **Tip:** Use numbered lists for step-by-step instructions and bullet points for general information.

6. Adding Hyperlinks for Navigation

Hyperlinks allow users to navigate between different pages of your site or external resources.

Linking to External Websites

To insert a hyperlink:

1. Select the text you want to hyperlink.

2. Click the **Insert Link** icon (⚭) in the toolbar.

3. Enter the **URL** and click **Apply**.

Linking to Internal Pages

To link to another page on your Google Site:

1. Highlight the text.

2. Click the **Insert Link** icon.

3. Choose a page from the available site pages.

✦ **Tip:** Use descriptive link text like *"Learn More About Our Services"* instead of generic text like *"Click Here"*.

7. Best Practices for Formatting Text in Google Sites

1. **Maintain a Clear Hierarchy** – Use headings and subheadings to organize content logically.

2. **Limit Font Styles** – Avoid using too many different text styles in one page.

3. **Keep Text Readable** – Use adequate contrast between text and background.

4. **Use Emphasis Sparingly** – Only bold or italicize important information.

5. **Organize with Lists** – Use bullet points and numbered lists for easy scanning.

6. **Ensure Mobile-Friendly Formatting** – Preview your site on different devices to check readability.

Conclusion

Applying styles and formatting options in Google Sites is essential for creating visually appealing and structured content. By utilizing text styles, adjusting colors and alignment, and incorporating hyperlinks and lists, you can make your site both engaging and professional.

In the next section, we will explore how to add and format images and multimedia content to further enhance your Google Site.

3.2.3 Organizing Content with Bullet Points and Tables

Clear and well-structured content is essential for creating an engaging and easy-to-navigate website. Google Sites provides built-in tools to help you organize your text using **bullet points and tables**, making your content more readable, scannable, and visually appealing. This section will guide you through the process of using these formatting options effectively to improve the structure and clarity of your Google Site.

1. Why Use Bullet Points and Tables?

The Benefits of Bullet Points

Bullet points help break up large blocks of text, making your content easier to read and understand. Here are some key benefits:

- Enhanced readability – Visitors can quickly scan information without reading long paragraphs.

- Better organization – Lists help categorize information logically.

- Improved engagement – Users are more likely to stay on your site if the content is structured well.

- Effective call-to-actions – You can highlight important points or instructions.

The Benefits of Tables

Tables are useful when you need to display structured data in a way that is easy to compare. They offer:

- Clear data presentation – Helps in organizing structured information such as pricing, schedules, or feature comparisons.

- Logical grouping – Allows users to quickly locate relevant data.

- Improved accessibility – Aids in presenting numerical data, schedules, and structured information more efficiently than plain text.

Now, let's explore how to use these tools in Google Sites.

---

2. How to Add and Use Bullet Points in Google Sites

Inserting Bullet Points

Adding bullet points in Google Sites is simple and follows a similar process to Google Docs.

Step-by-Step Guide

1. Select the text box – Click on an existing text box or insert a new one.

2. Highlight the text – If you already have a list of items, highlight them.

3. Click the bullet point icon – In the toolbar, click the bullet list button (●) to format your text into a list.

4. Adjust list settings – You can press "Enter" to add a new bullet or press "Tab" to create a sub-bullet.

Creating a Numbered List

If you prefer a structured sequence, you can use numbered lists instead of bullets. The steps are the same as above, but you need to click the numbered list icon (1, 2, 3) instead of the bullet list button.

Customizing Bullet Points

While Google Sites does not offer extensive customization options for bullet points, you can make your lists more visually appealing by:

- Using bold or italic text for key points.

- Adding colors to differentiate list items.

- Using indentation to create sub-lists (pressing "Tab" moves an item to a sub-level).

Best Practices for Using Bullet Points

- Keep each bullet concise – Aim for short, clear points (ideally one sentence).

- Maintain parallel structure – Start each bullet with the same type of word (e.g., all verbs or all nouns).

- Use bullets instead of long paragraphs when listing multiple ideas.

- Avoid excessive bullet points – If a list is too long, consider breaking it into sections.

3. How to Add and Use Tables in Google Sites

Tables help organize information into structured rows and columns. They are useful for presenting schedules, product comparisons, and other structured data.

Inserting a Table in Google Sites

Unlike Google Docs, Google Sites does not have a built-in table tool in the text editor, but you can still add tables using Google Docs or Google Sheets.

Method 1: Adding a Table via Google Docs

1. **Open Google Docs** and create a table by clicking **Insert > Table**.

2. **Format the table** with headers, colors, and styles.

3. **Copy the table** by selecting it and pressing **Ctrl + C (Cmd + C on Mac)**.

4. **Paste it into your Google Site** where you want the table to appear.

Method 2: Adding a Table via Google Sheets

If your data is numerical or requires calculations, Google Sheets is a better option.

1. **Create a table in Google Sheets** with your data.

2. **Format the table** with bold headers and cell colors.

3. **Embed the table** by clicking **Insert > Embed > Google Sheets** in Google Sites.

4. **Adjust visibility settings** so visitors can view the data without needing access permissions.

3.2 Customizing Tables in Google Sites

Once your table is added, you can:

- **Adjust column widths** to ensure data fits properly.

- **Use color-coding** to highlight important sections.
- **Add images inside table cells** (if inserted via Google Docs).

3.3 When to Use a Table Instead of Bullet Points

Content Type	Best Format
Listing general points	Bullet points
Step-by-step instructions	Numbered list
Data comparison (e.g., pricing plans)	Table
Schedules or event details	Table
Multiple categories of items	Table

4. Advanced Techniques for Organizing Content

4.1 Using a Combination of Lists and Tables

In some cases, using both bullet points and tables together can improve readability.

- Use **tables** for structured data.
- Use **bullet points** to summarize key takeaways.

Example:

Plan Type	Features
Basic	- Free hosting - Limited customization
Premium	- Custom domain - Advanced analytics

4.2 Embedding Interactive Tables

If your website needs **dynamic content**, consider embedding Google Sheets. This allows users to interact with your data directly from the site.

Steps to Embed a Google Sheet

1. Open Google Sheets and **format your data**.

2. Click **File > Share > Publish to the web**.

3. Copy the embed link and **paste it into Google Sites** using the Embed tool.

---

5. Summary and Best Practices

Key Takeaways

- **Use bullet points** for short, scannable content.

- **Use numbered lists** for step-by-step instructions.

- **Use tables** to organize structured information effectively.

- **Combine bullet points and tables** for better visual hierarchy.

Common Mistakes to Avoid

✕ Using too many bullet points in a single list.
✕ Creating tables without clear column headers.
✕ Failing to test how tables display on mobile devices.

By effectively using bullet points and tables, you can enhance readability, improve user experience, and ensure your Google Site delivers information clearly and efficiently.

3.3 Adding Images and Multimedia

Multimedia elements such as images, videos, and interactive content play a crucial role in making a website visually appealing and engaging. Google Sites provides several ways to incorporate images into your site, ensuring a seamless and user-friendly experience. This section will focus on **uploading and inserting images**, covering different methods, best practices, and customization options.

3.3.1 Uploading and Inserting Images

See what's new with the Thomsons

Family Photos

Check out some of our favorite snapshots over the years! Our kids sure love to explore.

Stories & Updates

Have we told you what's going on recently? Read about some of our favorite family adventures and find out whats new.

Parenting Tips

Through trial and error learned a few things along the way. Blowouts, bandages, and boredom... it never stops! Have a look at some helpful things we've discovered.

Adding images to your Google Site can enhance its design, make content more visually appealing, and provide better communication of ideas. Whether you want to upload images from your computer, insert them from Google Drive, or use web-based images, Google Sites offers various ways to achieve this.

Why Use Images on Your Google Site?

Before diving into the technical aspects, let's explore the key benefits of using images on your website:

- **Visual Appeal:** Images make your site more engaging and break up long blocks of text.

- **Improved Communication:** A picture can convey complex ideas quickly and effectively.

- **Professional Look:** High-quality images enhance the credibility and aesthetics of your site.

- **Better Engagement:** Visitors are more likely to stay on your page if there are relevant visuals.

Now, let's explore the different methods of uploading and inserting images into your Google Site.

Uploading Images from Your Computer

The most straightforward method to insert images is uploading them directly from your computer. This method allows you to use custom images, graphics, or photographs stored on your device.

Steps to Upload an Image from Your Computer:

1. **Open Your Google Site:**

   o Navigate to Google Sites and open the site you want to edit.

2. **Select the Section Where You Want to Insert the Image:**

   o Click on the page or section where the image should appear.

3. **Click the "Insert" Panel:**

   o On the right-hand sidebar, click **"Insert"** to open the content menu.

4. **Choose the "Images" Option:**

   o Click **"Images"** and select **"Upload"** to browse your files.

5. **Select and Upload the Image:**

   o   Locate the image file on your computer and click **"Open"** to upload it to your site.

6. **Resize and Adjust Placement (Optional):**

   o   Once the image is uploaded, you can drag it to reposition, resize it using the corner handles, or align it within the section.

Inserting Images from Google Drive

If your images are stored in Google Drive, you can easily add them to your Google Site. This is useful for shared images, frequently updated graphics, or collaborative projects.

Steps to Insert an Image from Google Drive:

1. **Click "Insert" on the Sidebar**

   o   Open the right-side menu and select **"Images."**

2. **Choose "Select from Drive":**

   o   Click **"Select from Drive"** to open your Google Drive.

3. **Find and Select the Image:**

   o   Navigate to the folder where your image is stored.

   o   Click on the image file and select **"Insert."**

4. **Adjust and Position the Image (Optional):**

   o   Once inserted, resize and move the image as needed.

5. **Set Permissions for Visibility (If Necessary):**

   ○ Ensure the image is set to **"Anyone with the link can view"** if you want public access.

Advantages of Using Google Drive:

✓☐ Easy access to shared images.

✓☐ Cloud storage prevents accidental deletion.

✓☐ Direct updates if the image is replaced in Drive.

Adding Images via URL (Web-Based Images)

Google Sites allows you to add images from the web using a direct URL. This method is ideal for embedding images from an external source, such as royalty-free image websites or your own online hosting service.

Steps to Insert an Image Using a URL:

1. Open the Insert Panel and Click "Images"

2. Select "By URL"

3. Paste the Image URL:

   ○ Copy the direct link to the image (ensure it ends in .jpg, .png, .gif, etc.).

4. Click "Insert" to Add the Image

5. Resize and Position the Image as Needed

Important Considerations:

✓☐ Make sure the image is **publicly accessible.**

✓☐ Avoid linking to copyrighted images without permission.

✓☐ Web-hosted images may **break** if the source changes.

Using Google Search to Find Images

Google Sites allows you to search for images directly within its interface. This is helpful for quickly finding royalty-free and Creative Commons images.

Steps to Insert an Image via Google Search:

1. Click "Insert" and Select "Images"

2. Choose "Search"

3. Enter Keywords to Find an Image

4. Select an Image and Click "Insert"

5. Adjust the Image as Needed

Benefits of Using Google Search for Images:

✓☐ Quick and easy way to find relevant visuals.

✓☐ Filters images that are free to use (always double-check licenses).

✓☐ Saves time compared to manually searching in a separate tab.

Customizing and Formatting Images

After inserting an image, you can customize it to better fit your website's design.

Resizing and Positioning

- Drag the corner handles to resize while maintaining proportions.

- Use the blue alignment grid to center the image.

- Click and drag to reposition within the section.

Cropping and Adjusting Aspect Ratio

Google Sites doesn't offer built-in cropping, but you can:

- Edit the image before uploading.

- Use Google Drawings to modify images before inserting them.

Adding Captions and Alternative Text (Alt Text)

For accessibility and SEO purposes, you should add alt text.

1. Click on the Image

2. Select "Alt Text" from the Options Menu

3. Enter a Description of the Image

4. Click "Apply"

Linking Images to Other Pages or Websites

You can turn an image into a clickable link.

1. Click the Image

2. Click the "Insert Link" Icon

3. Enter a URL or Select a Page Within the Site

4. Click "Apply"

Best Practices for Using Images on Google Sites

✓ Use High-Quality Images: Avoid pixelated or stretched images.
✓ Optimize File Sizes: Large images slow down site loading speed.
✓ Maintain Consistency: Use similar styles for a professional look.
✓ Respect Copyright Rules: Only use images you have permission for.
✓ Ensure Accessibility: Add alt text for visually impaired users.

Conclusion

Uploading and inserting images is an essential step in designing an engaging and professional-looking Google Site. Whether you upload images from your computer, use Google Drive, search the web, or embed images via URL, Google Sites provides a variety of tools to help you create a visually appealing website. By following best practices and customizing images effectively, you can enhance your site's usability and aesthetic appeal.

In the next section, we will explore **embedding multimedia content**, including videos and interactive elements, to further enhance your Google Site.

3.3.2 Embedding YouTube Videos

Videos can be a powerful tool to enhance the effectiveness of your Google Site. Whether you want to include tutorial videos, promotional content, educational materials, or engaging multimedia presentations, embedding YouTube videos in your Google Site can improve user experience and make your content more dynamic.

This section will guide you through the process of embedding YouTube videos into your Google Site, explain various customization options, and provide best practices to ensure seamless integration.

1. Why Embed YouTube Videos in Google Sites?

Embedding YouTube videos in your Google Site can provide several benefits:

- **Enhances User Engagement** – Videos make content more interactive and visually appealing.

- **Reduces Page Clutter** – Instead of filling your website with long text explanations, a video can summarize complex topics efficiently.

- **Improves Learning and Retention** – Studies show that people retain more information through video content than text alone.

- **Seamless Google Integration** – Since YouTube is a Google product, embedding videos in Google Sites is simple and requires no additional software.

- **Saves Storage Space** – Uploading videos directly to Google Sites isn't possible, but embedding them from YouTube avoids storage issues.

2. Methods for Embedding a YouTube Video in Google Sites

Google Sites provides a built-in method to embed YouTube videos quickly. There are two primary ways to do this:

1. **Using the YouTube Insert Tool** – The simplest and most direct method.

2. **Using the Embed URL Option** – Allows for embedding YouTube videos with iframe code.

2.1 Using the YouTube Insert Tool

This is the recommended method for embedding YouTube videos in Google Sites as it is the most user-friendly and requires no coding.

Steps to Embed a YouTube Video Using the Insert Tool:

1. Open **Google Sites** and navigate to the page where you want to add the video.

2. Click on the section where you want to insert the video.

3. In the right-hand panel, select **"Insert"** → **"YouTube"**.

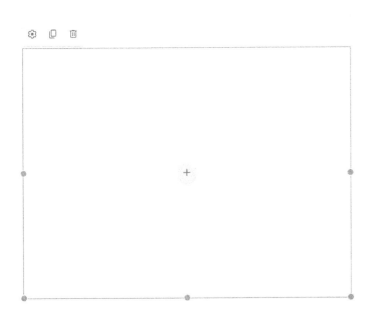

4. A pop-up window will appear. Use the search bar to find your video, or paste the **YouTube URL** directly.

5. Select the desired video and click **"Insert"**.

6. Adjust the size and position of the video by dragging its corners or repositioning it within the page.

2.2 Using the Embed URL Option

This method is useful if you need more control over how the video appears on your site.

Steps to Embed a YouTube Video Using the Embed Code:

1. Open **YouTube** and go to the video you want to embed.

2. Click on **"Share"** below the video.

3. Select **"Embed"** from the sharing options.

4. Copy the **iframe embed code** provided by YouTube.

5. Open **Google Sites**, navigate to the desired page, and click on the section where you want to embed the video.

6. In the right-hand panel, click **"Embed"**, then choose the **"Embed Code"** option.

7. Paste the copied iframe code into the box and click **"Insert"**.

8. Resize or reposition the video as needed.

---

3. Customizing Your Embedded YouTube Video

After embedding a YouTube video in Google Sites, you can customize its appearance and functionality.

Adjusting Video Size and Position

- Click on the embedded video to reveal resizing handles.

- Drag the corners to resize the video while maintaining its aspect ratio.

- Use alignment guides to center or align the video within the content section.

Setting Start and End Times

If you want the video to start or end at a specific timestamp:

1. Open **YouTube** and navigate to the video.

2. Click **"Share"**, then **"Embed"**.

3. In the embed code, modify the URL by adding parameters:

   o ?start=30 (starts at 30 seconds)

      o   &end=120 (ends at 120 seconds)

4. Paste the modified embed code into Google Sites.

Disabling Related Videos

By default, YouTube shows suggested videos after your embedded video finishes playing. To prevent this:

1. In the YouTube embed code, add ?rel=0 at the end of the video URL.

2. Paste the updated code into Google Sites.

Enabling Autoplay and Looping

- To make the video **autoplay**, add ?autoplay=1 to the embed URL.

- To make the video **loop**, add &loop=1 along with a playlist ID (playlist=VIDEO_ID).

Example:

```
<iframe width="560" height="315"
src="https://www.youtube.com/embed/VIDEO_ID?autoplay=1&loop=1&playlist=VIDEO
_ID" frameborder="0" allowfullscreen></iframe>
```

4. Best Practices for Using YouTube Videos in Google Sites

To ensure a smooth experience for your website visitors, follow these best practices:

Choose High-Quality and Relevant Videos

- Ensure that the videos are **clear, high-resolution (at least 720p or 1080p)**, and relevant to your site's topic.

- Avoid outdated or poorly produced videos.

Keep Load Times Fast

- Embedding multiple YouTube videos on one page may slow down site performance. Use only necessary videos.

- Place longer videos on separate pages if needed.

Optimize for Mobile Users

- Google Sites automatically makes YouTube videos **responsive**, but always preview your site on different devices to ensure optimal display.

Avoid Copyright Issues

- Only embed videos that you own or have permission to use.

- If you are embedding third-party videos, check their copyright status to avoid legal issues.

Use Video Captions for Accessibility

- Enable **YouTube subtitles** to improve accessibility for users with hearing impairments.

- Avoid embedding videos with excessive background noise or unclear speech.

5. Troubleshooting Common Issues

Video Not Showing Up

- Ensure the video is **public** on YouTube. Private videos won't display on Google Sites.

- Refresh the Google Sites editor and try re-embedding the video.

Video Not Playing on Mobile Devices

- Some embedded videos may be blocked on mobile due to YouTube restrictions. Consider linking to the video instead.

Incorrect Video Size or Cropping Issues

- Resize the video manually using Google Sites' drag-and-drop feature.

- Ensure the iframe width and height parameters are set correctly.

6. Conclusion

Embedding YouTube videos in Google Sites is an excellent way to enhance your website's content, making it more engaging and visually appealing. With Google Sites' built-in **YouTube insert tool** and **embed code options**, adding videos is simple and customizable.

By following best practices—such as optimizing for mobile users, ensuring fast load times, and using high-quality content—you can create an interactive and professional-looking website.

Now that you've mastered embedding videos, you're ready to explore the next step: **configuring navigation and page organization** in Google Sites!

3.3.3 Using Google Drive for Multimedia Content

Google Sites allows seamless integration with Google Drive, making it easy to embed multimedia content such as images, videos, documents, and presentations. By using Google Drive, you can keep your website dynamic, organized, and up to date without the need to re-upload files every time changes are made. In this section, we will explore how to use Google Drive effectively within Google Sites.

---

1. Why Use Google Drive for Multimedia in Google Sites?

Google Drive integration in Google Sites provides several advantages:

- **Cloud Storage Convenience**: Store and access multimedia files from anywhere without consuming local storage.

- **Automatic Updates**: Any updates made to a file in Google Drive will be reflected on your Google Site without re-uploading.

- **Easy Collaboration**: Share and edit files with team members, ensuring everyone has the latest version.

- **Embedding Large Files**: Instead of slowing down your website with large media files, you can link or embed them directly from Google Drive.

- **File Access Control**: Set permissions to control who can view, edit, or download embedded files.

Now, let's explore how to add different types of Google Drive content to your Google Site.

---

2. How to Add Google Drive Content to Google Sites

2.1 Embedding Google Drive Files (Images, PDFs, Documents, etc.)

Google Sites allows you to embed any file stored in Google Drive, including images, PDFs, Google Docs, Google Sheets, and Google Slides. Here's how:

Step 1: Open Google Sites Editor

1. Navigate to Google Sites and open the site you want to edit.

2. Select the page where you want to add a Google Drive file.

Step 2: Insert a Google Drive File

1. Click on the **"Insert"** tab in the right-hand menu.

2. Scroll down and click **"Drive"** to open your Google Drive.

3. Locate the file you want to embed (image, PDF, Google Docs, etc.).

4. Click **"Insert"** to add the file to your page.

Step 3: Adjust the File Display

- Resize the embedded file by dragging its corners.

- Click on the embedded file to access additional settings, such as alignment and linking options.

- Customize visibility settings to allow public or restricted access.

2.2 Adding Google Drive Videos to Google Sites

If you have video files stored in Google Drive, you can embed them directly into your Google Site.

Step 1: Upload a Video to Google Drive

1. Open Google Drive.

2. Click the **"+" (New)** button and select **"File Upload."**

3. Choose your video file and wait for it to upload.

Step 2: Embed the Video in Google Sites

1. In Google Sites, click on the **"Insert"** tab.

2. Click **"Drive"** and locate the video file.

3. Click **"Insert"** to embed the video into your site.

Step 3: Customize Video Playback

- Resize the video frame as needed.

- Allow users to play the video directly from the site without downloading it.

- Ensure the video permissions in Google Drive are set to **"Anyone with the link can view"** to make it accessible.

2.3 Adding Google Slides from Google Drive

Google Slides presentations can be embedded in Google Sites to showcase reports, tutorials, or interactive slideshows.

Step 1: Open Google Slides and Copy the File Link

1. Open your **Google Slides** presentation.

2. Click on **"File" > "Publish to the web."**

3. Select **"Embed"** and adjust auto-play and loop settings.

4. Copy the generated embed code.

Step 2: Embed the Google Slides Presentation

1. In Google Sites, go to the **"Insert"** tab.

2. Click **"Embed"**, then paste the copied code into the embed box.

3. Click **"Insert"** to add the presentation to your site.

Step 3: Customize the Display

- Adjust the size of the presentation frame.

- Enable autoplay for slides to run automatically.

- Use the **manual navigation** setting for users to control the slideshow.

2.4 Embedding Google Sheets for Live Data

Google Sheets is useful for displaying live data, charts, and interactive tables.

Step 1: Prepare Your Google Sheet

1. Open your **Google Sheets** document.

2. Ensure that data is formatted clearly.

3. Set sharing permissions so visitors can **view but not edit** the data.

Step 2: Embed the Google Sheet in Google Sites

1. In Google Sites, click on **"Insert"** > **"Drive"**.

2. Select your Google Sheet file and click **"Insert"**.

3. Resize the table to fit the page layout.

Step 3: Adjust Display Options

- Use filters in Google Sheets to allow users to view specific data sets.

- Update data in Google Sheets to reflect changes automatically on your website.

- Embed **specific charts** from Google Sheets rather than the entire spreadsheet for a cleaner look.

2.5 Embedding Google Forms for Surveys and Data Collection

Google Forms is useful for creating surveys, feedback forms, and registration pages.

Step 1: Create a Google Form

1. Go to Google Forms.

2. Design your form with questions, dropdowns, and checkboxes.

3. Click **"Send"**, then choose **"Embed"** to get the HTML embed code.

Step 2: Embed the Form in Google Sites

1. In Google Sites, click **"Insert"** > **"Embed"**.

2. Paste the Google Form embed code into the box.

3. Click **"Insert"** to add it to your page.

Step 3: Customize the Form Display

- Resize the embedded form to ensure all fields are visible.

- Use form settings to enable notifications and auto-responses.

- Monitor responses in **Google Sheets** for real-time analytics.

---

3. Managing Google Drive File Permissions

Proper file permissions are crucial to ensure that your embedded content is accessible to the right audience.

3.1 Setting File Access Levels

1. Open the file in **Google Drive**.

2. Click **"Share"** in the top-right corner.

3. Choose from the following options:

   o **Restricted** (only invited users can access)

   o **Anyone with the link can view**

   o **Anyone with the link can edit** (not recommended for public sites)

3.2 Ensuring Public Accessibility

- If your Google Site is public, make sure embedded files have **view permissions enabled for all users**.

- For internal team sites, restrict access only to organization members.

4. Conclusion

Using Google Drive to embed multimedia content in Google Sites is a powerful way to create an interactive, dynamic website. By integrating images, videos, Google Slides, Sheets, and Forms, you can enhance user engagement and streamline content updates without manually re-uploading files.

To summarize, you've learned how to:
✓ Embed Google Drive files (PDFs, Docs, Sheets, etc.).
✓ Add and customize videos from Google Drive.
✓ Embed Google Slides presentations.
✓ Display live data using Google Sheets.
✓ Insert Google Forms for surveys and feedback.
✓ Manage file permissions for secure and effective sharing.

By leveraging these features, your Google Site can become an efficient and professional-looking platform for education, business, or personal projects.

CHAPTER IV
Working with Pages and Navigation

4.1 Adding and Managing Pages

4.1.1 Creating New Pages

When building a website with Google Sites, adding pages is one of the fundamental steps in structuring your content. Whether you're creating an informational site, a portfolio, or a business page, organizing your content into multiple pages improves navigation and user experience. This section will guide you through creating new pages, understanding different page types, and structuring your site effectively.

Understanding the Role of Pages in Google Sites

Before diving into the technical steps, it's important to understand how pages function within Google Sites. Unlike traditional website builders, Google Sites offers a simple, streamlined approach to managing content through pages. Pages serve as containers for text, images, embedded files, and other multimedia elements, allowing you to present information in a structured way.

Key benefits of using pages in Google Sites include:

- **Better Organization:** Instead of cramming all your content onto a single homepage, you can create dedicated pages for different topics or sections.

- **Enhanced Navigation:** A well-structured site with multiple pages makes it easier for visitors to find relevant information.

- **Improved Readability:** By spreading content across multiple pages, you prevent information overload and create a more pleasant reading experience.

- **Scalability:** As your site grows, adding pages ensures that your content remains manageable and well-organized.

Types of Pages in Google Sites

Google Sites allows you to create different types of pages depending on your needs. While all pages function similarly, understanding how to use them effectively can help in designing a user-friendly website.

1. Standard Pages

These are the most common type of pages used in Google Sites. They contain text, images, videos, and other embedded content. You can fully customize their layout and appearance.

2. Nested (Sub) Pages

Subpages are pages that exist under a parent page. They are useful for organizing content hierarchically. For example, if you have a "Services" page, you can create subpages for "Consulting," "Training," and "Support."

3. Redirect Pages

While Google Sites does not have built-in redirect functionality, you can create a page that acts as a link to an external website or another section within your site. This can be useful for guiding users to external resources or integrating with other platforms.

Step-by-Step Guide to Creating a New Page

Now that we understand the role and types of pages, let's go through the process of creating a new page in Google Sites.

Step 1: Open Your Google Site

1. Go to Google Sites and open the site where you want to add a new page.
2. Make sure you're in the **Edit Mode** by clicking on the "Edit" button if needed.

Step 2: Access the Pages Panel

1. On the right-hand menu, click on the **"Pages"** tab.

2. This section displays all existing pages in your site, along with their hierarchy.

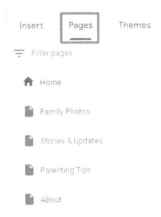

Step 3: Add a New Page

1. Click the **"+" button** at the bottom of the "Pages" panel.

2. Select **"New page"** from the options.

3. A dialog box will appear, prompting you to enter a **name for the new page**.

4. Type the desired name (e.g., "About Us," "Contact," or "Portfolio").

5. Click **"Done"** to create the page.

Step 4: Customize Your New Page

Once the new page is created, it will appear in the site's navigation menu and be automatically added to the list of pages in the "Pages" panel. You can now:

- **Edit the content** by adding text, images, and other elements.

- **Adjust the layout** using section dividers and columns.

- **Embed files** from Google Drive, YouTube, or other sources.

Organizing Your Pages for Better Navigation

Simply adding pages is not enough; organizing them properly ensures a smooth user experience. Here are some best practices:

1. Group Similar Pages Together

If your website has multiple sections, consider creating parent and subpages. For example:

- **Main Page:** Services
    - Consulting
    - Training
    - Support

2. Keep the Page Names Clear and Concise

Avoid long and complex page names. Instead of "Information About Our Company's History," simply use "Our History."

3. Use a Logical Page Order

Think about how users will navigate your site. Common pages should be easily accessible from the main menu, while less frequently used pages can be placed in dropdowns.

Managing and Editing Pages

Editing an Existing Page

To edit an existing page:

1. Open your Google Site and go to the **Pages** panel.

2. Click on the page you want to edit.

3. Make changes using the text editor, layout options, or by adding new content blocks.

4. Changes are saved automatically, but you need to **publish** the site for visitors to see updates.

Rearranging Pages

To change the order of pages:

1. Go to the "Pages" panel.

2. Click and **drag a page** to move it to a different position in the navigation structure.

Deleting or Restoring a Page

- To delete a page, click on the **three-dot menu** next to the page name and select **"Delete."**

- If you delete a page by mistake, go to the **"Site Versions"** to restore a previous version of your site.

Common Mistakes to Avoid When Creating Pages

1. **Adding Too Many Pages at Once** – Start small and expand as needed to keep your site organized.

2. **Using Generic Page Names** – A page called "Page 1" or "Untitled" doesn't help users understand its purpose.

3. **Not Testing Navigation** – Always preview your site to check if pages are accessible and easy to find.

4. **Ignoring Mobile Responsiveness** – Google Sites automatically adjusts for mobile, but test how your pages look on different devices.

5. **Forgetting to Publish** – Changes in Edit Mode are not visible to users until you click "Publish."

Conclusion

Creating pages in Google Sites is a straightforward process, but thoughtful planning can significantly improve the functionality and readability of your website. By structuring content effectively, using logical navigation, and keeping page names clear, you ensure a smooth user experience.

In the next section, we will explore **how to configure navigation** to enhance usability and accessibility. Stay tuned!

4.1.2 Organizing Pages in the Site Structure

Organizing pages effectively in Google Sites is essential for creating a user-friendly and well-structured website. A clear and logical site structure improves navigation, enhances user experience, and ensures that visitors can find the information they need quickly. In this section, we will explore best practices for structuring pages, managing the site hierarchy, using subpages, and maintaining consistency in your website's layout.

Understanding the Importance of a Well-Organized Site Structure

A well-structured website is not just visually appealing but also functional. A clear site hierarchy provides the following benefits:

- **Enhanced User Experience:** Visitors can navigate your site effortlessly and find information without frustration.

- **Improved Navigation:** A logical layout makes it easier for users to move between pages.

- **Better Content Management:** When pages are organized correctly, maintaining and updating content becomes more manageable.

- **SEO Benefits:** A well-structured site with proper internal linking can improve search engine rankings.

To create an effective site structure in Google Sites, it's essential to define a clear layout before adding and arranging pages.

Defining Your Website's Structure

Before organizing your pages in Google Sites, take some time to outline the structure of your website. Consider the following steps:

Step 1: Identify the Core Sections of Your Website

Think about the primary categories or sections your site will have. Common sections for different types of websites include:

- **Business Websites:** Home, About Us, Services, Products, Contact

- **Educational Websites:** Home, Courses, Resources, Assignments, Contact

- **Portfolio Websites:** Home, Portfolio, Blog, Testimonials, Contact

- **Team or Internal Websites:** Home, Departments, Announcements, Resources, Policies

Clearly defining your sections will help you determine how to structure your pages logically.

Step 2: Create a Sitemap

A sitemap is a visual representation of your website's hierarchy. This can be a simple sketch or a detailed diagram using tools like **Lucidchart, Microsoft Visio, or Google Drawings**. A sitemap typically includes:

- **Top-Level Pages (Main Categories)**

- **Subpages (Related Topics or Sections)**

- **Internal Links (Connections Between Pages)**

For example, a business website may have the following structure:

- **Home**

    o About Us

    o Services

        ▪ Web Design

        ▪ SEO

        ▪ Marketing

    o Portfolio

     ○   Blog

     ○   Contact

By defining this structure beforehand, you can easily translate it into Google Sites.

Adding and Organizing Pages in Google Sites

Once you have a clear idea of your website's layout, follow these steps to organize your pages effectively.

Step 1: Creating Main Pages

To add a new page in Google Sites:

1. Open your **Google Sites editor**.

2. Click on the **Pages tab** in the right-side panel.

3. Click the **+ button** at the bottom to create a new page.

4. Enter the page name and click **Done**.

This will create a **top-level page**, which appears in the navigation menu automatically.

Step 2: Creating Subpages (Child Pages)

Subpages help break down large topics into smaller sections, making your site easier to navigate. To create a subpage:

1. In the **Pages tab**, locate the main page under which you want to add a subpage.

2. Click the **three-dot menu** (:) next to the page.

3. Select **Add subpage**.

4. Name the subpage and click **Done**.

The new subpage will now appear nested under its parent page, both in the **Pages panel** and in the site's navigation menu.

Step 3: Drag and Drop to Reorder Pages

If you need to rearrange your site structure:

1. Go to the **Pages panel**.

2. Click and drag a page to move it to a different position.

3. Drop it where needed (either as a main page or as a subpage under another page).

This drag-and-drop functionality makes restructuring pages quick and intuitive.

Best Practices for Organizing Pages

1. Keep the Navigation Simple

Avoid adding too many pages to the top-level navigation. Ideally, limit the number of **main pages** to **5-7** for clarity. Subpages can be used for additional content.

2. Use Descriptive Page Names

Each page title should clearly describe its content. Instead of vague names like *"Info"*, use precise names like *"Our Services"* or *"Client Testimonials"*.

3. Maintain Consistency in Page Layouts

For a professional look, use consistent **fonts, colors, and layouts** across pages. You can create a standard template for similar sections.

4. Utilize Drop-Down Menus for Better Organization

Google Sites automatically generates **drop-down menus** when you create subpages. This helps group related topics while keeping the navigation bar uncluttered.

5. Link Pages for Better Connectivity

To help users navigate your site, use **internal links** within pages:

- Link relevant pages together (e.g., *Services → Web Design*).

- Add a **"Back to Home"** button or breadcrumbs for easy navigation.

Using Sections and Layouts for Better Page Organization

1. Divide Content into Logical Sections

Instead of one long page, break content into **smaller sections** with headings. This makes it easier to scan and read.

2. Use Layouts for a Professional Look

Google Sites provides pre-designed **section layouts** (text + images, multi-column, etc.). These layouts help organize content effectively without additional design effort.

3. Add a Table of Contents for Long Pages

For text-heavy pages, use the **Table of Contents** widget in Google Sites. This automatically generates a clickable list of headings, improving readability.

Managing and Updating Your Site Structure Over Time

A well-organized website needs **regular updates**. Follow these tips to keep your site structured and relevant:

1. Review and Update the Navigation Periodically

- As your site grows, reassess if pages need to be **merged, split, or reorganized**.
- Remove outdated or unnecessary pages.

2. Ensure Consistency Across Sections

- Use similar formatting and styles for all pages.
- Keep page layouts uniform for a seamless experience.

3. Test Your Navigation on Different Devices

Since Google Sites is **mobile-friendly**, check how the site appears on **desktop, tablet, and phone** screens to ensure smooth navigation.

4. Get Feedback from Users

Ask **visitors, team members, or customers** for feedback on navigation ease. This helps identify areas for improvement.

Conclusion

Organizing pages in Google Sites is essential for creating a structured, user-friendly website. By planning your **site structure**, using **subpages**, and optimizing **navigation**, you can ensure a seamless experience for your visitors.

By following these best practices, you'll be able to manage your site efficiently and provide users with an intuitive and accessible browsing experience.

4.1.3 Deleting and Restoring Pages

When working with Google Sites, managing your pages effectively includes not only adding and organizing them but also knowing how to delete and restore them when needed. Whether you want to remove outdated content, restructure your website, or recover accidentally deleted pages, understanding these functions is essential.

This section will cover the following:

- How to delete a page in Google Sites

- What happens when a page is deleted

- How to restore a deleted page

- Best practices for managing deletions and recoveries

Deleting a Page in Google Sites

Deleting a page in Google Sites is a straightforward process, but it should be done carefully to avoid losing important content. Follow these steps to remove a page:

Steps to Delete a Page

1. **Open Google Sites**

   o   Go to Google Sites and open the website you want to edit.

2. **Access the Page Management Panel**

   o   In the right-hand menu, click on **Pages** to view the list of pages in your site's structure.

3. **Select the Page to Delete**

o   Hover over the page you wish to delete.

o   Click the **three-dot menu (⋮)** next to the page name.

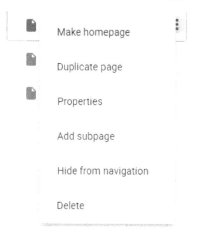

4. **Choose "Delete"**

o   In the dropdown menu, select **Delete**.

o   A confirmation message will appear, asking if you want to proceed with the deletion.

5. **Confirm Deletion**

o   Click **Delete** again to confirm.

o   The page will be removed from the site structure.

What Happens When You Delete a Page?

When a page is deleted in Google Sites, it is **permanently removed** from the site. Unlike Google Drive, where deleted files move to the trash and can be recovered later, **Google Sites does not have a built-in trash or recycle bin**. This means that once a page is deleted, you cannot restore it directly.

However, there are workarounds to recover lost content:

•   **Using Version History** – You can revert the site to a previous version where the page still existed.

- **Recreating the Page** – If you have a backup or previous draft, you can manually create the page again.

Restoring a Deleted Page in Google Sites

Since Google Sites does not provide a "restore" function for deleted pages, you need to rely on **Version History** to recover lost content. Version History allows you to **rollback your site to an earlier version** where the deleted page still exists.

Steps to Restore a Deleted Page Using Version History

1. **Open Your Google Site**

   o   Go to Google Sites and open the website where the page was deleted.

2. **Access Version History**

   o   In the top-right corner, click the **three-dot menu (⋮)**.

   o   Select **Version History**.

   o   A panel will appear on the right, showing different saved versions of your site.

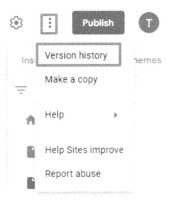

3. **Find the Version with the Deleted Page**

   o   Scroll through the available versions.

   o   Click on an earlier version before the page was deleted.

   o   Preview the content to confirm the page is still there.

4. **Restore the Previous Version**

   o   Click **Restore this version** to revert your site to the selected version.

   o   The deleted page will be restored along with any other content from that version.

Note: Restoring a version affects the entire site, not just a single page. If you made other changes after deleting the page, you may need to redo them after restoring.

Alternative Methods to Recover Deleted Content

If Version History does not work or you do not want to restore an entire site version, consider these alternative solutions:

1. Recreating the Page Manually

- If you have **screenshots** or **offline backups**, use them to manually reconstruct the deleted page.

- Check **Google Drive** or other sources where you might have saved copies of the page content.

2. Checking Google Search Cache

- If your site was **publicly available**, Google Search might have cached a version of the page.

- Search for your site in Google and click **Cached** to view an older version.

3. Using Third-Party Backup Services

- If you frequently update your Google Site, consider using third-party tools to **back up** content for easier recovery in the future.

Best Practices for Managing Deletions and Recoveries

To minimize the risk of losing important content, follow these best practices:

1. Always Double-Check Before Deleting

- Before removing a page, **review its content** to ensure you do not need it anymore.

- Consider **unpublishing** a page instead of deleting it permanently.

2. Use Version History Regularly

- Check **Version History** before deleting pages to know what backup options are available.

- If working on a **large-scale update**, save multiple versions for better recovery options.

3. Make Copies of Important Pages

- Before deleting, consider **duplicating** the page and saving it elsewhere.

- Store critical information in **Google Docs or Drive** for backup.

4. Train Your Team on Page Management

- If multiple people manage the site, ensure they understand the consequences of deleting pages.

- Set permissions carefully to prevent accidental deletions by unauthorized users.

Conclusion

Managing pages effectively in Google Sites involves not only adding and organizing them but also handling deletions carefully. Since **Google Sites does not have a built-in "undo delete" function**, users must rely on **Version History** or **manual backups** to recover lost content.

By following the best practices outlined in this chapter, you can minimize the risk of accidental deletions and ensure smooth website management.

4.2 Configuring Navigation

4.2.1 Automatic vs. Manual Navigation

Navigation plays a crucial role in the usability and structure of a website. In Google Sites, the navigation system helps visitors move between different pages efficiently, ensuring a smooth user experience. Google Sites offers two main navigation options: **automatic navigation** and **manual navigation**. Choosing the right type of navigation depends on how much control you want over the structure and layout of your site.

This section will explain the differences between automatic and manual navigation, their advantages and limitations, and how to configure them effectively.

1. Understanding Automatic Navigation

What is Automatic Navigation?

Automatic navigation is the default setting in Google Sites. When you create a new page, it is automatically added to the site's navigation menu. This feature simplifies site management, as you don't need to manually update the navigation every time you add or remove a page.

In automatic navigation, Google Sites organizes the pages based on the site hierarchy. The order of the pages in the navigation menu matches their arrangement in the site's page structure.

How Automatic Navigation Works

- Each new page is automatically placed in the navigation menu.

- Subpages (child pages) are nested under their parent pages.

- The navigation menu updates dynamically when pages are added, removed, or renamed.

- The menu appears as a **horizontal navigation bar** (top of the site) or a **sidebar navigation** (left side of the site), depending on the site's layout.

Advantages of Automatic Navigation

✓ Easy to use – Ideal for beginners, as it requires no manual setup.

✓ Time-saving – The menu updates itself when changes are made to pages.

✓ Consistent structure – The navigation always follows the logical page hierarchy.

✓ Reduces errors – No risk of forgetting to link a new page.

Limitations of Automatic Navigation

✗ Limited customization – You cannot reorder pages freely without adjusting the site structure.

✗ All pages appear in the menu – If you want to hide certain pages, you must configure their visibility settings.

✗ Lack of design flexibility – You cannot change the style or appearance of individual menu items.

2. Configuring Automatic Navigation

Enabling Automatic Navigation

By default, automatic navigation is turned on when you create a Google Site. However, if you have switched to manual navigation and want to revert to automatic, follow these steps:

1. Open your Google Site in **edit mode**.

2. Click on **Settings** (⚙☐) in the top-right corner.

3. Select **Navigation** from the menu.

4. Under **Navigation Mode**, choose **Automatic**.

5. Click **Done** to save changes.

Adjusting the Navigation Layout

Even with automatic navigation, you can modify its appearance:

- **Top Navigation Bar:** Pages appear in a horizontal menu at the top of the site.

- **Sidebar Navigation:** Pages appear in a collapsible menu on the left.

To change the navigation layout:

1. Click **Settings** (⚙️☐).

2. Select **Navigation**.

3. Under **Navigation Position**, choose **Top** or **Side**.

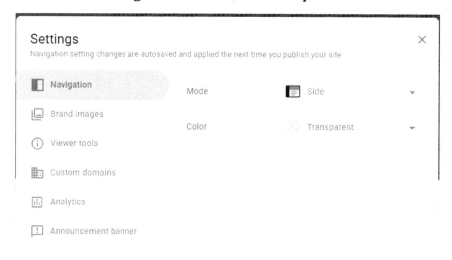

2.3 Hiding Pages from Automatic Navigation

If you want to remove a page from the navigation while keeping it published, follow these steps:

1. Click **Pages** in the right sidebar.

2. Find the page you want to hide.

3. Click the **More options (⋮)** button next to the page name.

4. Select **Hide from Navigation**.

The page will remain active but won't appear in the navigation menu.

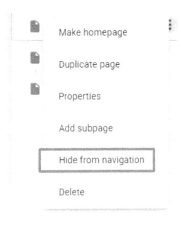

3. Understanding Manual Navigation

What is Manual Navigation?

Manual navigation gives you full control over the menu structure. Instead of Google Sites automatically adding new pages to the navigation menu, you manually define which pages appear, their order, and how they are structured.

How Manual Navigation Works

- Pages do **not** automatically appear in the menu when created.
- You manually add links to pages in the navigation menu.
- You can organize the menu items in any order.
- Subpages are added manually as dropdown items.

Advantages of Manual Navigation

✓ Full customization – You can arrange pages in any order.
✓ More design flexibility – You can add external links, rename menu items, or create custom structures.
✓ Better control over visibility – You decide which pages appear in the menu.

Limitations of Manual Navigation

✗ More time-consuming – You must manually update the navigation when adding new pages.

✗ Risk of broken links – If a page URL changes, you must manually update the menu.
✗ Requires planning – If the site has many pages, maintaining manual navigation can be difficult.

4. Configuring Manual Navigation

Switching to Manual Navigation

To enable manual navigation:

1. Open your Google Site in **edit mode**.

2. Click **Settings** (⚙☐).

3. Select **Navigation**.

4. Under **Navigation Mode**, choose **Manual**.

5. Click **Done** to save changes.

Adding Custom Menu Items

Once manual navigation is enabled, you need to add pages manually:

1. Click the **Pages** tab in the right sidebar.

2. Click the **Add Page (+)** button.

3. Enter a **name for the page**.

4. Click **Done** to create the page.

5. Drag the page into the **navigation menu** to place it where you want.

To add an **external link** to the menu:

1. Click the **Add Link** button.

2. Enter the **link text** and **URL**.

3. Click **Done**.

Organizing the Menu Structure

To create a dropdown menu with subpages:

1. Drag a page **below** another page in the Pages list.

2. Indent it slightly to the right.

3. The page will now appear as a **submenu item**.

Removing Pages from Manual Navigation

To remove a page from the navigation:

1. Click the **More options (:)** button next to the page.

2. Select **Remove from Navigation**.

The page remains on the site but is no longer in the menu.

5. Choosing Between Automatic and Manual Navigation

Feature	Automatic Navigation	Manual Navigation
Ease of Use	✅ Very easy	❌ Requires setup
Customization	❌ Limited	✅ Full control
Updates Automatically	✅ Yes	❌ No, must update manually
Allows External Links	❌ No	✅ Yes
Supports Hidden Pages	✅ Yes	✅ Yes
Best for Beginners	✅ Yes	❌ No
Best for Large Sites	❌ No	✅ Yes

Recommendation:

- **Use Automatic Navigation** if you want a simple, hands-free approach.

- **Use Manual Navigation** if you need more control over menu items.

- **Hybrid Approach:** You can use automatic navigation for most pages but manually add key pages or links as needed.

Conclusion

Navigation is essential for any website, and Google Sites provides both **automatic** and **manual** navigation options. Automatic navigation is best for simplicity and efficiency, while manual navigation allows for greater customization. By understanding both methods, you can configure your Google Site's navigation to provide the best experience for your visitors.

In the next section, we will explore **Creating Drop-down Menus**, which allows you to organize content more effectively.

4.2.2 Creating Drop-down Menus

Navigation plays a crucial role in user experience, making it easy for visitors to find the information they need. Drop-down menus are a great way to organize content hierarchically, allowing users to access different sections of your Google Site efficiently. In this section, we will explore what drop-down menus are, why they are useful, and how to create and manage them in Google Sites.

What Are Drop-down Menus?

A drop-down menu in Google Sites is a navigation element that expands when clicked or hovered over, revealing a list of subpages or links. It helps keep the top navigation bar clean and organized while allowing easy access to multiple sections of your site.

Key Features of Drop-down Menus in Google Sites:

- **Hierarchical Structure** – Organize pages into parent-child relationships.

- **Space-Saving Design** – Keeps the navigation bar uncluttered.

- **Easy Accessibility** – Visitors can access pages without too much scrolling or searching.

- **Customizable Order** – Pages in drop-down menus can be rearranged easily.

Why Use Drop-down Menus?

If your website has multiple pages, a structured navigation system improves usability. Here are a few key benefits of using drop-down menus:

1. Improved User Experience

Instead of listing all pages at the top level, drop-down menus allow you to group related pages, making navigation intuitive and reducing clutter.

2. Enhanced Organization

With a drop-down menu, you can categorize content efficiently. For example, a company website might have:

- **Products**
    - Software
    - Hardware
    - Accessories
- **Services**
    - Consulting
    - Support
    - Training
- **Resources**
    - Blog
    - Documentation
    - FAQs

This hierarchy helps visitors find relevant content without excessive clicking or searching.

3. Aesthetic Appeal

A well-structured drop-down menu improves the visual design of your website, making it appear more professional and organized.

How to Create Drop-down Menus in Google Sites

Now that we understand the benefits, let's go step by step to create a drop-down menu in Google Sites.

Step 1: Access the Navigation Menu

1. Open your Google Site in editing mode.

2. Click on the **Pages** tab in the right-hand panel.

3. Identify the pages that you want to organize under a drop-down menu.

Step 2: Create a Parent Page

Drop-down menus in Google Sites are created by nesting pages under a parent page.

1. If you don't already have a page to act as a parent, create one:

    o Click the **+ New Page** button at the bottom of the **Pages** panel.

    o Give your page a relevant name (e.g., "Services").

    o Click **Done** to create the page.

2. If you already have a page that you want to use as the parent, proceed to the next step.

Step 3: Add Subpages to the Drop-down Menu

To create a drop-down effect, you must nest subpages under the parent page.

1. Locate the page you want to move under the parent page.

2. Drag the page and drop it onto the parent page.

3. The page will now appear indented under the parent page, indicating that it is a subpage.

4. Repeat the process for additional subpages.

Once you've nested all necessary pages, Google Sites automatically creates a drop-down menu when you publish the site.

Step 4: Customize the Drop-down Menu Order

By default, pages appear in the order they were added. To rearrange them:

1. Open the **Pages** panel.

2. Click and drag a subpage to a new position within the drop-down hierarchy.

3. Release the page when it reaches the desired position.

This reordering is reflected immediately in the navigation bar.

Customizing the Appearance of Drop-down Menus

While Google Sites has limited styling options, you can still customize the look and feel of your drop-down menus.

Changing Navigation Style

1. Click on the **Settings (gear icon)** in the top-right corner of the site editor.

2. Select **Navigation** from the menu.

3. Choose between different styles:

   o **Top navigation** (menu appears at the top of the site).

   o **Side navigation** (menu appears as a collapsible sidebar).

4. Save your changes.

Using Icons and Titles for Better Readability

Google Sites allows you to use icons for certain pages to make the menu visually appealing.

1. Click on a page in the **Pages** panel.

2. Select **Properties** and upload an icon or logo.

3. The selected icon will appear next to the page title in the navigation menu.

Best Practices for Drop-down Menus in Google Sites

To ensure an optimal navigation experience, follow these best practices when using drop-down menus:

1. Keep the Menu Structure Simple

Avoid creating too many levels in your navigation. Ideally, stick to one or two levels deep to prevent confusion.

2. Use Clear and Concise Labels

Each menu item should have an intuitive label that clearly describes the content. For example:

✗ "Info" → ✓ "Company Overview"

3. Maintain Consistent Naming

If your site has multiple sections, keep naming conventions consistent. For example, all service pages should follow a similar format:

- **Web Development Services**

- **SEO Services**

- **Marketing Services**

4. Limit the Number of Menu Items

Too many menu options can overwhelm users. Keep the number of top-level items minimal, grouping related pages under drop-down menus.

5. Test on Different Devices

Google Sites automatically makes menus responsive, but it's always good to test how your drop-down menus function on:

- Desktops

- Tablets

- Mobile devices

Ensure that menus are easy to tap and navigate, especially on mobile screens.

Troubleshooting Drop-down Menu Issues

Even though Google Sites is user-friendly, you may encounter issues while setting up drop-down menus. Here's how to fix some common problems:

Problem: Subpages Are Not Appearing in the Drop-down Menu

Solution:

- Check if the subpages are properly nested under the parent page in the **Pages** panel.

- Ensure that the **Navigation settings** are configured to display drop-down menus.

Problem: Drop-down Menu Items Are Out of Order

Solution:

- Manually rearrange them by dragging pages in the **Pages** panel.

Problem: Drop-down Menu Not Working on Mobile

Solution:

- Test the menu in a mobile browser.

- Consider switching to **Side Navigation** if the drop-down menu is too complex.

Conclusion

Drop-down menus in Google Sites are an effective way to organize and simplify website navigation. By creating a structured menu with a parent-child hierarchy, you can enhance usability, improve aesthetics, and make content easier to find.

With the right setup and best practices, your Google Site will provide a seamless browsing experience for visitors. Now that you've mastered drop-down menus, let's move on to the next section: **Using Anchor Links for Better Navigation.**

4.2.3 Customizing Navigation Appearance

Navigation plays a crucial role in the usability and accessibility of any website. Google Sites offers several ways to customize the appearance of your site's navigation, allowing you to create a professional and user-friendly experience. In this section, we will explore how to customize your navigation bar, adjust menu styles, change placement, and enhance the visual appeal of your site's navigation.

1. Understanding Google Sites Navigation Options

Google Sites provides a built-in navigation system that automatically updates as you add pages to your site. You can choose between horizontal and sidebar navigation, adjust colors and fonts, and control how users interact with your menu. Customizing the navigation appearance ensures your website is easy to use and visually appealing.

Key Elements of Navigation in Google Sites

- **Primary navigation menu** – The main menu that helps users browse through different pages.

- **Submenus (Dropdown menus)** – Allow grouping related pages under a main category.

- **Navigation placement** – Can be set to the top of the page (horizontal) or on the side (sidebar).

- **Customization options** – Includes fonts, colors, transparency, and alignment.

2. Changing Navigation Placement and Style

By default, Google Sites places the navigation bar at the top of the page (horizontal layout). However, you can switch it to a sidebar layout or customize its appearance based on your design preferences.

Switching Between Horizontal and Sidebar Navigation

1. **Open your Google Site** and go to the **Site Editor**.

2. Click on the **Settings (⚙□) icon** in the top right corner.

3. Select **Navigation** from the menu.

4. Choose between **Top Navigation** (horizontal) or **Side Navigation** (sidebar).

5. The changes will be applied instantly, and you can preview how it looks.

When to Use Each Navigation Style

- **Top Navigation (Horizontal Menu):**
  - Best for websites with fewer pages.

- o Provides a clean and modern look.

- o Works well for business, portfolio, and small websites.

- **Side Navigation (Sidebar Menu)**:

  - o Ideal for websites with multiple pages and subpages.

  - o Helps users navigate complex structures.

  - o Commonly used for educational sites and internal company portals.

3. Customizing Colors, Fonts, and Transparency

Google Sites allows you to customize the navigation bar's appearance to match your website's theme.

Changing the Navigation Bar Color

1. Click on **Themes** in the **Site Editor**.

2. Select the theme you are using or customize it.

3. Scroll down to **Navigation** settings.

4. Choose a **Navigation Color** that fits your site's design.

5. Adjust the **Transparency** slider to make the menu more or less visible.

Best Practices for Navigation Bar Colors

- Use a **high-contrast color** for better visibility.

- Ensure the color matches your **brand identity**.

- Avoid using colors that blend into the background.

- Use transparency carefully to maintain readability.

Changing the Navigation Font and Style

1. Go to **Themes > Text Style** in the Site Editor.

2. Select **Navigation Text** from the available options.

3. Choose a font that is **easy to read** and matches your site's design.

4. Adjust the font **size, weight (bold/regular), and color**.

5. Preview the changes before publishing.

Recommended Font Styles for Navigation

- **Sans-serif fonts** (e.g., Roboto, Open Sans) for a modern look.

- **Serif fonts** (e.g., Times New Roman) for a traditional and formal style.

- **Bold or larger fonts** for better readability.

4. Creating Drop-down Menus for Better Organization

If your site has multiple pages, using **drop-down menus** (submenus) can improve navigation by grouping related content together.

How to Create a Drop-down Menu in Google Sites

1. In the **Site Editor**, go to the **Pages** panel.

2. Click on the **page you want to move under another page**.

3. Drag and drop it **underneath another page** (indent it slightly).

4. The subpage will now appear as a **drop-down menu** in the navigation bar.

5. Preview your site to see the updated menu structure.

Benefits of Using Drop-down Menus

- Keeps the navigation bar clean and organized.

- Helps users find information more easily.

- Prevents clutter, especially on large websites.

5. Adding Custom Navigation Buttons

In addition to the built-in navigation bar, you can create **custom navigation buttons** to guide users to specific pages or external links.

How to Add a Navigation Button

1. Click on **Insert > Button** in the Site Editor.

2. Enter a **Button Label** (e.g., "Contact Us" or "Start Here").

3. Link it to an **internal page** or **external URL**.

4. Choose a button **style (filled, outlined, text only)**.

5. Adjust **size, alignment, and positioning** as needed.

Best Practices for Navigation Buttons

- Use **clear and actionable labels** (e.g., "Get Started" instead of "Click Here").

- Place important buttons **above the fold** (visible without scrolling).

- Keep button **size consistent** across your site.

---

6. Enhancing Mobile Navigation for Better Usability

Since many users will access your site from mobile devices, it's important to ensure your navigation is **mobile-friendly**.

Checking Mobile Navigation on Google Sites

1. Click on **Preview** in the Site Editor.

2. Select the **Mobile View** option.

3. Test how the navigation **collapses into a mobile-friendly menu**.

4. Ensure that **buttons, links, and menus** are easy to tap.

5. Adjust **font sizes and spacing** if necessary.

Optimizing Navigation for Mobile Users

- Use a **hamburger menu (☰)** for compact navigation.

- Ensure buttons and links are **large enough to tap easily**.

- Keep the menu **short and simple** for quick access.

7. Final Tips for a Well-Designed Navigation

- **Keep the navigation menu simple** – Avoid too many items in the main menu.

- **Use clear labels** – Page titles should be easy to understand.

- **Maintain consistency** – Navigation should look the same across all pages.

- **Test before publishing** – Ensure links and menus work properly.

- **Update as needed** – Modify navigation as your site grows.

By following these customization techniques, you can create an intuitive and visually appealing navigation system that enhances user experience.

4.3 Using Anchor Links for Better Navigation

What Are Anchor Links?

Anchor links, also known as "jump links" or "internal page links," allow users to navigate quickly to a specific section of a webpage. Instead of scrolling manually, visitors can click on an anchor link to jump directly to relevant content. This feature is particularly useful for long pages with multiple sections, such as FAQs, tutorials, or reports.

In Google Sites, anchor links improve user experience by making navigation more intuitive and efficient. Although Google Sites does not have a built-in anchor link feature like traditional HTML-based websites, you can still create them using headings and manual link settings.

Why Use Anchor Links in Google Sites?

There are several benefits to using anchor links in your Google Site:

- **Enhanced User Experience**: Visitors can quickly find the information they need without excessive scrolling.

- **Improved Readability**: Large pages become easier to navigate when sections are clearly accessible.

- **Professional Appearance**: Proper navigation demonstrates good design and organization.

- **SEO Benefits**: Anchor links can help search engines understand content structure, potentially improving ranking for specific sections.

If you're creating a website with long pages—such as a help center, blog, or educational resource—anchor links can significantly improve usability.

How to Create Anchor Links in Google Sites

Google Sites does not provide an automatic anchor link feature, but you can manually create anchor links using a combination of section headings and text links.

Method 1: Using Headings as Anchors

One of the easiest ways to create anchor links in Google Sites is by using section headings. Each heading automatically generates a unique URL that you can use as an anchor link.

Step 1: Add a Heading to the Section You Want to Link To

1. Open your Google Site in edit mode.

2. Navigate to the section where you want to create an anchor.

3. Click on the text box and select the text you want to use as a heading.

4. Change the text format to a **Heading (H2, H3, or H4)** from the formatting options.

Step 2: Get the URL of the Heading

1. Click the **Preview** button to view your published site.

2. Scroll to the section where you added the heading.

3. Right-click on the heading text and select **Copy Link Address** (or copy the URL from the browser address bar).

4. This copied link is your anchor link.

Step 3: Create a Link to the Anchor

1. Go back to the Google Sites editor.

2. Select the text or button where you want to insert the anchor link.

3. Click the **Insert Link** option (chain icon).

4. Paste the copied URL.

5. Click **Apply** to save the link.

Now, clicking this link will take users directly to the selected heading on your page.

Creating a Table of Contents with Anchor Links

If your page contains multiple sections, you can use anchor links to create a **Table of Contents (TOC)** at the top of the page. This allows users to jump directly to specific parts of the content.

Step 1: Add a Table of Contents Section

1. Create a text box at the top of your page.

2. Title it **Table of Contents** or **Jump to Section**.

Step 2: Insert Anchor Links for Each Section

1. List the major sections of your page as bullet points or a numbered list.

2. Highlight each section title, then click **Insert Link**.

3. Paste the corresponding heading URL that you copied earlier.

4. Repeat this process for all sections.

Example TOC:

◆ Table of Contents

- Introduction

- How to Use Anchor Links

- Creating a TOC

- Best Practices

Once published, clicking any of these links will take users directly to the specified section.

Best Practices for Using Anchor Links

While anchor links can greatly improve navigation, following best practices ensures they function effectively:

1. Use Descriptive Link Text

Avoid vague text like "Click Here." Instead, use meaningful anchor text that describes the section, such as:
✅ *Jump to Creating a Table of Contents*
🚫 *Click Here*

2. Keep URLs Clean and Readable

When copying heading URLs, Google Sites may generate long links. If possible, use URL shorteners or clear labels for easier navigation.

3. Test Links After Publishing

Always preview your site and test anchor links to confirm they navigate correctly. If a link doesn't work, check that the heading is properly formatted.

4. Limit Anchor Links Per Page

Using too many anchor links can overwhelm users. Focus on linking only essential sections.

5. Ensure Mobile Compatibility

Test anchor links on mobile devices to ensure smooth scrolling and navigation.

Troubleshooting Anchor Link Issues

Although anchor links in Google Sites are straightforward, you may encounter a few challenges. Here's how to fix common problems:

Issue	Possible Cause	Solution
Link doesn't jump to the section	Incorrect URL or missing heading	Recopy and reinsert the heading URL
Anchor links don't work on mobile	Google Sites may load differently on mobile	Test on different devices and adjust formatting
Table of Contents links don't update	Google Sites doesn't auto-update links	Manually update links if you rename sections

Alternative Methods for Anchor Links

If the built-in method does not work as expected, you can try alternative techniques:

Using Google Docs for Advanced Anchor Links

- Create a Google Doc with the same content as your Google Site.

- Insert section headers and generate a **Table of Contents** in Google Docs.

- Embed the Google Doc in your Google Site.

- This method allows for dynamic TOC updates without manually managing links.

Using Button Links Instead of Text Links

If you prefer a visual approach, use Google Sites' **button element** to create anchor links.

1. Insert a button from the **Insert** menu.

2. Label the button with the section title.

3. Paste the heading URL into the button's link field.

Conclusion

Anchor links are a valuable tool for improving navigation in Google Sites, especially for content-heavy pages. By using heading-generated URLs, creating a table of contents, and following best practices, you can enhance user experience and make your site more accessible.

Key Takeaways:
✓ Anchor links allow users to jump to specific sections of a page.

✓ Google Sites does not have a built-in feature, but heading links can serve as anchors.

✓ Creating a Table of Contents improves navigation.

✓ Testing links ensures they work correctly on all devices.

✓ Alternative methods include Google Docs integration and button links.

By implementing these strategies, you can create a more user-friendly and professional Google Site!

CHAPTER V
Enhancing Your Site with Google Workspace Integration

5.1 Embedding Google Docs, Sheets, and Slides

Google Sites seamlessly integrates with other Google Workspace tools, allowing you to embed documents, spreadsheets, and presentations directly into your website. This feature is particularly useful for businesses, educators, and teams that need to share important files without requiring visitors to download them.

By embedding Google Docs, Sheets, and Slides, you can:

- Display important documents, reports, or guides in real-time.

- Share live data from Google Sheets that updates automatically.

- Present slideshows and visual presentations directly on your site.

This section will guide you through the process of embedding Google Docs into your Google Site.

5.1.1 Adding Google Docs to Your Site

What is Google Docs Embedding?

Google Docs embedding allows you to display a document directly on your website without requiring users to open it in a separate window. Visitors can view the document's content as if it were part of the webpage, ensuring a smooth and interactive experience.

Some common use cases for embedding Google Docs include:

- Displaying a company policy or employee handbook.
- Sharing a research paper, case study, or educational material.
- Providing a step-by-step guide or instruction manual.
- Making a collaborative document available to the public.

Step-by-Step Guide to Embedding Google Docs

Step 1: Prepare Your Google Doc

Before embedding, ensure that your document is properly formatted and ready for public or internal viewing.

1. Open **Google Docs** and navigate to the document you want to embed.
2. Format the document using headings, bullet points, and images for readability.
3. If necessary, remove any confidential or unnecessary information.

Step 2: Adjust Document Sharing Settings

To allow others to view the document, you must adjust its sharing settings.

1. Click the **"Share"** button in the top right corner.
2. Under **"General Access"**, select one of the following options:
   o **Restricted** – Only specific users can view the document.
   o **Anyone with the link** – Anyone with the link can view the document.
   o **Public** – The document is available to everyone on the internet.
3. Choose **"Viewer"** as the access level to prevent edits by unauthorized users.

Step 3: Embed the Google Doc into Your Google Site

Once your document is ready and sharing permissions are set, follow these steps to embed it into Google Sites:

1. Open **Google Sites** and navigate to the page where you want to embed the document.

2. Click on the **"Insert"** tab in the right-hand panel.

3. Scroll down and select **"Drive"** to access your Google Drive files.

4. Locate and select the Google Doc you wish to embed.

5. Click the **"Insert"** button to place the document on your site.

Step 4: Adjust the Display Settings

After inserting the Google Doc, you can customize how it appears on your site:

- **Resize the document**: Click and drag the corners of the embedded document to adjust its size.

- **Enable full-screen viewing**: Allow visitors to open the document in a separate tab for easier reading.

- **Positioning**: Move the embedded document to different sections of the page for better layout.

Alternative Method: Embedding with an iFrame Code

If you want more control over how your document appears, you can use an **iFrame code** instead of the built-in Google Sites embed feature.

Steps to Generate an iFrame Embed Code:

1. Open your Google Doc.

2. Click **"File"** > **"Share"** > **"Publish to the web"**.

3. In the pop-up window, click **"Embed"**.

4. Copy the generated HTML **iFrame code**.

Steps to Insert the iFrame Code in Google Sites:

1. In Google Sites, go to the page where you want to embed the document.

2. Click **"Embed"** from the right-hand menu.

3. Select **"Embed Code"** and paste the iFrame code.

4. Click **"Insert"** to place the document on the site.

This method allows for more flexibility, such as adjusting the width and height of the embedded document.

Best Practices for Embedding Google Docs

To ensure that your embedded documents provide the best user experience, follow these best practices:

✅ **Keep Documents Well-Formatted** – Use proper headings, spacing, and bullet points to enhance readability.

✅ **Use Descriptive Titles** – Clearly label your documents so visitors know their purpose.

✅ **Regularly Update Content** – Since embedded Google Docs update in real time, ensure the information remains relevant.

✅ **Check Permissions Regularly** – Ensure that the document is accessible to the intended audience.

✅ **Optimize for Mobile** – Test your embedded document on different devices to confirm that it displays correctly.

Common Issues and How to Fix Them

Issue	Cause	Solution
Document does not appear on the site	Sharing settings are too restrictive	Change document settings to "Anyone with the link can view"
Visitors cannot scroll through the document	The embedded frame is too small	Resize the document box in Google Sites
Formatting appears different from the original	Some elements are not fully supported in embedded view	Use the "Publish to the web" iFrame method instead
Users cannot edit the document	View mode is enabled instead of edit mode	Ensure you have shared the editable link (if needed)

Conclusion

Embedding Google Docs into your Google Site is an effective way to share information, collaborate with teams, and present content in an accessible format. Whether you use the standard Google Sites embed tool or the advanced iFrame method, ensuring proper permissions and formatting is crucial.

In the next section, we will explore how to embed **Google Sheets** into your site, allowing you to display dynamic, real-time data effortlessly.

5.1.2 Displaying Google Sheets for Live Data

Google Sheets is a powerful tool for managing data, creating reports, and collaborating in real time. When embedded into a Google Site, Google Sheets can display live data that updates automatically whenever the original spreadsheet is modified. This feature is particularly useful for businesses, educators, project managers, and anyone who wants to share dynamic content on their website without manually updating it.

This section will guide you through the steps to embed a Google Sheet into your Google Site, explore customization options, and discuss best practices for displaying live data effectively.

1. Why Embed Google Sheets in Google Sites?

Embedding Google Sheets into Google Sites provides several advantages, including:

- **Real-time Updates**: Any changes made to the original Google Sheet are automatically reflected on your site.

- **Collaboration**: Multiple users can edit the spreadsheet, and the updated data will be instantly available.

- **Visualization**: Google Sheets allows the creation of charts and tables that can be displayed interactively.

- **Centralized Data Management**: Instead of updating data manually on a web page, users can update the sheet, and the site will display the latest information.

- **Improved Accessibility**: Data can be viewed on any device without requiring the viewer to access Google Sheets separately.

Common use cases for embedding Google Sheets include:

- **Project Dashboards**: Display project status updates, team assignments, and deadlines dynamically.

- **Financial Reports**: Share live financial summaries with stakeholders.

- **Event Schedules**: Publish real-time schedules for conferences, workshops, or meetings.

- **Student and Course Data**: Share assignments, grades, or other important data with students.

- **Inventory and Stock Updates**: Keep a real-time record of available stock levels.

2. How to Embed Google Sheets into Google Sites

Step 1: Prepare Your Google Sheet for Embedding

Before embedding a Google Sheet, ensure the data is formatted correctly:

1. **Organize Your Data**: Use clear headers and structured tables for better readability.

2. **Use Filters and Named Ranges**: Filters help users view specific data sets, while named ranges make referencing data easier.

3. **Ensure Proper Sharing Settings**: The sheet should be accessible to your intended audience.

Step 2: Change Sharing Permissions

By default, Google Sheets are private. You need to modify the sharing settings:

1. Open the **Google Sheet** you want to embed.

2. Click on **"Share"** in the top right corner.

3. Under **"General Access,"** select one of the following:

   o *Restricted*: Only specific people can view the sheet.

   o *Anyone with the link*: Anyone can view the sheet (useful for public websites).

4. Choose the appropriate permission:

- o **Viewer**: Users can see but not edit the data.

- o **Commenter**: Users can leave comments but cannot modify the content.

- o **Editor**: Users can make changes (not recommended unless necessary).

5. Click **"Done"** to save the changes.

Step 3: Insert Google Sheets into Google Sites

1. Open your **Google Site**.

2. Navigate to the page where you want to embed the Google Sheet.

3. Click the **"Insert"** tab in the right-hand panel.

4. Select **"Sheets"** from the options.

5. A window will appear displaying all your Google Sheets. Choose the sheet you want to embed.

6. Click **"Insert"**, and the sheet will appear on your page.

Step 4: Customize the Embedded Sheet

Once the sheet is inserted, you can adjust its appearance:

- **Resize the Sheet**: Click and drag the corners of the embedded sheet to fit your page layout.

- **Select Display Options**: Choose whether to display only part of the sheet or the full document.

- **Enable Scrollbars**: Allow users to scroll through data if needed.

Step 5: Publish and Test Your Site

1. Click **"Publish"** to make your changes live.

2. Open your Google Site in a new browser tab to verify that the sheet displays correctly.

3. Make changes to the Google Sheet and check if they reflect automatically on your site.

3. Best Practices for Displaying Live Data in Google Sheets

To ensure that your embedded Google Sheet is user-friendly and effective, consider these best practices:

1. Optimize Readability

- Use **clear column headers** and row labels to make data easy to understand.
- Apply **alternating row colors** to improve visibility.
- Use **bold text** for important information.

2. Limit Data Displayed

- If your sheet has a large dataset, consider embedding only a specific range instead of the full sheet.
- Hide unnecessary columns and rows before embedding.
- Use **filters** to let users explore data interactively.

3. Use Charts for Better Visualization

Instead of displaying raw data, you can insert **Google Sheets charts** into your Google Site:

1. In Google Sheets, create a **chart** based on your data.
2. Click on the chart and select **"Publish chart"** under the three-dot menu.
3. Copy the embed link and paste it into Google Sites using the **"Embed"** option.

4. Protect Sensitive Data

- Do not share confidential or personal data publicly.
- Adjust **sharing permissions** to prevent unauthorized edits.
- Use **Google Sheets' "Protected Ranges"** to restrict certain data from being modified.

5. Keep Your Data Updated

- Set up **automated updates** using Google Sheets formulas.
- Use **Google Apps Script** to fetch live data from external sources.

- Check your site regularly to ensure that embedded sheets are displaying the correct information.

4. Troubleshooting Common Issues

If your embedded Google Sheet isn't displaying correctly, consider these solutions:

Issue 1: Embedded Sheet Doesn't Load

- Ensure that the sheet's **sharing settings** allow public access.
- Refresh the Google Sites page and check for updates.
- Clear browser cache and cookies.

Issue 2: Data Doesn't Update in Real-Time

- Check if the embedded sheet is loading a **cached version**.
- Reload the page to see the latest data.
- Confirm that changes are saved in Google Sheets.

Issue 3: Formatting Issues in the Embedded Sheet

- Adjust column widths to prevent data from being cut off.
- Use text wrapping options in Google Sheets for better display.
- Resize the embedded window in Google Sites.

5. Conclusion

Embedding Google Sheets into Google Sites is an excellent way to display live data dynamically. Whether you're creating a financial dashboard, project tracker, or educational resource, integrating spreadsheets ensures that your website remains up to date without manual intervention.

By following the steps outlined in this chapter, you can successfully insert and manage live data in your Google Site, making your website more interactive and functional.

Now that we've covered Google Sheets, the next section will explore how to integrate **Google Slides** to enhance your site with presentations and visual content.

5.1.3 Presenting Google Slides on a Page

Google Slides is a powerful tool for creating presentations, and integrating it into your Google Site can enhance the way you share information with your audience. Whether you're embedding a company presentation, an educational slideshow, or an interactive sales pitch, Google Sites makes it easy to display Google Slides seamlessly.

This section will guide you through the entire process of embedding Google Slides on your site, customizing its display, and ensuring that visitors have the best viewing experience possible.

Why Embed Google Slides on Your Google Site?

There are many reasons to add a Google Slides presentation to your Google Site, including:

1. Professional and Engaging Content

Google Slides allows you to present content in an organized and visually appealing way, making it easier for your audience to understand complex ideas.

2. Seamless Google Workspace Integration

Since Google Sites is part of Google Workspace, embedding Google Slides is quick and efficient, requiring no extra software or coding.

3. Interactive and Dynamic Presentations

Unlike static images or PDFs, Google Slides allow users to interact with the content by clicking through slides at their own pace.

4. Easy Updates and Live Changes

If you make changes to your Google Slides presentation, the embedded version on your Google Site updates automatically, ensuring that visitors always see the latest content.

5. Ideal for Multiple Use Cases

- **Educational Purposes** – Teachers can upload lecture slides, study materials, and classroom instructions.
- **Corporate Websites** – Businesses can display training materials, reports, and client presentations.

- **Event Promotion** – Organizers can showcase event schedules, speaker profiles, or promotional slideshows.

- **Portfolios and Personal Websites** – Individuals can present their work in a structured and engaging manner.

How to Embed Google Slides on Your Google Site

Step 1: Open Your Google Site

1. Go to Google Sites.

2. Open the Google Site where you want to embed the presentation.

3. Navigate to the page where you want to insert the Google Slides presentation.

Step 2: Insert the Google Slides Presentation

1. Click on the **"Insert"** tab in the right-hand panel.

2. Scroll down and click **"Drive"** (since Google Slides files are stored in Google Drive).

3. A file picker window will open. Search for or select the Google Slides file you want to embed.

4. Click **"Insert"** to add it to your Google Site.

Step 3: Adjust the Size and Position

Once the Google Slides presentation appears on your page:

- **Resize it** by clicking and dragging the edges of the embedded slide window.

- **Reposition it** by clicking and dragging it to a different location on the page.

- **Align it** with other elements on the page for a more organized layout.

Step 4: Configure Display Settings

Google Sites provides different display options for embedded presentations:

- **Start on Slide #** – Choose which slide the presentation starts from.

- **Auto-Advance Slides** – Set slides to advance automatically every few seconds.

- **Loop Slideshow** – Have the presentation restart automatically when it reaches the last slide.

- **Enable Fullscreen** – Allow viewers to expand the presentation for better visibility.

To configure these settings:

1. Click on the embedded Google Slides presentation.

2. Select the **"Settings"** or **"Gear"** icon.

3. Adjust the display settings according to your preferences.

Step 5: Publish Your Site

1. Click the **"Publish"** button in the top-right corner of Google Sites.

2. If your site is already published, simply refresh the page to see the embedded Google Slides in action.

Alternative Method: Using Embed Code

If you need more control over the way Google Slides appears on your site, you can use the **embed code** method instead of the built-in Google Drive insertion.

Step 1: Get the Embed Code from Google Slides

1. Open your Google Slides presentation.

2. Click **"File"** → **"Publish to the Web"**.

3. Go to the **"Embed"** tab.

4. Configure your slideshow settings:

   o **Auto-start slideshow**

   o **Loop playback**

   o **Slide transition speed**

5. Click **"Publish"** and confirm.

6. Copy the **embed code** that appears.

Step 2: Insert the Embed Code into Google Sites

1. Go to your Google Site.

2. Navigate to the page where you want to embed the presentation.

3. Click **"Embed"** in the **"Insert"** menu.

4. Switch to the **"Embed Code"** tab.

5. Paste the embed code you copied from Google Slides.

6. Click **"Insert"** and adjust the size and position as needed.

Customizing the Embedded Presentation

1. Adjusting the Display Size

- Click and drag the corners of the embedded slide window to adjust its size.

- Ensure the slides are large enough for readability but not overwhelming to the site layout.

2. Choosing the Right Auto-Advance Setting

- For informational slideshows, set a longer duration between slides (e.g., 10 seconds).

- For rapid presentations or animations, use a shorter transition time.

3. Using Hyperlinks for Additional Navigation

- If your slides contain hyperlinks, ensure that they open in a new tab so visitors don't navigate away from your site.

4. Embedding Multiple Presentations

- If your site requires multiple presentations, consider placing them in separate sections for better organization.

Troubleshooting Common Issues

Problem 1: Google Slides Not Displaying Properly

- Ensure the presentation is **shared publicly** (or with specific users).

- Check your Google Drive permissions to confirm that visitors can view the file.

Problem 2: Slides Are Cut Off or Not Fully Visible

- Adjust the **size of the embedded frame** within Google Sites.

- Ensure that your slide dimensions are properly formatted in Google Slides.

Problem 3: Presentation Not Updating After Edits

- Refresh the Google Sites page to see the latest changes.

- If using an embedded link, unpublish and republish the Google Slides file.

Problem 4: Auto-Advance and Loop Settings Not Working

- Double-check the settings in **"Publish to the Web"** in Google Slides.

- Ensure that your browser allows embedded media to auto-play.

Best Practices for Presenting Google Slides on Google Sites

1. **Ensure Readability** – Use large fonts and high-contrast colors for accessibility.

2. **Optimize for Mobile Users** – Test the embedded slides on mobile devices to ensure they are responsive.

3. **Keep Slides Concise** – Avoid long paragraphs; focus on key points.

4. **Use High-Quality Images** – Ensure graphics and charts are clear and not pixelated.

5. **Regularly Update Your Presentation** – If the content is dynamic, set reminders to review and refresh it.

Conclusion

Embedding Google Slides into your Google Site is a great way to present information in an engaging and interactive format. Whether you're showcasing a project, providing learning materials, or delivering a business presentation, Google Slides enhances your site's effectiveness.

By following the steps outlined in this section, you can seamlessly integrate slideshows, customize their appearance, and troubleshoot common issues. Now that you've mastered embedding Google Slides, you're ready to explore further customization options to make your site even more dynamic.

5.2 Integrating Google Forms and Surveys

5.2.1 Creating and Embedding a Google Form

Google Forms is a powerful tool that allows you to create surveys, quizzes, feedback forms, and more. When integrated with Google Sites, it enables you to collect and manage data efficiently. Whether you're gathering customer feedback, conducting employee surveys, or creating event registrations, embedding Google Forms into your website ensures a seamless user experience.

In this section, we will guide you through the process of creating a Google Form and embedding it into your Google Site. We will also explore customization options and best practices to optimize user engagement.

Step 1: Accessing Google Forms

To create a Google Form, you first need to access the Google Forms platform. Follow these steps:

1. Open your web browser and go to Google Forms. https://forms.google.com/

2. Sign in with your Google account if you haven't already.

3. Click on the **Blank Form** option to start from scratch or choose a template from the **Template Gallery**.

Once you have opened Google Forms, you are ready to start designing your form.

Step 2: Creating a Google Form

Google Forms provides a user-friendly interface for creating forms. Here's how to create a basic form:

2.1 Adding a Form Title and Description

- Click on the **Untitled Form** field at the top and enter a name for your form.
- Add a brief description to provide instructions or context for respondents.

2.2 Adding Questions to Your Form

Google Forms supports various types of questions, including:

- **Short Answer** – For open-ended responses.
- **Paragraph** – For longer text responses.
- **Multiple Choice** – Allows users to select one answer from a list.
- **Checkboxes** – Allows users to select multiple answers.
- **Dropdown** – A compact list where users select one option.
- **File Upload** – Allows users to upload files to Google Drive.
- **Linear Scale** – Used for rating responses (e.g., 1 to 5).
- **Multiple Choice Grid** – A table format for selecting options.

To add a question:

1. Click on the ⊕ **Add Question** button.
2. Select the **question type** from the dropdown menu.
3. Enter the **question text** and provide answer choices (if applicable).
4. Toggle the **Required** option if you want to make the question mandatory.

2.3 Adding Sections and Organizing Your Form

- Click the **Add Section** button (two rectangles icon) to create different sections.
- This helps organize long forms and improves readability.
- Users can navigate between sections using "Next" and "Back" buttons.

2.4 Customizing Form Settings

Google Forms offers customization settings under the **Settings** tab:

- **Collect email addresses** – Useful for authentication or follow-ups.

- **Limit to one response per user** – Prevents duplicate submissions.

- **Allow respondents to edit responses after submission** – Useful for corrections.

- **Enable response summary** – Shows results to participants after submission.

Step 3: Customizing the Form's Appearance

To match your form with your Google Site's design, you can customize its appearance:

1. Click on the **Palette (Paintbrush Icon)** in the top right corner.

2. Choose a **header image** or upload your own.

3. Select a **theme color** that matches your website.

4. Adjust the **background color** and **font style** for better readability.

These customizations help maintain brand consistency and make your form visually appealing.

Step 4: Generating the Embed Code for Google Sites

Once your form is ready, you need to generate the embed code:

1. Click on the **Send** button in the top-right corner.

2. Select the **<> Embed HTML** option.

3. Adjust the form **width and height** to fit your site's layout (default is 640x800 pixels).

4. Click **Copy** to save the embed code to your clipboard.

Step 5: Embedding the Google Form into Google Sites

Now, let's embed the Google Form into your Google Site:

1. Open **Google Sites** and navigate to the page where you want to embed the form.

2. Click on **Insert** from the right-hand menu.

3. Select **Embed** and switch to the **Embed Code** tab.

4. Paste the HTML code copied from Google Forms.

5. Click **Next**, then **Insert** to add the form to your site.

After embedding, you can **resize the form** by dragging its corners to fit your page layout.

Step 6: Testing and Publishing the Form

Before making your form live, it's essential to test it:

1. Click **Preview (Eye Icon)** in Google Forms to check the user experience.

2. Submit a test response to ensure the form functions correctly.

3. Verify if responses are correctly recorded in **Google Forms > Responses tab**.

Once satisfied, **publish your Google Site** by clicking the **Publish** button.

Step 7: Managing and Analyzing Form Responses

After embedding the form, you can track responses in real time:

- **View responses in Google Forms**: Navigate to the **Responses** tab to see summaries and individual submissions.

- **Export data to Google Sheets**: Click on the **Google Sheets icon** to analyze data more effectively.

- **Enable email notifications**: Turn on notifications under **More options (⋮ menu) > Get email notifications for new responses**.

If needed, you can disable the form by clicking **Responses > Accepting Responses** toggle.

Best Practices for Using Google Forms in Google Sites

1. **Keep Forms Short and Simple** – Avoid overwhelming users with too many questions.

2. **Use Conditional Logic** – Utilize **"Go to section based on answer"** to improve user experience.

3. **Ensure Mobile-Friendliness** – Test on multiple devices to ensure readability.

4. **Maintain Brand Consistency** – Match the form design with your site's theme.

5. **Regularly Monitor Responses** – Review data periodically to keep insights up to date.

Conclusion

Integrating Google Forms into Google Sites is an effective way to collect feedback, manage registrations, and enhance user engagement. By following this guide, you can easily create, customize, and embed forms into your website, ensuring a seamless and interactive experience for your audience.

In the next section, we will explore how to collect and view responses efficiently, as well as how to use Google Forms for registrations and feedback collection.

5.2.2 Collecting and Viewing Responses

Google Forms is a powerful tool that allows you to collect and analyze data efficiently. Once you have embedded a Google Form into your Google Site, the next critical step is managing the responses. This section will guide you through the process of collecting, viewing, and analyzing responses to make the most of your data.

1. How Google Forms Collects Responses

Google Forms automatically collects responses as users submit them. These responses are stored in the **Responses** tab of the form and can also be linked to a Google Sheet for advanced analysis.

When a user fills out and submits a form, Google Forms records their answers and updates the response data in real time. This allows form owners to monitor incoming responses instantly.

Key Features of Google Forms Response Collection:

- Automatic data recording without manual input

- Real-time updates of new responses

- The ability to view responses directly in Google Forms or link them to a spreadsheet

- Options for email notifications upon new submissions

- Built-in data visualization tools, such as charts and graphs

2. Accessing Responses in Google Forms

Once responses start coming in, you can easily access them by following these steps:

Step 1: Open the Google Form

1. Go to Google Forms and log in with your Google account.

2. Select the form for which you want to view responses.

Step 2: Navigate to the Responses Tab

At the top of the form, you'll see three main tabs:

- **Questions** – where you build and edit the form

- **Responses** – where all submitted data is collected

- **Settings** – where you configure response options

Click on the **Responses** tab to access the submitted answers.

Step 3: Reviewing Response Summary

Google Forms automatically generates a summary of all responses, including:

- The total number of responses

- Graphical summaries (charts, pie charts, bar graphs) for multiple-choice and rating-scale questions

- A list of submitted answers for short-answer and paragraph questions

This feature provides an easy way to analyze trends and common answers without needing additional tools.

Step 4: Viewing Individual Responses

If you want to look at each response separately:

1. In the **Responses** tab, click on the **Individual** sub-tab.

2. Use the left and right arrows to navigate between individual submissions.

3. If needed, you can print or delete specific responses.

---

3. Linking Google Form Responses to Google Sheets

For better data organization and analysis, you can link your Google Form to a Google Sheet. This allows you to:

- Store responses in a structured format

- Use formulas and filters to analyze data

- Share response data with team members

Step 1: Link the Form to a Google Sheet

1. Open the **Responses** tab of your Google Form.

2. Click the green **Google Sheets icon** in the top-right corner.

3. Choose:

   o **Create a new spreadsheet** – if you want to start fresh.

   o **Select an existing spreadsheet** – if you want to merge responses with another dataset.

4. Click **Create** or **Select** to confirm.

Step 2: Access and Manage the Spreadsheet

Once linked, the spreadsheet will automatically update as new responses are submitted. Each column represents a question, and each row corresponds to a respondent.

You can now:

- Sort and filter responses using Google Sheets tools.

- Create custom charts for deeper analysis.

- Use conditional formatting to highlight key data points.

Step 3: Unlinking or Changing the Linked Spreadsheet

If you need to unlink or change the destination spreadsheet:

1. Go to the **Responses** tab in Google Forms.

2. Click the **More options (:)** menu.

3. Select **Unlink form** or **Change destination**.

Note: Once you unlink the form, no new responses will be recorded in the original spreadsheet, but existing data will remain.

4. Enabling Email Notifications for New Responses

If you want to stay updated every time someone submits a response, Google Forms offers email notifications.

How to Enable Email Notifications:

1. Open the **Responses** tab in Google Forms.

2. Click on the **More options (:)** menu.

3. Select **Get email notifications for new responses**.

This ensures that you or your team members receive an email alert whenever a new response is submitted.

Tip: If you're working with a team, you can forward these email notifications or set up filters in Gmail to organize them automatically.

5. Managing and Exporting Responses

Sometimes, you may need to export response data for further analysis or reporting.

Exporting Responses as a CSV File

If you need to share responses outside Google Sheets, you can export them as a CSV file:

1. Open the **Responses** tab in Google Forms.
2. Click the **More options (⋮)** menu.
3. Select **Download responses (.csv)**.
4. Open the file in Excel or another data analysis tool.

Printing Responses

To print responses directly from Google Forms:

1. Go to the **Responses** tab.
2. Click the **More options (⋮)** menu.
3. Select **Print all responses**.

Tip: If you only want to print individual responses, use the **Individual** view in the Responses tab.

Deleting Responses

If you need to clear all collected responses without affecting the form structure:

1. Open the **Responses** tab.
2. Click the **More options (⋮)** menu.
3. Select **Delete all responses**.

Warning: This action is irreversible, so ensure you have backed up the data first.

6. Analyzing Responses with Google Forms' Built-In Tools

Google Forms provides **automatic visual reports** for quick analysis. These include:

- Pie charts for multiple-choice and checkbox questions

- Bar graphs for rating scale responses

- Line graphs for tracking trends over time

To access these insights:

1. Open the **Responses** tab.

2. Scroll down to view the **Summary** section.

3. Hover over graphs to see specific data points.

Using Google Data Studio for Advanced Reporting

If you need more advanced analysis, consider importing the response data into **Google Data Studio** for custom dashboards and interactive reports.

Conclusion

Managing responses in Google Forms is essential for collecting and analyzing data effectively. Whether you prefer using the built-in tools in Google Forms or exporting responses to Google Sheets for deeper insights, the platform offers multiple ways to handle data efficiently.

By linking your form to a spreadsheet, enabling email notifications, and using response analysis tools, you can streamline data collection and make informed decisions based on real-time feedback.

In the next section, we will explore **how to use Google Forms for event registrations and feedback collection**, making your Google Site an even more interactive and engaging platform.

5.2.3 Using Google Forms for Registrations and Feedback

Google Forms is a powerful tool that allows users to create online forms for various purposes, including registrations, surveys, and feedback collection. When integrated with Google Sites, it provides a seamless way to gather information from visitors, track responses, and even automate workflows.

In this section, we will explore how to effectively use Google Forms for **event registrations, feedback collection, and other interactive purposes** within your Google Site.

1. Why Use Google Forms for Registrations and Feedback?

Google Forms is an ideal solution for managing registrations and collecting feedback due to the following reasons:

Ease of Use

- Google Forms has an intuitive drag-and-drop interface that makes it easy to create and customize forms.

- Users can add various question types, such as multiple-choice, dropdowns, and open-ended responses, without any coding knowledge.

Seamless Integration with Google Sites

- Google Forms can be embedded directly into a Google Site, allowing visitors to submit their responses without being redirected elsewhere.

- Responses are automatically stored in **Google Sheets**, making it easy to organize and analyze data.

Real-Time Response Tracking

- Submissions are recorded instantly, allowing site owners to track registrations and feedback in real time.

- Notifications can be set up to alert administrators whenever a new response is received.

Customization and Automation

- Forms can be **customized with branding**, including logos and colors, to match your website's theme.

- Google Forms can be linked with **Google Sheets and Google Scripts** for automation, such as sending confirmation emails.

2. Creating a Google Form for Registrations

Common Use Cases for Registration Forms

Google Forms can be used for a variety of registration needs, including:

- **Event registrations** (webinars, workshops, conferences)
- **Membership sign-ups** (clubs, courses, online communities)
- **Job applications** (internship programs, hiring forms)

Steps to Create a Registration Form

Step 1: Access Google Forms

1. Go to Google Forms.
2. Click on the **"Blank"** form to start from scratch or choose a template.

Step 2: Add Essential Fields

A well-structured registration form should include:

- **Name** (Short answer question)
- **Email Address** (Short answer with email validation)
- **Phone Number** (Short answer with number validation)
- **Event Date & Time Preference** (Dropdown or Multiple Choice)
- **Additional Comments** (Paragraph text)

Step 3: Customize Form Settings

- Enable **response validation** for fields like email and phone number.
- Set required questions to ensure all necessary information is collected.
- Add **confirmation messages** to let users know their submission was successful.

Step 4: Enable Notifications and Response Collection

- Click the **"Responses"** tab and enable **Google Sheets linking** for easy tracking.
- Enable **email notifications** to get alerts when a new response is submitted.

3. Embedding the Registration Form in Google Sites

After creating the form, you need to embed it in your Google Site:

Step 1: Open Google Sites

1. Navigate to your **Google Site editor**.
2. Choose the page where you want to embed the form.

Step 2: Insert the Form

1. Click **"Insert"** > **"Forms"** from the right-hand menu.
2. Select your form from the list.
3. Click **"Insert"**, and adjust the size and positioning on the page.

Step 3: Publish and Test

1. Click **"Publish"** to make changes live.
2. Test the form submission to ensure everything works properly.

4. Creating a Google Form for Feedback Collection

Common Use Cases for Feedback Forms

Feedback forms help gather insights on:

- Website usability (User experience, navigation ease)
- Event satisfaction (Opinions on workshops, seminars)
- Customer service feedback (Reviews on product or service quality)

Steps to Create a Feedback Form

Step 1: Define the Purpose

Before creating a feedback form, decide what information you want to collect:

- Are you gathering general opinions or specific feedback?

- Will responses be anonymous or require user details?

Step 2: Choose the Right Question Types

A good feedback form includes a mix of:

- Likert Scale Questions (e.g., "Rate your experience from 1 to 5")

- Multiple Choice Questions (e.g., "Which feature did you use most?")

- Open-Ended Questions (e.g., "What improvements would you suggest?")

Step 3: Add Conditional Logic for Better Engagement

- Use **"Go to section based on answer"** logic to tailor the form experience.

- Example: If a user rates an event **5 stars**, the form skips the complaint section.

Step 4: Customize the Appearance

- Add your **company logo** and change the **theme color** to match your website.

- Enable **progress bars** for long surveys.

5. Automating Responses and Analyzing Data

Sending Automatic Confirmation Emails

To send a confirmation email after form submission:

1. Install the **Google Forms add-on "Form Notifications"**.

2. Set up an **email template** for responses.

3. Customize the message with details like **event date and time**.

Viewing and Analyzing Responses

- Responses are stored in **Google Sheets** for better organization.

- Use **filters and charts** to analyze feedback trends.

- Export results in **CSV format** for advanced reporting.

Using Google Forms Data to Improve Your Site

- Identify common **pain points** based on feedback.

- Improve **website design** based on navigation suggestions.

- Adjust **event planning** based on user preferences.

6. Best Practices for Using Google Forms on Google Sites

1. **Keep Forms Short and Simple**

   o Limit the number of questions to **increase response rates**.

2. **Ensure Mobile Compatibility**

   o Test forms on **smartphones and tablets** for a smooth experience.

3. **Use Required Fields Wisely**

   o Only mark **critical questions** as required to avoid user frustration.

4. **Regularly Update Forms**

   o Modify forms based on **user feedback** to keep them relevant.

5. **Follow Data Privacy Guidelines**

   o Inform users how their data will be used to **build trust**.

Conclusion

Using Google Forms for registrations and feedback enhances the functionality of Google Sites by making it interactive and user-friendly. Whether you're collecting **event sign-ups** or improving your site through **user feedback**, integrating Google Forms ensures a smooth, automated process.

By following this guide, you can create professional forms, embed them seamlessly, and use response data to optimize your website experience.

5.3 Using Google Calendar and Maps

5.3.1 Embedding a Google Calendar for Scheduling

Google Sites allows you to integrate Google Calendar, making it easy to share events, schedules, and availability with your audience. Whether you're managing a business, an educational platform, or a personal project, embedding Google Calendar enhances organization and communication. In this section, we will explore how to add Google Calendar to your Google Site, customize its display, and optimize its functionality for different use cases.

Why Embed Google Calendar in Google Sites?

Embedding a Google Calendar in your site offers multiple benefits, including:

- **Centralized Scheduling:** Display upcoming events, deadlines, or meetings in one place.

- **Real-Time Updates:** Any changes made to the calendar reflect instantly on the site.

- **Improved Communication:** Helps teams, students, or clients stay informed.

- **Simplified Event Management:** Reduces the need for manual event notifications.

Now, let's go through the steps to embed Google Calendar into your Google Site.

Step 1: Preparing Your Google Calendar

Before embedding Google Calendar, ensure it is properly configured for sharing:

1. **Open Google Calendar**

   o Go to Google Calendar. https://calendar.google.com/

   o Sign in with your Google account if you haven't already.

2. **Select or Create a Calendar**

   o On the left panel, you will see "My calendars." Click on an existing calendar or create a new one by selecting the "+" icon next to "Other calendars" and choosing "Create new calendar."

   o Give the calendar a name, description, and time zone.

3. **Make the Calendar Public (If Needed)**

   o If your site is publicly accessible and you want everyone to view the calendar:

     ▪ Click the **gear icon (⚙️⬜)** in the top-right corner and select **Settings**.

     ▪ Choose your calendar from the left panel.

     ▪ Scroll to **Access permissions for events** and check **Make available to public**.

   o If you only want specific people to view the calendar, click **Add people and groups** and enter their email addresses.

4. **Get the Embed Code**

   o Scroll down to the **Integrate calendar** section.

   o Copy the provided **iframe embed code** or the **Calendar ID** if using Google Sites' built-in embed feature.

Step 2: Adding Google Calendar to Your Google Site

Once your calendar is ready, follow these steps to add it to your Google Site:

Method 1: Using the Google Sites Calendar Integration

1. Open your **Google Site** and navigate to the page where you want to add the calendar.

2. Click on **"Insert"** in the right-hand panel.

3. Scroll down and select **"Calendar"**.

4. A list of your Google Calendars will appear. Click on the one you want to embed.

5. Click **"Insert"** to add it to your page.

6. Resize or reposition the calendar as needed by dragging the edges.

Method 2: Using the Embed Code

If you prefer to embed Google Calendar manually:

1. In **Google Sites**, click on **"Embed"** from the right panel.

2. Choose the **"Embed Code"** tab.

3. Paste the **iframe embed code** copied from Google Calendar.

4. Click **"Insert"**, then adjust the calendar's size and position.

Step 3: Customizing the Display of Google Calendar

Google Sites allows you to modify how the calendar appears on your page.

Adjusting Calendar Size and Layout

- Click on the embedded calendar in **Google Sites**.

- Drag the corners to **resize** it as needed.

- Use the settings menu to adjust the **view mode** (Month, Week, or Agenda).

Showing or Hiding Specific Calendars

- If you've embedded a calendar with multiple event types (work, personal, holidays), you can toggle which ones are displayed:

  o Open **Google Calendar** and go to **Settings**.

- o Under **Integrate calendar**, modify the embed code to remove specific calendars.

Changing the Default View (Month, Week, or Agenda)

- To modify how events appear:

  - o Open **Google Calendar** settings.

  - o Under **Embed code**, find mode="MONTH" and change it to:

    - "WEEK" (for a week view)

    - "AGENDA" (for a list of events)

Step 4: Optimizing the Google Calendar Experience

To enhance user engagement and ensure a smooth experience, consider these best practices:

1. Keep Your Calendar Updated

- Regularly update events to ensure accuracy.

- Use Google Calendar's **recurring event** feature for repeating events.

2. Use Color-Coding for Better Organization

- Assign different colors to different types of events (e.g., work meetings, deadlines, holidays).

3. Enable Notifications and Reminders

- Users can **subscribe** to your calendar to receive notifications directly.

4. Create Event Links for Easy Access

- In the **event details**, add links to registration pages, meeting rooms, or documents.

5. Sync with Other Calendar Apps

- Ensure users can sync the embedded calendar with their personal Google or Outlook calendars.

Real-World Applications of Google Calendar in Google Sites

Here are some practical ways to use Google Calendar in your site:

Business Use Cases

- Display office hours, meetings, or company events.

- Provide an appointment booking calendar for customers.

Educational Use Cases

- Share class schedules or exam dates for students.

- Embed a school-wide event calendar for parents and staff.

Personal Use Cases

- Manage a personal blog's content schedule.

- Create a family calendar for important dates and vacations.

Troubleshooting Common Issues

Problem 1: Calendar Not Displaying Properly

Solution: Ensure the calendar is set to **public visibility** in Google Calendar settings.

Problem 2: Embed Code Not Working

Solution: Double-check the copied embed code and ensure it's properly formatted.

Problem 3: Calendar Events Not Updating on Google Sites

Solution: Refresh the page or clear browser cache to reflect the latest changes.

Conclusion

Embedding Google Calendar into Google Sites is a powerful way to enhance scheduling and communication. By following the steps outlined in this section, you can create an organized and visually appealing event display that keeps your audience informed. Whether you're using Google Calendar for business, education, or personal use, integrating it into your site ensures that event management is seamless and effective.

5.3.2 Adding Google Maps for Location Sharing

Google Maps is a powerful tool that allows users to locate addresses, get directions, and explore geographic areas. When integrated into Google Sites, Google Maps enhances the user experience by providing location-based information directly on your web pages. Whether you want to share the location of your business, a conference venue, or an event, embedding Google Maps can make navigation easy for your visitors.

This section will walk you through the process of embedding Google Maps into your Google Site, customizing the map, and ensuring that it effectively serves your purpose.

1. Why Use Google Maps on Your Site?

Embedding Google Maps on your Google Site offers several benefits:

- **Enhanced User Experience**: Visitors can find locations quickly without leaving your website.

- **Accurate Directions**: Users can get real-time navigation and directions to your location.

- **Professional Appearance**: A Google Map makes your website look polished and informative.

- **Customizable Options**: You can highlight multiple locations, add markers, and adjust map views.

- **Google Ecosystem Integration**: Since Google Maps is part of Google Workspace, it works seamlessly with your Google Sites project.

Common use cases include:

- Displaying a business or office location

- Providing directions to an event or conference

- Showcasing multiple store branches

- Highlighting tourist spots or landmarks

2. How to Embed Google Maps in Google Sites

There are two primary ways to add Google Maps to a Google Site:

1. **Using the Built-in Google Maps Embed Feature** (Easiest method)

2. **Embedding a Custom Google Map with an HTML Embed Code** (More customization options)

Method 1: Using the Built-in Google Maps Feature

This is the quickest way to embed a map into your Google Site.

Step 1: Open Google Sites Editor

- Navigate to Google Sites.

- Open your existing site or create a new one.

Step 2: Select the Page for Your Map

- Click on the page where you want to add the map or create a new section.

Step 3: Insert a Google Map

- Click on the **Insert** tab from the right-hand sidebar.

- Scroll down and select **Maps**.

- A Google Maps window will appear where you can search for a location.

Step 4: Search for a Location

- In the Google Maps search bar, type the address or place name.

- Click **Select** once you find the correct location.

- The map will now be inserted into your Google Site.

Step 5: Resize and Adjust the Map

- Click on the embedded map to resize or reposition it within your site layout.

- You can drag the corners to adjust its dimensions.

Step 6: Publish Your Site

- Click **Publish** to make the map visible to your visitors.

Pros of Using the Built-in Google Maps Feature

✓☐ Fast and easy to embed
✓☐ No need for additional configuration
✓☐ Works seamlessly within Google Sites

Cons

✗ Limited customization (no custom markers or routes)
✗ Cannot display multiple locations easily

---

3. How to Embed a Custom Google Map Using an HTML Embed Code

If you need advanced customization, such as multiple locations, custom pins, or different map styles, you can generate an embed code from Google Maps and insert it into your Google Site.

Step 1: Open Google Maps and Create a Custom Map

- Go to Google Maps. https://www.google.com/maps

- Search for your desired location.

- Click on **Share** → **Embed a Map**.

Step 2: Copy the Embed Code

- Choose the **Map Size** (Small, Medium, Large, or Custom).

- Click **Copy HTML** to get the embed code.

Step 3: Insert the Code into Google Sites

- Go to Google Sites and open your page.

- Click **Embed** (found in the right-hand panel).

- Select the **Embed Code** option.

- Paste the copied HTML code and click **Insert**.

Step 4: Adjust the Map on Your Page

- Click on the embedded map to resize or reposition it as needed.

Pros of Using the Custom Embed Code

✓☐ Allows for multiple locations and custom markers
✓☐ More customization (routes, layers, map styles)
✓☐ Advanced display options

Cons

✗ Requires manually copying and pasting the embed code
✗ Limited real-time editing compared to the built-in method

4. Customizing Your Google Maps Embed

To make your map more interactive and informative, consider the following customizations:

Adding Multiple Locations (Custom Markers)

If you need to highlight multiple places (e.g., branch offices, event locations), use **Google My Maps**:

1. Open Google My Maps. https://www.google.com/maps/d/

☰ Google My Maps

⚘ CREATE A NEW MAP

2. Click **Create a New Map**.

3. Add multiple pins by searching locations and clicking **Add to Map**.

4. Customize marker icons and colors.

5. Click **Share** → **Get Embed Code** → Paste into Google Sites.

Changing the Map Style

Google Maps offers different styles such as:

- **Default Roadmap** (best for directions)
- **Satellite View** (real-world imagery)
- **Terrain View** (useful for hiking or elevation maps)

To change the style:

1. In **Google My Maps**, click **Base Map**.
2. Choose the preferred style.
3. Embed the updated map into Google Sites.

5. Best Practices for Using Google Maps on Your Site

- **Ensure the Map is Mobile-Friendly**

  o Google Sites automatically makes embedded maps responsive, but always preview your site on mobile devices.

- **Keep the Map Visible and Accessible**

  o Place the map in an easy-to-find section, such as the **Contact Us** or **Location** page.

- **Use Custom Labels for Clarity**

  o Instead of just showing a pin, label locations with descriptions like "Main Office" or "Event Venue."

- **Test the Map Before Publishing**

  o Open the embedded map and test navigation links to ensure they work correctly.

- **Use Google Maps API for Advanced Features**

  o If you need real-time traffic updates or user location detection, consider using Google Maps API (requires coding).

6. Troubleshooting Common Issues

The Map is Not Displaying Properly

✓ Check if the map is correctly embedded using the **Preview** feature.

✓ Ensure the URL or embed code is copied correctly.

✓ If using a custom map, verify that **public access** is enabled.

The Map is Not Updating

✓ Refresh the page or republish the site.

✓ If using Google My Maps, make sure the latest version is embedded.

Map Takes Too Long to Load

✓ Use a smaller map size to improve loading speed.

✓ Ensure a stable internet connection when embedding large maps.

---

7. Conclusion

Adding Google Maps to your Google Site is a simple yet powerful way to enhance user experience and provide valuable location-based information. Whether you're showcasing a single location or multiple points of interest, using the built-in feature or embedding a custom map can significantly improve your site's navigation and accessibility.

By following the steps outlined above, you can seamlessly integrate Google Maps and ensure that your visitors can easily find the locations they need. Experiment with customization options and best practices to make your site both informative and visually appealing.

5.4 Connecting Google Drive Files and Folders

Google Sites seamlessly integrates with Google Drive, allowing you to embed and display various files and folders directly on your website. Whether you need to share documents, presentations, spreadsheets, images, or even videos, embedding Google Drive content enhances accessibility and ensures that your audience always sees the latest version of your files.

In this section, we will explore the benefits of integrating Google Drive with Google Sites, provide step-by-step instructions for embedding files and folders, and discuss best practices for managing permissions and security.

Why Connect Google Drive to Your Google Site?

Google Drive integration in Google Sites offers several key advantages:

1. **Automatic Updates:** Since files are linked directly from Google Drive, any changes made to the original file are automatically reflected on your website.

2. **Easy File Sharing:** You can share important documents, presentations, and reports with your visitors without needing to upload and update them manually.

3. **Improved Collaboration:** If your website is used for team collaboration, embedding shared folders allows team members to access necessary files in one centralized location.

4. **Seamless Google Workspace Integration:** Google Drive works effortlessly with other Google tools such as Docs, Sheets, Slides, Forms, and more.

5. **Organized Content Management:** Instead of cluttering your site with multiple file uploads, you can embed folders that dynamically update as you add or remove files in Google Drive.

Embedding Individual Google Drive Files

Embedding a file from Google Drive into your Google Site is a simple process. You can add documents, spreadsheets, slides, PDFs, images, and even videos.

Step-by-Step Guide to Embedding a Google Drive File:

1. **Open Your Google Site**

   o Navigate to Google Sites and open the site where you want to embed the file.

2. **Select the Page**

   o Choose the page where you want to insert the Google Drive file.

3. **Insert a Google Drive File**

   o Click on the **"Insert"** tab in the right-hand menu.

   o Scroll down and click on **"Drive."**

   o A pop-up window will appear, allowing you to browse and select a file from your Google Drive.

4. **Choose the File to Embed**

   o Locate the file you want to embed and click **"Insert."**

   o The file will appear on your Google Site as a preview.

5. **Resize and Adjust the File Display**

   o Click on the embedded file to resize it or move it within the page layout.

   o You can adjust the width and height to make the content fit appropriately.

6. **Publish Your Site**

   o Click **"Publish"** to make the embedded file visible to your site visitors.

◆ **Tip:** Ensure that your file's sharing settings in Google Drive allow the appropriate level of access. If a visitor does not have permission, they will see a "You need access" message instead of the file preview.

Embedding Google Drive Folders

Instead of embedding individual files, you can embed an entire Google Drive folder. This is useful when you want to share a collection of documents, images, or resources that may be updated regularly.

Steps to Embed a Google Drive Folder:

1. **Open Your Google Site**

   o Go to Google Sites and select your website.

2. **Navigate to the Desired Page**

   o Choose the page where you want to insert the folder.

3. **Insert a Google Drive Folder**

   o Click on **"Insert"** in the right-hand menu.

   o Select **"Drive."**

   o In the pop-up window, navigate to the folder you want to embed.

4. **Insert and Adjust Folder Display**

   o Click **"Insert"** to add the folder to your Google Site.

   o Resize and position the folder display for better visibility.

5. **Check Folder Permissions**

   o Ensure that the folder's sharing settings allow your audience to view its contents.

6. **Publish Your Site**

   o Click **"Publish"** to update your site with the embedded folder.

♠ **Tip:** When you update files in Google Drive, the changes will automatically reflect on your site without needing to re-upload or re-embed anything.

Managing File and Folder Permissions

Before embedding Google Drive content into your site, you need to configure the appropriate sharing settings to ensure your audience can view the files.

Adjusting File Permissions in Google Drive:

1. **Go to Google Drive**

   o   Open Google Drive and locate the file or folder you want to embed.

2. **Right-click and Select "Share"**

   o   A sharing settings window will appear.

3. **Set Viewing Permissions**

   o   Choose who can access the file:

   ▪   **Restricted:** Only specific people you invite can view it.

   ▪   **Anyone with the link:** Anyone with the link can view the file.

   ▪   **Public:** The file is accessible to anyone on the internet.

4. **Copy the Sharing Link (If Needed)**

   o   If you want to share the file directly, click **"Copy Link"** and paste it into your site.

◆ **Important:** If you embed a file with restricted access, visitors may see a "Request access" message instead of the file preview.

Best Practices for Using Google Drive with Google Sites

To make the most of Google Drive integration, follow these best practices:

✓ **Use Organized Folders:** Keep your Google Drive structured by organizing files into folders before embedding them on your site.

✓ **Check Permissions Regularly:** Ensure that all embedded files and folders have the correct sharing settings to avoid access issues.

✓ **Use Descriptive File Names:** Name your files clearly to help visitors understand the content without opening each one.

✓ **Update Content Dynamically:** Take advantage of Google Drive's live updates to keep site content fresh without republishing.

✅ **Consider Using View-Only Mode:** If sharing sensitive documents, ensure they are set to **"View Only"** to prevent unwanted edits.

✅ **Test Your Site Before Publishing:** Always preview your site to check that embedded files and folders display correctly for visitors.

Troubleshooting Common Issues

Here are some common problems and their solutions when embedding Google Drive content in Google Sites:

❖ **Issue:** Embedded file doesn't appear or shows a "You need access" message.
Solution: Check Google Drive permissions and set the file to "Anyone with the link can view."

❖ **Issue:** Folder contents are not updating on the site.
Solution: Refresh your browser or re-embed the folder to ensure it syncs properly.

❖ **Issue:** Embedded file is too large or loads slowly.
Solution: Optimize file size by compressing images and documents before uploading them to Google Drive.

❖ **Issue:** Visitors cannot download files from an embedded folder.
Solution: Ensure file sharing settings allow downloads or provide direct links to downloadable versions.

Conclusion

Integrating Google Drive with Google Sites is a powerful way to enhance your website by embedding documents, spreadsheets, slides, and folders. By following the steps outlined in this chapter, you can ensure seamless file sharing, improve collaboration, and keep your content up-to-date without manual updates.

In the next chapter, we will explore how to customize and optimize your Google Site further by working with custom URLs, embedding third-party content, and designing effective call-to-action buttons.

CHAPTER VI
Customizing and Optimizing Your Google Site

6.1 Working with Custom URLs and Domains

6.1.1 Assigning a Custom Domain to Your Site

A custom domain can give your Google Site a professional appearance, making it easier for visitors to remember and access. Instead of using the default Google Sites URL (e.g., sites.google.com/view/yoursitename), you can assign a custom domain like www.yourwebsite.com. This chapter will guide you through the process of setting up a custom domain for your Google Site, including purchasing a domain, configuring DNS settings, and linking it to Google Sites.

1. Why Use a Custom Domain?

Using a custom domain provides several benefits:

- **Branding** – A personalized domain helps establish a stronger brand identity.

- **Credibility** – Visitors perceive custom domains as more professional and trustworthy.

- **Easier Access** – A shorter and memorable domain makes it easier for users to find your site.

- **SEO Benefits** – Custom domains can improve search engine rankings and visibility.

2. Purchasing a Custom Domain

Before linking a custom domain to Google Sites, you need to purchase a domain from a domain registrar. Some popular domain registrars include:

- Google Domains
- GoDaddy
- Namecheap
- Bluehost
- Hover

Steps to Purchase a Domain:

1. **Visit a Domain Registrar** – Go to a domain provider's website (e.g., Google Domains).
2. **Search for an Available Domain** – Use the search function to check if your desired domain name is available.
3. **Select a Domain** – Choose a domain that fits your brand and is easy to remember.
4. **Register the Domain** – Follow the checkout process and pay for the domain.
5. **Set Up Domain Management** – After purchasing, access the domain's DNS settings in the registrar's dashboard.

3. Connecting a Custom Domain to Google Sites

Once you have a domain, you can connect it to your Google Site using Google's built-in domain mapping feature.

Steps to Link Your Domain to Google Sites:

Step 1: Open Google Sites

1. Navigate to Google Sites.
2. Open the site you want to assign a custom domain to.

Step 2: Access the Custom Domain Settings

1. Click on the **Settings (⚙☐)** icon in the top-right corner.

2. Select **Custom Domains** from the menu.

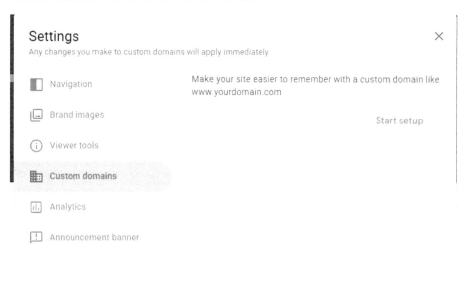

3. Click **Start Setup**.

Step 3: Verify Domain Ownership

Google requires verification to ensure you own the domain before linking it.

1. Select **Use a Domain from a Third-Party Provider** if your domain was purchased outside Google Domains.

2. Google will provide a TXT record that you need to add to your domain registrar's DNS settings.

3. Go to your domain provider's dashboard and locate the **DNS Settings** or **DNS Management** section.

4. Add the provided TXT record to verify ownership.

5. Save changes and return to Google Sites. Click **Verify** to complete the process.

💡 *Note: Verification may take a few minutes to a few hours, depending on your domain provider.*

4. Configuring DNS Settings for Your Custom Domain

After verification, you need to update your DNS settings to point your domain to Google Sites.

Adding CNAME Records

A **CNAME record** (Canonical Name Record) tells the internet that your domain should redirect to Google's servers.

1. Go to your domain registrar's DNS settings.

2. Locate the section for **CNAME records**.

3. Add the following CNAME records:

Hostname / Name	Type	Value / Target
www	CNAME	ghs.googlehosted.com

4. Save the changes.

Adding A Records (Optional for Naked Domains)

If you want visitors to access your site using yourwebsite.com (without "www"), you need to add **A records** to point to Google's IP addresses.

1. Find the **A Records** section in your domain settings.

2. Add the following A records:

Hostname / Name	Type	Value / Target
@	A	216.239.32.21
@	A	216.239.34.21
@	A	216.239.36.21
@	A	216.239.38.21

3. Save the changes.

💡 Note: DNS updates may take up to 24 hours to fully propagate across the internet.

5. Finalizing the Domain Connection in Google Sites

After configuring DNS settings, return to Google Sites and complete the setup:

1. Go back to **Settings > Custom Domains**.

2. Click **Use a Domain You Own** and enter your domain name.

3. Google will check the DNS settings and confirm if they are correct.

4. Click **Save and Publish** to finalize the setup.

Your site is now accessible via your custom domain!

6. Troubleshooting Common Issues

Issue: Domain Not Verifying

- Double-check that you copied and pasted the TXT record correctly.

- Wait 15-30 minutes and try verifying again.

- If using Cloudflare, disable proxy mode (set DNS records to **DNS only**).

Issue: Site Not Loading After Updating DNS

- DNS changes can take up to 24 hours to propagate.

- Make sure your CNAME and A records are entered correctly.

- Clear your browser cache and test again.

Issue: HTTPS Not Working

- Google Sites automatically enables HTTPS, but it may take some time.

- Ensure that **Force HTTPS** is enabled in Google Sites settings.

7. Maintaining and Managing Your Custom Domain

Once your domain is connected, keep these best practices in mind:

- **Renew Your Domain Annually** – Avoid losing your domain by enabling auto-renewal.

- **Update DNS Records When Necessary** – If you switch site platforms, update DNS settings accordingly.

- **Monitor Website Performance** – Use Google Analytics to track visitor engagement.

8. Summary and Key Takeaways

- A **custom domain** improves branding and professionalism.

- Purchase a domain from a trusted registrar like **Google Domains or GoDaddy**.

- Use **CNAME and A records** to point your domain to Google Sites.

- **Verification and DNS propagation** may take a few hours to complete.

- Regularly **maintain and update** your domain settings for security and performance.

By following these steps, you can successfully assign a custom domain to your Google Site, ensuring a professional and accessible online presence!

★ **Next Section:** *6.1.2 Using Google Domains for Registration*

6.1.2 Using Google Domains for Registration

When customizing your Google Site, one of the most effective ways to establish a professional and recognizable online presence is by using a custom domain. Google Domains is a service that allows you to purchase, register, and manage domain names directly from Google. By using Google Domains, you can easily link your domain to your Google Site, enhancing your website's credibility and making it easier for users to find and remember your site.

In this section, we will cover:

- What Google Domains is and its benefits

- How to search for and purchase a domain

- Managing domain settings

- Connecting your Google Site to a Google Domains-registered domain

- Additional domain settings and configurations

What is Google Domains?

Overview of Google Domains

Google Domains is a domain registration service provided by Google, offering a straightforward and reliable way to purchase and manage domain names. Unlike other domain registrars, Google Domains seamlessly integrates with Google Sites, Google Workspace, and other Google services, making it an excellent choice for users who want a hassle-free setup.

Benefits of Using Google Domains for Your Google Site

1. **Seamless Integration with Google Services**

   o Google Domains is designed to work effortlessly with Google Sites, Google Workspace, and other Google tools, eliminating compatibility issues.

2. **User-Friendly Interface**

   o The interface is intuitive and easy to navigate, making domain registration and management simple, even for beginners.

3. **Free Privacy Protection**

   o Unlike many other registrars that charge extra for privacy protection, Google Domains includes WHOIS privacy protection at no additional cost.

4. **Automatic Domain Renewal**

   o You can enable automatic renewal to prevent your domain from expiring unexpectedly.

5. **Reliable DNS and Security**

- o   Google Domains uses Google's own DNS infrastructure, ensuring fast and secure domain resolution.

6. **Custom Email with Google Workspace**

    - o   If you need a professional email address (e.g., yourname@yourdomain.com), Google Domains integrates with Google Workspace, making email setup easy.

7. **No Hidden Fees**

    - o   The pricing is transparent, and there are no unexpected fees for domain management.

How to Search for and Purchase a Domain on Google Domains

Step 1: Access Google Domains

1. Open a web browser and go to Google Domains.

2. Sign in with your Google account if you are not already logged in.

Step 2: Search for an Available Domain

1. In the search bar, type the desired domain name.

2. Click the **Search** button to see available options.

3. Browse the list of available domains and choose the one that best suits your website.

    - o   Google Domains offers multiple domain extensions such as **.com, .net, .org, .site, .tech**, etc.

4. If your preferred domain is unavailable, consider alternative domain extensions or modify the domain name slightly.

Step 3: Add the Domain to Your Cart

1. Once you find an available domain, click the **Add to cart** button.

2. Review the details of your selection, ensuring that WHOIS privacy protection is enabled (this is free with Google Domains).

Step 4: Complete the Purchase

1. Click **Proceed to checkout** and enter your payment details.

2. Provide any required information, such as your name and contact details (this is required for domain registration).

3. Choose whether to enable auto-renewal to keep your domain active without manual renewal.

4. Click **Buy** to finalize the transaction.

5. Once the purchase is complete, Google will confirm your domain registration via email.

Managing Your Domain in Google Domains

Accessing Your Domain Settings

1. Go to Google Domains.

2. Click **My domains** to view the list of your registered domains.

3. Select the domain you want to manage.

Key Domain Management Features

- **DNS Settings**: Manage Domain Name System (DNS) settings, including records for website and email configuration.

- **Subdomains**: Create and manage subdomains like blog.yourdomain.com.

- **Privacy Protection**: Enable or disable WHOIS privacy settings.

- **Auto-Renewal**: Enable auto-renewal to avoid losing your domain due to expiration.

- **Domain Transfers**: Transfer your domain to another registrar if needed.

Connecting Your Google Site to a Google Domains-Registered Domain

After purchasing a domain, you need to link it to your Google Site so that visitors can access your site using your custom domain.

Step 1: Open Your Google Site

1. Go to Google Sites.

2. Open the website you want to connect to your custom domain.

Step 2: Open the Custom Domains Settings

1. Click on **Settings (⚙□)** in the top-right corner.

2. Select **Custom domains** from the menu.

3. Click **Start setup**.

Step 3: Verify Domain Ownership

1. Choose **Use a domain from Google Domains**.

2. If you're signed into the same Google account used to purchase the domain, your domain should appear in the list.

3. Select your domain and click **Next**.

4. Google will automatically verify ownership, so you won't need to manually update DNS records.

Step 4: Publish Your Site with the Custom Domain

1. Click **Save** and **Publish** your Google Site.

2. Your site will now be accessible at your custom domain (e.g., www.yourdomain.com).

Additional Domain Settings and Configurations

Setting Up Custom Email with Google Workspace

If you want a professional email address (e.g., contact@yourdomain.com), you can set up Google Workspace with Google Domains:

1. In **Google Domains**, go to **Email** settings.

2. Click **Get Google Workspace** and follow the setup instructions.

Creating Subdomains

1. In **Google Domains**, navigate to **DNS Settings**.

2. Under **Custom Records**, add a new **CNAME** record for the subdomain.

3. Point the subdomain to your Google Site or another web service.

Configuring Advanced DNS Settings

For more control over how your domain resolves:

1. Go to **Google Domains > DNS**.

2. Modify **A, CNAME, MX, TXT, and other DNS records** as needed.

Troubleshooting Common Issues

Domain Not Linking to Google Sites

- Ensure you selected **"Use a domain from Google Domains"** in the custom domain settings.

- Check if your domain is active and not expired.

Website Not Loading with Custom Domain

- Wait up to 24 hours for DNS changes to propagate.

- Verify that your Google Site is published.

Google Workspace Email Not Working

- Double-check MX record settings in **Google Domains > DNS**.

- Ensure that Google Workspace has been correctly linked to your domain.

Conclusion

Using Google Domains to register and link a custom domain to your Google Site is an effective way to enhance your site's professionalism and credibility. With seamless integration, robust security, and easy management, Google Domains is an excellent choice for personal, business, and educational websites. By following the steps outlined in this section, you can set up and manage your custom domain with confidence.

6.1.3 Managing URL Redirects

Introduction to URL Redirects

When building and managing a website, you may need to change page URLs, move content, or consolidate pages. However, when users or search engines try to visit the old URL, they may encounter a "Page Not Found" (404) error. This is where **URL redirects** come into play. A URL redirect automatically forwards visitors from one URL to another, ensuring a seamless user experience and maintaining search engine rankings.

While Google Sites does not have a built-in URL redirection feature like traditional content management systems (CMS), there are several methods to set up redirects effectively. In this section, we will explore how to implement URL redirects within Google Sites, why they are important, and alternative solutions.

Why Use URL Redirects?

URL redirects are essential for various reasons, including:

1. Maintaining User Experience

- If a page URL changes, users should be automatically directed to the new page instead of seeing a "404 Page Not Found" error.

- Redirects ensure that users do not get lost when navigating your site.

2. Preserving SEO (Search Engine Optimization)

- Search engines rank pages based on their URLs and content. Changing a URL without a redirect may cause a loss in search engine ranking.

- Redirects help maintain SEO value by signaling search engines that content has been moved rather than removed.

3. Consolidating or Updating Content

- If you merge multiple pages into one, redirects ensure that old URLs point to the new location.

- Redirects prevent duplicate content issues, improving website structure.

4. Rebranding and Domain Changes

- If you migrate your Google Site to a custom domain, redirects ensure visitors land on the new domain instead of outdated links.

Types of URL Redirects

There are different types of redirects, each serving a specific purpose:

1. 301 Redirect (Permanent Redirect)

- This is used when a page has been permanently moved to a new location.

- Search engines transfer the SEO ranking of the old URL to the new one.

2. 302 Redirect (Temporary Redirect)

- Used when a URL change is temporary, such as during website maintenance or A/B testing.

- Search engines keep the original URL indexed and do not transfer SEO value.

3. Meta Refresh Redirect

- This uses HTML code to refresh the page and redirect users after a few seconds.

- Less effective for SEO but can be useful when no other redirect options are available.

4. JavaScript Redirect

- Uses JavaScript to redirect users when they visit a page.

- Not ideal for SEO, but can work when editing HTML is allowed.

How to Set Up URL Redirects in Google Sites

Since Google Sites does not offer a built-in redirect feature, here are different ways to achieve URL redirection:

Method 1: Using a Custom Button or Link as a Manual Redirect

A simple but effective way to guide users from an old page to a new one is to place a prominent button or hyperlink.

Steps:

1. Open **Google Sites** and navigate to the page where you want the redirect to happen.

2. Click **"Insert" > "Button"** to add a navigation button.

3. Name the button (e.g., "Go to the New Page").

4. Enter the new URL in the link field.

5. Click **"Insert"** and move the button to a visible location.

6. Publish your site to apply changes.

While this method does not automatically redirect users, it provides a clear way for visitors to access the correct page.

Method 2: Redirecting via Google Domains (For Custom Domains Only)

 Google Domains

About the Squarespace purchase of Google Domains registrations

On 15 June 2023, Google entered into a definitive agreement with Squarespace, indicating their intent to purchase all domain registrations and related customer accounts from Google Domains. When the transaction between Google and Squarespace closed on 7 September 2023, all Google Domains users became customers of Squarespace. As of 10 July 2024, all domains have migrated to Squarespace.

Please contact Squarespace for further help.

For migrated Cloud Domains, contact Cloud support.

If you have a custom domain linked to your Google Site, Google Domains allows URL forwarding to redirect traffic from an old URL to a new one.

Steps:

1. Go to **Google Domains** (https://domains.google.com/).

2. Sign in with the account associated with your Google Site.

3. Select your domain name.

4. Navigate to **"Website" > "Forwarding"**.

5. Click **"Add a Forward"** and enter the old URL.

6. In the destination field, enter the new URL.

7. Choose **"Permanent Redirect (301)"** if the change is permanent.

8. Click **"Save"** to apply changes.

This method works well if you control the domain and need to redirect an entire website or specific pages.

Method 3: Using Google Analytics to Guide Visitors

While Google Analytics does not provide direct URL redirection, you can set up **Event Tracking** to detect when users visit an old page and then display a message guiding them to the new URL.

Steps:

1. Set up **Google Analytics** on your Google Site.

2. Create a tracking event for the old URL.

3. Display a pop-up or notification directing users to the new page.

This method requires some technical expertise and does not provide automatic redirection but helps improve navigation.

Method 4: JavaScript Redirects (Requires Embedding HTML Code)

Although Google Sites does not support direct HTML editing, you can embed JavaScript within an **"Embed Code"** block to create a redirect.

Steps:

1. Open the old page in **Google Sites**.

2. Click **"Insert" > "Embed" > "Embed Code"**.

3. Enter the following JavaScript code:

4. <script>

5.   window.location.href = "https://newpage.com";

6. </script>

7. Click **"Insert"** and publish your site.

This method works only if embedding scripts is allowed. However, some browsers and Google Sites security policies may block it.

Best Practices for Managing Redirects in Google Sites

To ensure smooth redirection and prevent user frustration, follow these best practices:

1. Test Your Redirects

- Before publishing, test the redirect to ensure it works as expected.
- Use **incognito mode** or a different device to verify functionality.

2. Update Internal Links

- If you redirect a page, update any internal links pointing to the old URL.
- This prevents unnecessary redirects and improves site navigation.

3. Inform Users About Changes

- If possible, add a notice on the old page stating it has moved.
- Provide a **manual link** for users who might face redirection issues.

4. Monitor Site Traffic

- Use **Google Analytics** to track how often the old URL is accessed.
- If traffic remains high, consider keeping the redirect active longer.

5. Avoid Redirect Loops

- A redirect loop happens when Page A redirects to Page B, which redirects back to Page A.
- Ensure each redirect follows a clear path to prevent infinite loops.

Conclusion

While Google Sites does not have a built-in redirect feature like traditional website builders, you can still manage URL redirections using **manual navigation links, Google Domains forwarding, JavaScript, or event tracking.** Each method has its pros and cons, so choosing the right approach depends on your specific needs.

Redirects are crucial for maintaining **user experience, SEO rankings, and content organization.** By implementing best practices and regularly testing your redirects, you can ensure a smooth transition when updating your Google Site.

6.2 Adding Buttons, Links, and Call-to-Actions

6.2.1 Creating Navigation Buttons

Introduction to Navigation Buttons in Google Sites

Navigation buttons are an essential part of any website, providing visitors with an easy way to move between pages, access key information, and engage with your content. In Google Sites, you can create navigation buttons to enhance user experience and improve site structure. These buttons help guide visitors to important sections, making your site more intuitive and efficient.

In this section, we will cover:

- The types of navigation buttons you can add in Google Sites

- How to create and customize buttons

- Best practices for using navigation buttons effectively

Understanding Navigation Buttons in Google Sites

Google Sites does not provide a built-in "button" element like some other website builders. However, you can create navigation buttons using **text links, image-based buttons, and embedded buttons from external tools**. These buttons can link to:

- Internal pages within your Google Site

- External websites or resources

- Documents and files stored in Google Drive

- Specific sections of a page using anchor links

By leveraging these methods, you can create visually appealing and functional navigation buttons tailored to your needs.

Creating Navigation Buttons in Google Sites

Method 1: Using the Built-in Button Feature

Google Sites offers a **button feature** that allows you to create clickable elements that direct users to a specific location. Here's how to add a button:

Step 1: Add a Button to Your Page

1. Open your **Google Site** in edit mode.

2. Navigate to the page where you want to add a button.

3. Click on the **"Insert"** tab in the right-hand menu.

4. Scroll down and click **"Button"**.

5. In the pop-up window:

   o Enter the **Button Name** (this will be the text displayed on the button).

   o Enter the **Link URL** (this could be an internal page, an external website, or a Google Drive file).

6. Click **"Insert"** to add the button to your page.

Step 2: Customize the Button

Once the button is added to your page, you can adjust its appearance:

- **Resize the Button**: Click and drag the edges to make it larger or smaller.

- **Align the Button**: Click on the button and use the alignment tools to center it, move it left, or move it right.

- **Change the Button Style**:

   o **Filled**: A solid-colored button.

   o **Outlined**: A button with a border but no background fill.

   o **Text only**: The button appears as a hyperlink without a button-like appearance.

- **Adjust Button Placement**: Drag the button to reposition it on the page.

Step 3: Publish Your Changes

Once you are satisfied with the button's appearance, click **"Publish"** to make the changes live.

Method 2: Creating Buttons with Hyperlinked Text

If you prefer a text-based navigation button, you can use hyperlinked text as an alternative.

Step 1: Insert a Text Box

1. Go to the page where you want the button.

2. Click **"Insert"** → **"Text box"**.

3. Type the text that will act as a button (e.g., **"Go to Contact Page"**).

Step 2: Add a Hyperlink

1. Highlight the text you just entered.

2. Click on the **link icon** in the text editing toolbar.

3. Enter the URL of the destination (this could be another page on your site, an external website, or a Google Drive file).

4. Click **Apply**.

Step 3: Format the Text to Look Like a Button

- **Make the text bold** to make it stand out.

- **Increase the font size** for better visibility.

- **Change the background color** of the text box to simulate a button appearance.

This method is useful for a minimalistic design and works well in text-heavy sections of your site.

Method 3: Using Images as Buttons

You can also use **clickable images** to function as navigation buttons. This method is particularly useful for making visually appealing call-to-action elements.

Step 1: Add an Image

1. Click **"Insert"** → **"Images"**.

2. Upload an image or choose one from Google Drive or Google Search.

Step 2: Link the Image

1. Click on the inserted image.

2. Select the **link icon** in the toolbar.

3. Enter the URL of the page or resource you want to link to.

4. Click **Apply**.

Step 3: Resize and Position the Image

- Drag the corners of the image to adjust its size.

- Align the image for a clean and structured look.

Using images as buttons is ideal for creating engaging and interactive navigation elements.

Best Practices for Using Navigation Buttons

1. Keep Buttons Clear and Descriptive

- Use **action-oriented** text like *"Learn More"*, *"Sign Up"*, or *"Visit Our Blog"*.

- Avoid vague text like *"Click Here"*—instead, describe the action clearly.

2. Maintain Consistency

- Use the **same style** for all buttons to create a unified design.

- Ensure buttons are positioned consistently across all pages.

3. Prioritize Accessibility

- Choose **contrasting colors** so buttons are visible against the background.

- Ensure buttons are **large enough** to be tapped on mobile devices.

- Add **alt text** for image-based buttons to assist visually impaired users.

4. Test Your Buttons

- Click on each button before publishing to ensure the links work correctly.

- Check the button behavior on **mobile, tablet, and desktop** to ensure responsiveness.

Conclusion

Navigation buttons are a powerful way to enhance the usability of your Google Site. Whether using the built-in button feature, hyperlinked text, or images, each method allows you to create a **seamless and engaging navigation experience**.

By following best practices and customizing buttons to match your site's branding, you can ensure visitors can easily access important content and take meaningful actions.

Next Steps

Now that you have learned how to create navigation buttons, the next section (**6.2.2 Inserting Hyperlinks and Internal Links**) will explore additional ways to connect pages and improve your site's navigation.

6.2.2 Inserting Hyperlinks and Internal Links

Creating an effective website is not just about adding content; it's also about ensuring visitors can navigate smoothly. One of the most powerful ways to improve navigation is by using **hyperlinks and internal links**. These links allow users to move between pages, access external resources, and interact with your content seamlessly.

This section will cover:

- The different types of links you can use in Google Sites

- How to insert hyperlinks to external websites

- How to create internal links for better site navigation

- Best practices for using links effectively

Understanding Hyperlinks and Internal Links

Before diving into the technical aspects, let's define the key types of links used in Google Sites:

1. Hyperlinks (External Links)

Hyperlinks, also known as **external links**, direct users to a website outside your Google Site. These are useful for referencing resources, linking to related content, or directing users to social media or partner sites.

Example of an external hyperlink:

- A link to an industry-related article: Google's official blog

- A link to a YouTube tutorial: Watch this tutorial

2. Internal Links (Page-to-Page Navigation)

Internal links help users navigate within your Google Site by linking to other pages in your site. These links are useful for:

- Connecting related pages

- Improving user experience and site structure

- Creating a table of contents or quick access links

Example of an internal link:

- A link to your site's "About Us" page

- A link to a specific section on the same page (anchor link)

Now that we understand the types of links, let's explore how to insert them.

How to Insert Hyperlinks in Google Sites

Hyperlinks are essential for directing users to external websites. Here's how to add them in Google Sites:

Step 1: Select the Text or Image for the Link

- Open your Google Site in editing mode.
- Click on the **text box** where you want to add the hyperlink.
- Highlight the text you want to turn into a link (e.g., "Click here to learn more").

Step 2: Insert the Link

- Click on the **Insert link icon** in the text toolbar.
- A pop-up will appear asking for the **URL**.
- Type or paste the external website link (e.g., https://www.google.com).
- Click **Apply** to save the link.

Step 3: Test the Link

- After applying the hyperlink, click **Preview** to see how it works.
- Click on the link to ensure it opens correctly in a new tab.

How to Insert a Hyperlink to an Image

You can also add hyperlinks to images:

- Click on an **image** in your Google Site.
- Click the **Insert link icon**.
- Paste the external URL and click **Apply**.

This is useful for linking banners, call-to-action images, or social media icons.

How to Create Internal Links in Google Sites

Internal links make navigation within your site seamless. They allow users to jump between pages or specific sections.

1. Linking to Another Page on Your Google Site

To link to another page within your Google Site:

- Highlight the text you want to link (e.g., "Visit our Contact Page").

- Click the **Insert link icon**.

- Instead of pasting a URL, select one of your site's pages from the list.

- Click **Apply**.

2. Creating Anchor Links (Jump Links) within a Page

Anchor links allow users to jump to a specific section of the same page. These are useful for long pages, FAQs, or tables of contents.

Step 1: Add a Heading or Section Title

Google Sites automatically assigns an anchor link to **titles and headings**. Use these for internal navigation.

Step 2: Copy the Section's Anchor Link

- Click on the **title or heading** of the section you want to link to.

- Right-click the **"Copy link to this section"** option.

- Paste this link where needed in your site.

Step 3: Create the Link

- Highlight the text that should act as the anchor link.

- Click **Insert link (∞)** and paste the copied anchor link.

- Click **Apply**.

Now, when users click this link, they will jump directly to the section within the page.

Best Practices for Using Links in Google Sites

To ensure an optimal user experience, follow these best practices when using hyperlinks and internal links:

1. Use Descriptive Link Text

Avoid generic terms like *"Click here."* Instead, use meaningful phrases:
✓ "Read our blog on Google Sites tips."
✗ *"Click here for more info."*

2. Open External Links in a New Tab

To prevent users from leaving your site, ensure external links open in a new tab. By default, Google Sites does this automatically.

3. Avoid Overloading Pages with Links

Too many links can overwhelm users. Keep your navigation simple and logical.

4. Keep Your Links Updated

Broken links hurt user experience. Regularly check and update external and internal links.

5. Optimize Links for SEO

- Use keyword-rich anchor text for better search rankings.

- Structure internal links to improve site navigation.

Conclusion

Adding hyperlinks and internal links in Google Sites is crucial for seamless navigation and engagement. By strategically placing links to external resources, internal pages, and specific sections, you enhance user experience and improve content accessibility.

To recap:

- **Hyperlinks** connect to external websites.

- **Internal links** navigate users within your site.

- **Anchor links** help users jump to sections on the same page.

- **Best practices** improve readability, SEO, and usability.

Now that you know how to insert and optimize links, let's explore more ways to enhance your Google Site in the next section: **6.2.3 Designing Effective Call-to-Actions**.

6.2.3 Designing Effective Call-to-Actions

A call-to-action (CTA) is an essential element of any website, guiding visitors toward a desired action. Whether you want users to subscribe to a newsletter, fill out a contact form, download a resource, or make a purchase, an effective CTA can significantly enhance user engagement and conversion rates.

In this section, we will cover:

- The importance of CTAs in website design

- Types of CTAs suitable for Google Sites

- Best practices for designing compelling CTAs

- How to create and customize CTAs in Google Sites

The Importance of CTAs in Website Design

A website without clear CTAs can lead to confusion, low engagement, and lost opportunities. CTAs serve as signposts that guide visitors through your site and encourage them to take specific actions. Here's why CTAs are important:

1. Increases User Engagement

CTAs encourage visitors to interact with your content rather than passively consuming it. Whether it's clicking a button, watching a video, or signing up for an event, CTAs keep users engaged.

2. Improves Conversion Rates

If your website has a goal (e.g., collecting leads, selling a product, or signing up users), CTAs are the direct pathways to achieving it. A well-placed CTA can significantly increase conversions.

3. Enhances User Experience (UX)

Good CTAs make website navigation easier. Instead of leaving visitors to guess what they should do next, a CTA provides clear direction, improving overall UX.

4. Reinforces Your Website's Purpose

Every website has a purpose—whether it's to inform, sell, or connect. CTAs reinforce that purpose by directing visitors toward meaningful interactions.

Types of CTAs Suitable for Google Sites

Depending on the goal of your website, different types of CTAs may be used. Here are some common types of CTAs that work well with Google Sites:

1. Clickable Buttons

- Used for primary actions such as signing up, contacting, or downloading a file.
- Example: "Get Started," "Download Now," "Join Us."

2. Hyperlinks within Text

- Useful for linking to additional resources, product pages, or contact forms.
- Example: "Learn more about our services here."

3. Image-Based CTAs

- Graphics or banners that act as a CTA when clicked.
- Example: A "Shop Now" image linked to an online store.

4. Contact Forms as CTAs

- Encourages visitors to get in touch directly.
- Example: A form titled "Request a Free Consultation."

5. Embedded Videos with CTAs

- A video explaining a product or service with a final CTA directing users to take action.

- Example: "Watch the demo and sign up for free."

Best Practices for Designing Compelling CTAs

Creating an effective CTA involves more than just adding a button or link. Below are key principles to follow when designing CTAs in Google Sites.

1. Use Action-Oriented Language

A good CTA should inspire action. Use strong, clear verbs that prompt immediate engagement. Examples:

- Weak: "Click here"

- Strong: "Start Your Free Trial"

2. Make Your CTA Visually Stand Out

Ensure your CTA stands out from the rest of the content by using contrasting colors, bold text, or buttons.

- **Color Contrast:** A CTA button should have a distinct color that stands out against the background.

- **Size & Placement:** The CTA should be large enough to notice but not overwhelming.

3. Keep CTAs Simple and Specific

Users should understand what will happen when they click. Avoid vague phrases like "Submit" or "Click Here." Instead, be specific:

- "Get Your Free eBook" instead of "Download"

- "Request a Demo" instead of "Learn More"

4. Place CTAs Strategically

The placement of your CTA affects its effectiveness. Here are some optimal locations:

- **Above the Fold:** The first visible area on a webpage.
- **End of a Page/Post:** After providing value, a CTA can guide the next step.
- **Sidebars or Floating Buttons:** Always visible options for action.

5. Use Urgency and Scarcity

People respond to urgency. If your CTA includes time-sensitive offers, it increases the likelihood of action.

- "Sign Up Today – Limited Spots Available"
- "Sale Ends in 24 Hours"

6. Mobile Optimization

Ensure your CTAs work well on mobile devices:

- Use large buttons for easy tapping.
- Keep text short and readable.
- Avoid placing CTAs too close to other clickable elements.

How to Create and Customize CTAs in Google Sites

Google Sites provides several ways to create and customize CTAs. Below, we outline step-by-step instructions for adding buttons, hyperlinks, and other CTA elements.

1. Creating a Button CTA in Google Sites

1. Open your Google Site and navigate to the page where you want to add a CTA.
2. Click the **Insert** tab on the right panel.
3. Select **Button** from the menu.
4. Enter the button **text** (e.g., "Sign Up Now").
5. Add a **link** (e.g., a signup form or another page).

6. Click **Insert**, then drag and resize the button as needed.

Customizing Your Button CTA

- **Change Color:** Click on the button and select a color that stands out.

- **Adjust Size:** Drag the edges of the button to resize.

- **Reposition:** Move the button to a more prominent location.

2. Adding Hyperlinks as CTAs

1. Highlight the text you want to link.

2. Click the **Link** icon in the toolbar.

3. Paste the URL and click **Apply**.

4. Format the linked text (bold, color change) to make it stand out.

3. Adding Image-Based CTAs

1. Click **Insert > Images** and upload an image.

2. Click on the image, then select the **Link** option.

3. Add the target URL and apply changes.

4. Resize and position the image to align with your design.

4. Using Google Forms as CTAs

1. Go to **Insert > Forms** and select an existing form or create a new one.

2. Customize the form to capture leads, registrations, or feedback.

3. Position the form where visitors can easily access it.

Conclusion

A well-designed CTA can transform your Google Site from a passive information hub into an interactive, goal-oriented platform. By using clear language, strategic placement, and compelling design, you can significantly improve user engagement and achieve your website's objectives.

Key Takeaways:

✅ Use strong, action-oriented language for your CTAs.

✅ Ensure CTAs visually stand out with contrasting colors and bold fonts.

✅ Place CTAs in high-visibility areas, such as above the fold and at the end of pages.

✅ Optimize for mobile users to ensure accessibility on all devices.

✅ Utilize Google Sites' built-in features like buttons, hyperlinks, and Google Forms for effective CTAs.

Now that you understand how to design effective CTAs, you can apply these strategies to create a more engaging and user-friendly Google Site.

6.3 Embedding Third-Party Content

6.3.1 Using HTML Code Snippets

Introduction to HTML Code Snippets in Google Sites

Google Sites offers a simple and user-friendly interface for building websites without any coding knowledge. However, if you want to extend its functionality and integrate advanced features, using **HTML code snippets** can be a powerful way to enhance your site.

With HTML code snippets, you can embed third-party widgets, interactive elements, custom forms, and even design enhancements that go beyond the built-in capabilities of Google Sites. This feature allows you to integrate external tools, such as social media feeds, countdown timers, chatbots, and even advanced styling effects.

In this section, we will explore how to use **HTML code snippets** in Google Sites, including where to insert them, best practices, common use cases, and troubleshooting tips.

Understanding HTML Code Snippets in Google Sites

Before we dive into how to insert HTML code snippets, it's important to understand how Google Sites handles them. Unlike traditional website builders or CMS platforms that allow full HTML, CSS, and JavaScript editing, Google Sites has certain restrictions:

- **No Full HTML Editing**: You cannot directly modify the full HTML structure of a Google Site.

- **Limited JavaScript Support**: While embedding HTML elements is possible, Google Sites **blocks most JavaScript code** for security reasons.

- **Allowed Embeds**: Google Sites supports iframe embeds, custom forms, and external content via HTML snippets.

Despite these limitations, you can still add useful functionality with properly formatted HTML embeds.

How to Insert HTML Code Snippets in Google Sites

Step 1: Open the Page Where You Want to Add HTML Code

1. Open **Google Sites** and navigate to the site where you want to insert the HTML snippet.

2. Select the **page** where you want the HTML content to appear.

Step 2: Insert an Embed Box

1. Click on the **"Insert"** tab in the right-hand menu.

2. Scroll down and select **"Embed"**.

3. A popup window will appear, giving you two options:

   o **By URL**: This allows you to embed external websites.

   o **By Code**: This is where you will paste your HTML code snippet.

Step 3: Add Your HTML Code

1. Select the **"By Code"** option.

2. Copy and paste your **HTML code snippet** into the box.

3. Click **"Next"** to preview the code output.

4. If everything looks good, click **"Insert"** to add it to your page.

5. Adjust the size and position of the embed box as needed.

Practical Use Cases for HTML Code Snippets in Google Sites

Now that you know how to insert HTML code, let's explore some common use cases where HTML snippets can significantly enhance your Google Sites experience.

1. Embedding Social Media Feeds

If you want to display a live feed from **Twitter, Instagram, or Facebook**, you can use their embed codes.

Example: Twitter Feed Embed

Go to Twitter Publish https://publish.twitter.com/# and enter the Twitter handle or hashtag you want to display. Copy the generated HTML code and embed it into Google Sites.

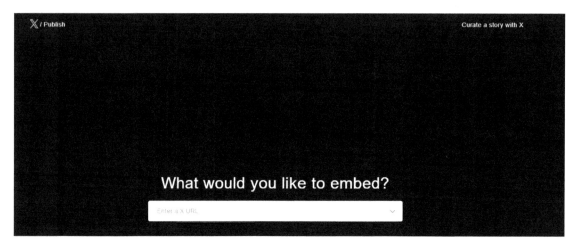

<a class="twitter-timeline"
href="https://twitter.com/TwitterDev?ref_src=twsrc%5Etfw">Tweets by
TwitterDev</a>

<script async src="https://platform.twitter.com/widgets.js" charset="utf-8"></script>

2. Adding a Countdown Timer

If you're hosting an event, you might want to add a countdown timer.

Example: Simple Countdown Timer Embed

You can use Countdown Timer Generator https://www.tickcounter.com/ to create an HTML snippet like this:

```
<iframe src="https://www.tickcounter.com/widget/countdown/123456" width="100%"
height="100"></iframe>
```

3. Embedding a Google Form

While Google Sites provides a built-in way to embed Google Forms, you can also use an HTML snippet for better customization.

Example: Google Form Embed Code

1. Open your Google Form.

2. Click **"Send"**, then choose the **embed icon (<>)**.

3. Copy the **iframe code** and paste it into Google Sites.

```
<iframe
src="https://docs.google.com/forms/d/e/YOUR_FORM_ID/viewform?embedded=true"
width="640" height="480" frameborder="0" marginheight="0"
marginwidth="0">Loading...</iframe>
```

4. Adding a Live Chat Widget

If you want to provide live customer support, you can integrate a chat widget from **Tawk.to, LiveChat, or Drift**.

Example: Tawk.to Live Chat Embed

1. Sign up for Tawk.to.

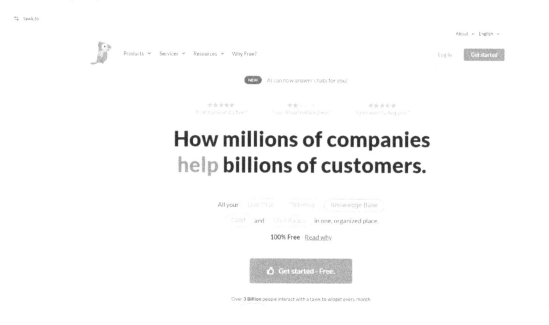

2. Copy the JavaScript snippet provided by Tawk.to.

3. Since Google Sites blocks JavaScript, you will need to embed it using an external HTML hosting service like CodePen or GitHub Pages.

Best Practices for Using HTML Code in Google Sites

1. Use Trusted Sources

Since Google Sites does not allow direct JavaScript execution, make sure you **embed HTML from trusted sources** to avoid security risks.

2. Use Iframes Where Possible

Google Sites supports **iframes**, which allow you to embed external content like forms, maps, videos, and widgets.

3. Keep Embeds Mobile-Friendly

Ensure that any embedded content is **responsive** so that it looks good on mobile devices.

<iframe src="YOUR_EMBED_URL" style="width:100%; height:400px;"></iframe>

4. Test Before Publishing

Always **preview** your site to make sure the embedded content works properly.

Troubleshooting Common Issues

Issue 1: Embedded Content Not Displaying

- Check if the **website source allows embedding** (some sites block iframes).
- Ensure that you are **pasting the correct HTML code**.
- Some widgets require additional permissions; check the settings.

Issue 2: The Embed Box is Too Small

- Manually **resize** the embed box in Google Sites.
- Use **CSS width and height attributes** to adjust the size.

Issue 3: Google Blocks JavaScript Code

- Google Sites does not support custom JavaScript execution.
- Use **external services like CodePen or GitHub Pages** to host scripts and embed them via an iframe.

Conclusion

Using **HTML code snippets** in Google Sites can unlock powerful features that enhance the functionality of your website. While Google Sites has limitations on full HTML and JavaScript customization, it still allows you to embed a variety of third-party tools, such as **social media feeds, forms, calendars, and widgets**.

By following best practices and troubleshooting common issues, you can seamlessly integrate **interactive elements** into your Google Site, creating a more engaging and dynamic user experience.

6.3.2 Adding Social Media Feeds

Introduction

Social media has become an essential part of modern websites, allowing businesses, bloggers, and educators to connect with their audience in real time. Embedding social media feeds in Google Sites can help you display dynamic content from platforms like Facebook, Twitter (now X), Instagram, LinkedIn, and YouTube. This integration enhances engagement, keeps your website content fresh, and provides visitors with the latest updates without requiring manual updates on your site.

In this section, we will explore how to embed different social media feeds into Google Sites, the benefits of doing so, and troubleshooting tips for common issues.

1. Why Embed Social Media Feeds in Google Sites?

Before diving into the technical aspects, let's discuss why embedding social media feeds can be beneficial for your Google Site.

Increased Engagement

Social media feeds provide dynamic and interactive content that encourages users to explore your social platforms directly from your site. This keeps your visitors engaged and increases your social media following.

Fresh and Automated Content

Instead of manually updating your website with recent news, promotions, or events, social media feeds update automatically. Whenever you post on your social media accounts, the latest content is reflected on your site.

Improved Credibility and Social Proof

Displaying social media posts, customer testimonials, or product updates from your official social accounts can help build trust and credibility with your audience.

Better SEO and Traffic Growth

When users engage with embedded social media content, they are more likely to share it, increasing traffic to both your website and social media accounts.

2. Methods for Embedding Social Media Feeds in Google Sites

Google Sites does not have built-in widgets for social media feeds, but you can embed them using **HTML embed codes**, **third-party tools**, and **Google Widgets**. Below are methods for integrating feeds from popular social media platforms.

3. Embedding Social Media Feeds Using Embed Codes

Most social media platforms provide an **"Embed"** feature, allowing you to copy and paste an HTML snippet into your website.

Facebook Feed

Step 1: Get the Facebook Page Plugin Embed Code

1. Go to the Facebook Page Plugin.

    https://developers.facebook.com/docs/plugins/page-plugin

2. Enter your Facebook Page URL.

3. Customize the settings (width, height, timeline display, etc.).

4. Click **"Get Code"** and copy the **iframe** code.

Step 2: Add to Google Sites

1. Open **Google Sites** and navigate to the page where you want to embed the Facebook feed.

2. Click **"Embed"** from the right sidebar.

3. Paste the **iframe** code into the embed box.

4. Click **"Insert"** and adjust the size as needed.

Twitter (X) Feed

Step 1: Get the Twitter Widget Embed Code

1. Go to Twitter Publish. https://publish.twitter.com/#

2. Enter your Twitter handle or the URL of a specific tweet.

3. Choose the **"Embedded Timeline"** option.

4. Copy the generated **HTML code**.

Step 2: Insert Twitter Feed in Google Sites

1. Open **Google Sites**.

2. Click **"Embed"** and select the **"Embed Code"** option.

3. Paste the Twitter embed code.

4. Adjust the display settings and save the changes.

3.3 Instagram Feed

Instagram does not provide an official way to embed a feed, but you can use a third-party tool like **Taggbox**, **Juicer**, or **EmbedSocial**.

Method Using EmbedSocial

1. Sign up for an account at EmbedSocial. https://embedsocial.com/

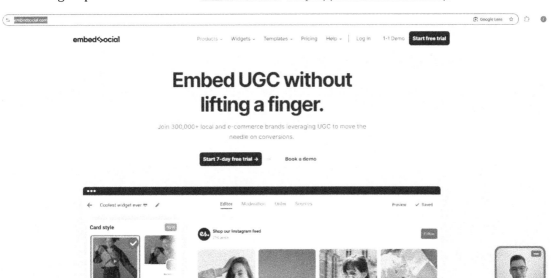

2. Connect your Instagram account.

3. Generate the **embed code** for your Instagram feed.

4. Copy and paste the embed code into **Google Sites** using the **"Embed"** feature.

YouTube Video or Playlist

Google Sites allows direct embedding of YouTube videos.

Method 1: Using the Built-in YouTube Feature

1. Click **"Insert"** in Google Sites.

2. Select **"YouTube"** and search for the video.

3. Click **"Insert"** to add it to your page.

Method 2: Using an Embed Code for Playlists

1. Open YouTube and go to a playlist.

2. Click **"Share"** → **"Embed"**.

3. Copy the **iframe** code and paste it into Google Sites.

4. Using Third-Party Social Media Widgets

If you want to display multiple social media feeds in one section, consider using a **social media aggregator tool**.

Best Social Media Aggregator Tools

- **Taggbox** – Supports Facebook, Instagram, Twitter, and YouTube feeds.

- **Juicer** – A free tool to embed multiple feeds.

- **Elfsight** – Offers beautiful, customizable social media widgets.

How to Embed a Social Media Widget in Google Sites

1. Sign up for a social media aggregator (e.g., **Taggbox**).

2. Connect your social media accounts.

3. Customize the feed layout.

4. Copy the **HTML embed code**.

5. Paste the code into Google Sites using **"Embed Code"**.

5. Troubleshooting Common Issues

Even though embedding social media feeds is straightforward, users sometimes face challenges.

Feeds Not Displaying Correctly

- Ensure that the embedded URL is publicly accessible.

- Some browsers block mixed content (HTTP vs. HTTPS). Use secure URLs.

Content Not Updating in Real-Time

- Some third-party tools update every few hours. Consider premium options for faster updates.

- Refresh your Google Site after embedding.

Permissions Errors

- Some social media platforms require authentication before embedding.

- Ensure your social media content is set to **"Public"** visibility.

6. Conclusion

Embedding social media feeds in Google Sites enhances engagement, keeps your content fresh, and builds a stronger online presence. Whether using **direct embed codes**, **third-party widgets**, or **Google-integrated solutions**, you can create a dynamic website that effectively connects with your audience.

By following the steps outlined in this chapter, you can integrate live feeds from Facebook, Twitter (X), Instagram, LinkedIn, YouTube, and more into your Google Site with ease.

6.3.3 Embedding External Widgets and Tools

Google Sites is a powerful platform for creating and managing websites, but its built-in functionality has some limitations. To extend your website's capabilities, you can embed external widgets and tools that add dynamic content, interactivity, and enhanced user engagement. Whether you want to display social media feeds, integrate customer service chatbots, or add interactive maps, embedding third-party tools can significantly improve the experience for your visitors.

This section will guide you through different types of external widgets and tools you can embed in your Google Site, the methods for embedding them, and best practices to ensure a seamless integration.

Understanding External Widgets and Tools

What Are External Widgets and Tools?

External widgets and tools are third-party applications or web-based services that can be embedded into a website to provide additional functionality. These can include:

- Social media feeds (e.g., Twitter, Instagram, Facebook)
- Chatbots and customer service tools (e.g., Tawk.to, Zendesk, Drift)
- Survey and feedback tools (e.g., Typeform, SurveyMonkey)
- Calendars and booking systems (e.g., Calendly, Eventbrite)
- E-commerce elements (e.g., PayPal buttons, Shopify product embeds)
- Live chat and forums (e.g., Disqus, Chatra)
- Analytics and tracking widgets (e.g., Google Analytics, Hotjar)

Embedding these tools allows you to expand the capabilities of Google Sites without needing to write custom code or host additional services elsewhere.

Methods for Embedding External Widgets in Google Sites

There are three main ways to embed third-party content into Google Sites:

1. Using the "Embed" Feature

Google Sites has a built-in **Embed** option that allows you to add external content by inserting a website URL or embedding custom HTML code.

Steps to Embed External Widgets via URL:

1. Open your **Google Site** in edit mode.

2. Navigate to the page where you want to embed the widget.

3. Click the **"Insert"** menu in the right-hand sidebar.

4. Select **"Embed"** from the available options.

5. Choose **"By URL"** and paste the web address of the widget you want to embed.

6. Click **"Insert"**, adjust the size, and position the widget on your page.

★ *Note: Some third-party tools provide shareable URLs specifically designed for embedding.*

Steps to Embed External Widgets via HTML Code:

If the widget provider gives you an HTML embed code (often an <iframe> or <script> snippet), follow these steps:

1. Follow steps 1-4 above.

2. Choose **"Embed Code"** instead of "By URL."

3. Paste the provided HTML <iframe> or JavaScript code snippet.

4. Click **"Next"**, then **"Insert"** to add the widget to your page.

5. Resize and position the widget as needed.

★ *Not all HTML codes will work with Google Sites, especially JavaScript-based widgets. If an embed fails, check whether the provider supports iframe embedding.*

Common Widgets and How to Embed Them

Here's how you can embed some of the most common third-party tools into Google Sites:

1. Embedding Social Media Feeds

Many websites benefit from displaying live social media feeds. You can embed a Twitter timeline, Instagram posts, or Facebook feeds to keep your content fresh.

Embedding a Twitter Feed:

1. Go to https://publish.twitter.com/.
2. Enter your Twitter profile URL (e.g., https://twitter.com/YourUsername).
3. Customize the appearance and copy the **embed code**.
4. Paste the embed code into Google Sites using the **"Embed Code"** option.

Embedding an Instagram Post:

1. Open the Instagram post you want to embed.
2. Click the **three-dot menu** and select **"Embed"**.
3. Copy the generated embed code.
4. Insert it into Google Sites using the **"Embed Code"** feature.

2. Embedding a Live Chat Widget (Tawk.to, Drift, or Zendesk Chat)

Live chat widgets improve customer engagement by providing real-time support.

Embedding a Tawk.to Chat Widget:

1. Sign up for a free account at https://www.tawk.to/.
2. Go to **Admin Panel > Channels > Chat Widget** and copy the provided embed code.
3. Paste the code into Google Sites under the **"Embed Code"** section.

3. Adding an Appointment Booking System (Calendly, Eventbrite)

If you need to allow visitors to book appointments, Calendly is a great tool.

Embedding Calendly:

1. Sign in at https://calendly.com/ and create an event.

2. Click **"Share" > "Embed on Your Website"**.

3. Copy the **iframe code** and paste it into Google Sites using the embed feature.

4. Embedding Surveys and Forms (Typeform, SurveyMonkey)

If Google Forms doesn't meet your needs, Typeform and SurveyMonkey offer more advanced options.

Embedding a Typeform Survey:

1. Create a survey at https://www.typeform.com/.

2. Click **"Share" > "Embed in a webpage"**.

3. Copy the iframe embed code and insert it into Google Sites.

5. Embedding Google Analytics for Traffic Tracking

Google Analytics helps you monitor visitor behavior on your site.

Steps to Integrate Google Analytics:

1. Go to **Google Analytics** and create a tracking ID.

2. Open **Google Sites**, click **"Settings"**, and find the **Analytics** section.

3. Enter your tracking ID and save the changes.

Best Practices for Embedding External Widgets

1. Ensure Mobile Responsiveness

Some embedded widgets may not display correctly on mobile devices. Test your site on different screen sizes and adjust widget sizes accordingly.

2. Optimize Page Load Speed

Too many embedded elements can slow down your website. Prioritize essential widgets and use compressed images to maintain performance.

3. Maintain Consistent Design and Layout

Ensure that embedded widgets blend well with your website's theme. Avoid widgets with clashing colors or fonts that disrupt user experience.

4. Verify Security and Privacy Policies

When embedding third-party tools, ensure they comply with data privacy regulations (e.g., GDPR, CCPA). Avoid embedding unknown or untrusted sources.

Troubleshooting Common Issues

Issue 1: Widget Not Displaying Properly

- Ensure the widget provider allows embedding on third-party sites.
- Try refreshing the page or testing in an incognito browser.
- Use the **"Preview"** mode to verify before publishing.

Issue 2: Embed Code Is Blocked by Google Sites

- Google Sites does not support some JavaScript-based widgets.
- Check if the provider offers an iframe alternative.
- Contact the widget provider for an approved embed method.

Issue 3: Widget Not Updating Automatically

- Some widgets require manual refreshes to display updates.
- Check the settings in the third-party tool to enable live updates.

Conclusion

Embedding external widgets and tools in Google Sites is a great way to enhance your website's functionality. By integrating social media feeds, live chat, appointment booking, surveys, and analytics, you can create a more interactive and engaging experience for your visitors. Always follow best practices to ensure seamless performance, mobile compatibility, and a professional appearance.

Now that you've mastered embedding external tools, let's move on to the next chapter, where we will explore publishing and sharing your Google Site!

CHAPTER VII
Publishing and Sharing Your Website

7.1 Previewing and Testing Your Site

7.1.1 Viewing Your Site on Different Devices

Creating a website using Google Sites is simple, but ensuring it looks great on all devices requires thorough testing. Websites are accessed through various devices, including desktops, laptops, tablets, and smartphones. Each of these has different screen sizes and resolutions, which can impact how your site appears and functions. This section will guide you through previewing and testing your Google Site on different devices to ensure an optimal user experience.

Why Testing on Multiple Devices is Important

A website that appears well-structured on a desktop might not necessarily display correctly on a mobile phone. Some reasons why testing on multiple devices is crucial include:

- **Responsive Design Adaptation:** Google Sites automatically adjusts layouts for different screen sizes, but it's important to verify that all elements align properly.

- **User Experience (UX):** A site that is difficult to navigate on a mobile device may drive users away. Ensuring intuitive navigation on all devices is key.

- **Content Visibility:** Font sizes, images, and buttons should remain clear and functional across different screen resolutions.

- **Performance Optimization:** Some elements may load differently on mobile compared to desktops. Testing allows you to detect slow-loading images or misaligned content.

How to Preview Your Google Site on Different Devices

1. Using the Built-in Google Sites Preview Mode

Google Sites provides a built-in preview feature that allows you to check how your website appears on different screen sizes. Follow these steps:

Step 1: Open the Site Editor

- Navigate to Google Sites and open your website in editing mode.

Step 2: Click the Preview Button

- In the top-right corner of the screen, locate the **Preview** icon (an eye-shaped icon). Click it to enter preview mode.

Step 3: Switch Between Different Device Views

- Once in preview mode, you will see three icons at the bottom-right:

    - **Desktop View** (default)

    - **Tablet View** (medium screen size)

    - **Mobile View** (small screen size)

- Click on each icon to see how your website adapts to different screens.

Step 4: Navigate and Check Responsiveness

- Click through your site's pages, test buttons, and ensure that images, text, and embedded elements resize correctly.

2. Manually Resizing Your Browser Window

If you want to quickly test responsiveness without switching devices, you can resize your browser window manually.

Steps to Resize the Browser Window:

1. Open your Google Site in a browser.

2. Click and drag the browser window from a corner to resize it.

3. Observe how the layout adjusts as the window shrinks or expands.

4. Ensure that images, text, and navigation menus are correctly displayed.

This method is a simple way to simulate how your site might look on smaller screens without using a mobile device.

3. Testing on Actual Devices

While Google Sites' preview mode is useful, it's always a good idea to test on real devices to see how your site behaves in a real-world scenario.

Steps to Test on Actual Devices:

1. **Publish Your Site:** Ensure that your site is published so it can be accessed from any device.

2. **Open the Website on a Mobile Device:**

   o On your smartphone or tablet, open a web browser (Chrome, Safari, Edge, etc.).

   o Enter the URL of your published Google Site.

3. **Check Responsiveness:** Scroll through the site, test menus, images, and buttons to ensure everything is functional.

4. **Rotate the Device:** Switch between portrait and landscape orientations to see if the content adjusts properly.

Key Areas to Check on Mobile Devices:

✓ **Navigation Menu:** Ensure that menus collapse into a mobile-friendly format (hamburger menu).
✓ **Text Readability:** Verify that text is neither too small nor too large.
✓ **Image Scaling:** Check that images are properly resized without being cropped awkwardly.

✓ **Buttons and Links:** Make sure interactive elements are easily clickable on smaller screens.

---

4. Using Developer Tools in a Web Browser

Most modern browsers include developer tools that allow you to test your website in different screen resolutions without needing multiple devices.

How to Use Developer Tools for Mobile Testing:

In Google Chrome:

1. Open your Google Site in **Google Chrome**.

2. Press **F12** or **Right-click > Inspect** to open Developer Tools.

3. Click the **"Toggle Device Toolbar"** icon (a small phone and tablet symbol).

4. Select a device type from the dropdown menu (e.g., iPhone, iPad, Galaxy, etc.).

5. Interact with your website as if you were using that device.

In Mozilla Firefox:

1. Open your site in **Firefox**.

2. Press **Ctrl + Shift + M** (Windows) or **Cmd + Option + M** (Mac).

3. Choose a device from the dropdown list.

4. Test how the site adapts to different resolutions.

In Microsoft Edge:

1. Open your site in **Edge**.

2. Press **F12** to open Developer Tools.

3. Click on the **"Emulation"** tab and select a device profile.

Using developer tools allows for quick and efficient testing without requiring physical devices.

Common Issues and Fixes When Viewing on Different Devices

1. Text is Too Small or Large on Mobile

✓ Solution: Use appropriately sized fonts and avoid excessive zooming. Stick to Google Sites' default styles for best results.

2. Images Are Cropped or Misaligned

✓ Solution: Use responsive images and avoid setting fixed pixel widths. Instead, use percentage-based sizing.

3. Navigation Menu is Difficult to Use on Small Screens

✓ Solution: Ensure that the navigation is set to "Automatic" so Google Sites optimizes it for mobile.

4. Embedded Content (Videos, Forms) Doesn't Display Correctly

✓ Solution: Check if third-party content is responsive. If not, consider using a responsive embed code or an iframe.

5. Buttons and Links Are Hard to Click on Mobile

✓ Solution: Make sure buttons are large enough and have enough spacing between them for touch-screen users.

Final Testing Checklist

Before publishing your Google Site, go through this checklist:

✓ Viewed the site on desktop, tablet, and mobile
✓ Tested all navigation links and buttons
✓ Checked text readability on smaller screens
✓ Verified image and media display correctly
✓ Ensured site is responsive and user-friendly

By following these steps, you can ensure that your Google Site is accessible, visually appealing, and user-friendly on all devices. This will help you create a professional and functional website that provides a great experience for all visitors.

7.1.2 Checking Navigation and Links

Ensuring that your website's navigation and links function correctly is an essential step before publishing your Google Site. A well-structured navigation system helps visitors find information easily, while properly working links ensure that users can access internal and external resources without frustration. In this section, we will cover how to test and verify your navigation menus, page links, anchor links, external links, and embedded links to ensure a smooth user experience.

1. Understanding the Importance of Navigation and Links

Navigation and links play a crucial role in how users interact with your website. If your navigation is confusing or your links are broken, visitors may become frustrated and leave your site. Here's why proper navigation and link checking is vital:

- **Enhances user experience** – Visitors can quickly find what they need without confusion.

- **Improves accessibility** – Proper navigation ensures that all users, including those using assistive technologies, can browse the site efficiently.

- **Boosts search engine ranking** – A well-structured navigation system helps search engines index your site properly.

- **Prevents frustration** – Broken or incorrect links can cause users to lose trust in your site.

2. Checking the Navigation Menu

The navigation menu is one of the primary ways users move around your site. It typically appears at the top of every page and provides quick access to important sections. To ensure that your navigation is working properly, follow these steps:

Reviewing Navigation Structure

- Click on the **Navigation Settings** in Google Sites to verify how pages are organized.

- Ensure that all important pages are included in the navigation menu.

- Check whether subpages appear correctly in dropdown menus (if applicable).

- Make sure the order of pages makes sense logically.

Testing Navigation on Desktop and Mobile

- Open your site on different devices (desktop, tablet, and smartphone).

- Click on each menu item to verify that it leads to the correct page.

- Check how the navigation menu behaves on mobile devices. Google Sites automatically optimizes for mobile, but it's important to confirm that dropdowns and links are easy to tap.

- Test both **automatic navigation** (default setting) and **manual navigation** (custom links) to confirm they work as expected.

Checking Sticky or Fixed Navigation (if applicable)

- Some websites use a **fixed navigation bar** that stays visible while scrolling.

- Test scrolling behavior to ensure the navigation remains accessible.

- Check whether the menu overlaps with content or disappears unexpectedly.

3. Testing Internal Page Links

Internal links direct users from one page on your site to another. These include navigation links, buttons, and text-based hyperlinks.

Manually Clicking Through All Links

- Visit each page on your site and manually click on all internal links.

- Verify that they lead to the correct destination.

- If a link is broken, update or remove it.

Checking Page URLs

- Hover over links to check their destination URL before clicking.

- Ensure that relative links (e.g., /about-us) and absolute links (e.g., https://yoursite.com/about-us) are correctly formatted.

Using Google Sites' Built-in Link Verification

- Google Sites does not have an automatic broken link checker, so manual testing is required.

- However, you can use third-party tools like **Broken Link Checker (online services)** or browser extensions to find dead links quickly.

4. Testing Anchor Links (Jump Links)

Anchor links allow users to jump to a specific section within a page. They are commonly used for long articles, FAQs, or documentation pages.

Verifying Anchor Links

- Click on each anchor link and ensure it scrolls to the correct section.

- If anchor links are not working, check whether they are set up correctly.

- Test the behavior on different browsers and devices to ensure consistency.

Checking URL Structure for Anchors

- Anchor links usually appear as https://yoursite.com/page#section-name.

- Ensure that the #section-name is correctly added to the target section's HTML ID.

5. Testing External Links

External links connect your Google Site to other websites, such as references, resources, or partner sites.

Ensuring External Links Open Correctly

- Click on each external link to verify that it opens the intended website.

- Ensure that links to third-party sites are not broken or outdated.

Setting External Links to Open in a New Tab

- Google Sites does not automatically open external links in a new tab.

- To prevent users from leaving your site entirely, you can instruct them to right-click and open links in a new tab, but ideally, you should use a button widget for external links.

6. Checking Embedded Links (Google Drive, YouTube, etc.)

Many Google Sites include embedded content such as Google Docs, YouTube videos, and external widgets. These elements often contain clickable links that should be tested.

Verifying Google Drive File Links

- If you embed Google Docs, Sheets, or Slides, test whether users can access the files.

- Adjust **sharing permissions** in Google Drive to ensure visitors have the appropriate access (view, comment, or edit).

- If a file is restricted, visitors may see an error message when trying to open it.

Testing YouTube Video Links

- Click on embedded YouTube videos to confirm they play correctly.

- Check if the video is restricted or private (unlisted videos work best for embedding).

- Test on both desktop and mobile to ensure compatibility.

7. Using Browser Developer Tools for Advanced Link Testing

If you want to perform an in-depth check of all links on your site, browser developer tools can be useful.

Inspecting Links with Developer Tools

- Open **Google Chrome** (or another modern browser).

- Right-click on any link and select **Inspect**.

- Look at the **HTML code** to verify the link structure.

Running a Console Log Check

- Open the **Developer Console** (F12 in Chrome).

- Click on the **Console** tab and refresh the page.

- If any broken links exist, they may appear as errors in red text.

8. Fixing Broken Links and Navigation Issues

If you find any problems during testing, follow these steps to fix them:

- **Update incorrect URLs** – If a link leads to the wrong page, edit it in Google Sites.

- **Remove broken links** – If a webpage no longer exists, remove the link or replace it with a new resource.

- **Reorganize navigation** – If the menu is confusing, restructure it using Google Sites' drag-and-drop navigation editor.

- **Adjust mobile navigation settings** – If the mobile menu is difficult to use, consider simplifying it.

9. Final Review Before Publishing

Once all links and navigation elements are tested and fixed, perform a final review:

- **Have someone else test your site** – A fresh pair of eyes may spot issues you missed.

- **Test links over a few days** – Sometimes, newly created sites need time to propagate across Google's systems.

- **Check for outdated links periodically** – Regular maintenance ensures long-term usability.

Conclusion

Checking navigation and links is a critical part of preparing your Google Site for publishing. By following a systematic approach—testing menus, internal and external links, anchor links, and embedded content—you can ensure a smooth browsing experience for visitors. Once your navigation and links are optimized, you're ready to move on to the next step: **Publishing Your Google Site!**

7.1.3 Testing Embedded Content and Forms

Introduction

When building a website with Google Sites, embedded content such as Google Forms, YouTube videos, Google Drive files, maps, and third-party widgets play a crucial role in making your site interactive and dynamic. However, just because the content appears correctly in the site editor doesn't guarantee it will function properly for your visitors. Testing embedded elements is essential to ensure that they load correctly, display properly on different devices, and function as expected when interacted with by users.

This section will guide you through the steps to effectively test embedded content and forms before publishing your site. By following these best practices, you can identify potential issues and fix them before your audience experiences any problems.

1. Understanding Embedded Content in Google Sites

Google Sites allows you to embed a variety of content types, including:

- **Google Forms** (for surveys, registrations, and feedback collection)
- **Google Docs, Sheets, and Slides** (for sharing files with visitors)
- **YouTube Videos** (for adding visual engagement)
- **Google Calendar** (for displaying events and schedules)
- **Google Maps** (for sharing locations)
- **Third-party Widgets** (such as social media feeds, countdown timers, and booking tools)

Each type of embedded content requires different testing methods to ensure it works correctly across various browsers and devices.

2. Testing Google Forms

Google Forms is a commonly used tool for collecting user responses on your website. Whether you are using it for surveys, event registrations, or feedback forms, you need to verify that it functions properly.

2.1 Steps to Test Google Forms on Your Site

1. **Check Form Display**

   o   Open your Google Site in preview mode.

   o   Navigate to the page where the form is embedded.

   o   Ensure the form appears fully loaded and properly aligned.

2. **Test Form Submission**

   o   Enter sample data in all fields, including required and optional ones.

   o   Test different answer formats (text, multiple choice, checkboxes, file uploads, etc.).

   o   Submit the form and check if the confirmation message appears.

3. **Verify Data Collection**

   o   Open the Google Form response sheet to confirm that the data was recorded correctly.

   o   Check if any fields are missing or not saving input properly.

4. **Test Form Behavior on Mobile Devices**

   o   Open your Google Site on a smartphone or tablet.

   o   Ensure the form adjusts well to smaller screens and is easy to interact with.

5. **Test With Different User Accounts**

   o   Try filling out the form as a guest user (without signing in).

   o   Log in with different Google accounts and test submission.

6. **Check Form Restrictions and Settings**

   o   If the form requires sign-in, verify that users with the required access can fill it out.

   o   Test settings like response limits, file upload restrictions, and required fields.

2.2 Common Google Forms Issues and Fixes

Issue	Possible Cause	Solution
Form does not load	Google Form link might be incorrect or restricted	Check and update the embed link or adjust access settings
Submit button not working	Required fields not filled out properly	Ensure all required fields are completed before submitting
File upload option not available	Form is restricted to specific accounts	Change form settings to allow external responses
Responses not appearing in the sheet	Form linked to the wrong spreadsheet	Verify form responses are being recorded in the correct sheet

3. Testing Other Embedded Google Content

Aside from Google Forms, many users embed Google Docs, Sheets, Slides, and other Google services into their websites. Testing these elements ensures they display correctly and are accessible to your intended audience.

Testing Embedded Google Docs, Sheets, and Slides

- Open your site in preview mode and verify that the document loads correctly.

- Ensure that users with the right permissions can view or edit the document.

- Test the document on different devices and screen sizes to check responsiveness.

- If the document does not appear, confirm that the sharing settings allow public viewing.

Testing Google Calendar Embeds

- Verify that events appear correctly on the embedded calendar.

- Ensure that time zones and event details are displayed accurately.

- Test on mobile devices to confirm proper scaling and interaction.

Testing Embedded Google Maps

- Check if the location pin is accurate.

- Verify that zooming and panning functions work as expected.

- Test map responsiveness on smaller screens.

4. Testing Third-Party Embedded Content

Many users embed third-party content such as social media feeds, booking widgets, or custom HTML elements. These require extra testing to ensure compatibility with Google Sites.

How to Test Third-Party Embeds

1. **Confirm that the embed code is correct**

   o Copy and paste the embed code into a separate test page to ensure it works before adding it to your Google Site.

2. **Check browser compatibility**

   o Test your site in multiple browsers (Chrome, Firefox, Safari, Edge) to ensure the embedded content loads correctly.

3. **Verify mobile responsiveness**

   o Open your site on a mobile device and test interactions with the embedded content.

4. **Monitor loading times**

   o Some third-party embeds can slow down your page. Test loading speed using tools like Google PageSpeed Insights.

5. **Check user permissions**

   o If the embedded content requires users to log in (e.g., private YouTube videos, Google Drive files), test it with a guest account to verify access.

Common Issues and Solutions for Third-Party Embeds

Issue	Possible Cause	Solution
Embedded widget does not appear	Incorrect embed code or unsupported script	Double-check the embed code and ensure it's compatible with Google Sites

Issue	Possible Cause	Solution
Slow page load time	Large or unoptimized embed	Reduce the number of embedded elements and use lightweight alternatives
Content not displaying on mobile	Non-responsive embed	Test on mobile devices and adjust embed settings if possible

5. Final Testing Checklist

Before publishing your Google Site, use this checklist to verify that all embedded content and forms function correctly:

✅ All embedded Google Forms load, accept responses, and store data correctly.
✅ Google Docs, Sheets, and Slides display properly with the correct sharing permissions.
✅ Google Calendar events are visible and correctly formatted.
✅ Google Maps functions properly with accurate location pins.
✅ Third-party embeds appear as expected on desktop and mobile devices.
✅ All embedded content loads quickly and does not negatively impact site performance.

Conclusion

Testing embedded content and forms is a crucial step in ensuring a smooth and engaging user experience. By thoroughly checking each element before publishing your Google Site, you can prevent technical issues and ensure that your website functions properly for all visitors.

By following this guide, you now have the tools to troubleshoot and fix common embedding problems, making your Google Site more interactive, functional, and professional.

7.2 Publishing Your Google Site

7.2.1 Setting Site Visibility Options

Once you have designed and built your website using Google Sites, the next crucial step is deciding who can view it. Google Sites provides multiple visibility options, allowing you to control who can access your content. Whether you are creating a personal website, an internal company portal, or a public-facing site, understanding the different visibility settings will help you ensure your site reaches the right audience.

Understanding Google Sites Visibility Options

When publishing a Google Site, you have three primary visibility settings:

1. Restricted (Private Access Only)
2. Anyone with the Link (Unlisted Access)
3. Public on the Web (Fully Public Access)

Each setting serves a different purpose and should be chosen based on the intended audience for your website.

1. Restricted (Private Access Only)

The *Restricted* setting means that only specific people you invite can view the site. This is ideal for internal projects, team collaboration, or confidential websites where you want to limit access.

How to Set Your Site to Restricted Mode

1. Click the **"Publish"** button in the top-right corner of Google Sites.
2. Under **"Who can view my site?"**, click **"Manage"**.
3. Choose **"Restricted"** from the dropdown menu.

4. Click **"Add people and groups"** to manually invite individuals.

5. Enter the email addresses of the people who should have access.

6. Choose their permission level:

    o **Viewer** (Can only view the published site)

    o **Editor** (Can edit the site if they have edit permissions)

7. Click **"Done"** to save your changes.

When to Use Restricted Visibility

- Company intranet or employee-only resources

- Private team collaboration pages

- Educational content for specific students or staff

- Client-specific websites with confidential data

Pros and Cons of Restricted Visibility

✓ **Pros:**

- Maximum security and privacy

- Control over who can access the site

- Prevents unauthorized users from viewing content

✗ **Cons:**

- Users need to sign in with a Google account

- Less convenient for large audiences

- Requires manual invitation management

2. Anyone with the Link (Unlisted Access)

The *Anyone with the link* option allows users to access your site if they have the direct URL. This setting is useful when you want to share your site with a group of people without making it publicly searchable.

How to Set Your Site to Unlisted Access

1. Click the **"Publish"** button in Google Sites.

2. Under **"Who can view my site?"**, click **"Manage"**.

3. Select **"Anyone with the link"**.

4. Click **"Done"** to apply the changes.

When to Use Unlisted Visibility

- Sharing event details with a select audience

- Providing access to an exclusive online portfolio

- Distributing content to a limited group without requiring Google account sign-ins

- Sharing drafts of your website before making it public

Pros and Cons of Unlisted Visibility

✅ **Pros:**

- No need for users to sign in

- Easier access without compromising full public visibility

- Can be shared via email, chat, or direct link

✖ **Cons:**

- Anyone who gets the link can access the site

- Less control over who shares the link further

- Not ideal for confidential or sensitive content

3. Public on the Web (Fully Public Access)

The *Public* setting makes your website accessible to anyone on the internet. It can be found on search engines like Google and is ideal for businesses, personal blogs, portfolios, or educational resources meant for a broad audience.

How to Set Your Site to Public

1. Click **"Publish"** in the Google Sites editor.

2. Under **"Who can view my site?"**, click **"Manage"**.

3. Select **"Public on the web"**.

4. Click **"Done"** and confirm your choice.

When to Use Public Visibility

- Business websites showcasing services or products

- Personal blogs or portfolios

- Public knowledge bases and educational resources

- Event pages or community announcements

Pros and Cons of Public Visibility

✅ **Pros:**

- Anyone can access the site without restrictions

- Search engines can index the site for discoverability

- No need for user authentication

✖ **Cons:**

- No control over who views the content

- Potential risk of unauthorized copying or sharing

- Must ensure no private or sensitive data is included

Changing Visibility Settings After Publishing

Google Sites allows you to modify visibility settings even after publishing. If you initially set your site to *Restricted* but later decide to make it public, follow these steps:

1. Open your Google Site.

2. Click **"Publish settings"** from the dropdown menu next to the **Publish** button.

3. Under **"Who can view my site?"**, click **"Manage"**.

4. Select the new visibility setting you want.

5. Click **"Done"** to save your changes.

Best Practices for Choosing the Right Visibility Option

Choosing the correct visibility setting depends on the purpose of your website. Here are some best practices to consider:

For Internal Use (Private Company Sites):

- Use **Restricted** visibility.

- Limit access to only essential team members.

- Regularly review and update permissions.

For Limited Sharing (Clients, Students, or Small Groups):

- Use **Anyone with the link** visibility.

- Keep the URL private and only share with the intended audience.

- Disable search engine indexing (found in Google Sites settings).

For Public-Facing Websites (Businesses, Blogs, or Portfolios):

- Use **Public** visibility.

- Optimize for SEO to increase discoverability.

- Ensure no confidential information is included.

Conclusion

Setting the correct visibility options in Google Sites is a crucial step in controlling access to your content. Whether you are building a private team portal, a limited-access project, or a fully public website, Google Sites provides flexible visibility settings to match your needs.

In the next section (**7.2.2 Configuring Access Permissions**), we will explore how to fine-tune permissions by inviting collaborators, assigning editing roles, and managing shared access effectively.

🚀 Key Takeaways

✓ **Restricted Visibility** is best for confidential or private content.

✓ **Anyone with the Link** provides easier sharing without full public exposure.

✓ **Public Visibility** is ideal for blogs, business sites, or educational resources.

✓ You can change visibility settings anytime from the Google Sites editor.

✓ Regularly review access settings to ensure security and privacy.

7.2.2 Configuring Access Permissions

Once you have created and designed your Google Site, it's crucial to configure access permissions properly. Google Sites offers flexible sharing and permission settings, allowing you to control who can view, edit, or manage your site. Whether you are working on a private project, a team collaboration, or a public-facing website, setting up the right permissions ensures security, accessibility, and efficient workflow.

Understanding Access Permissions in Google Sites

Google Sites uses a permission system similar to other Google Workspace tools like Google Docs, Sheets, and Slides. You can control access based on:

- **Who can view the site** – Decide if your site should be public, private, or restricted to specific users.

- **Who can edit the site** – Allow collaborators to modify content, structure, and settings.

- **Who can publish the site** – Control whether other users can make the site live or update published versions.

These settings help you manage your site efficiently while maintaining security and avoiding unwanted changes.

How to Access and Configure Sharing Settings

To configure permissions for your Google Site, follow these steps:

1. **Open Your Google Site** – Go to Google Sites and open the site you want to configure.

2. **Click the "Share" Button** – In the upper-right corner, click the **"Share"** button (represented by an icon of a person with a plus sign).

3. **Adjust Access Settings** – The sharing settings panel will appear, allowing you to specify permissions for different users.

4. **Select Access Level** – Choose whether users can edit or only view the site.

Understanding the Different Permission Levels

Google Sites provides two primary roles when configuring access:

1. **Editors** – Users who can edit and make changes to the site.

2. **Viewers** – Users who can only view the published version of the site but cannot make any edits.

Editor Role

- Can add, modify, and delete content.

- Can adjust site navigation and settings.

- Cannot publish the site unless explicitly granted permission.

- Cannot delete the site.

Viewer Role

- Can only view the published version of the site.

- Cannot edit, modify, or change any settings.

Adding and Managing Collaborators

If you want to share your site with specific individuals or groups, follow these steps:

1. **Enter Email Addresses** – In the sharing settings, type the email addresses of people you want to invite.

2. **Set Their Permissions** – Choose whether they should be **Editors** or **Viewers**.

3. **Send Invitations** – Click **"Send"** to notify users via email.

You can also share the site with Google Groups, making it easier to manage permissions for larger teams.

Removing or Changing Access for Collaborators

To update permissions for existing collaborators:

1. Open the **Share** settings.

2. Find the user's name in the list.

3. Click the **drop-down menu** next to their name to change their role or remove access.

Setting Up Public vs. Private Access

When configuring access, you need to decide whether your Google Site should be **public**, **private**, or restricted to a specific audience.

Public Access

- Anyone on the internet can view your site.

- Useful for business websites, portfolios, or public information sites.

Private Access

- Only users you invite can view the site.

- Ideal for internal documentation, company portals, or restricted educational content.

Restricted Access (Within an Organization or Specific Users)

- Available for Google Workspace users.

- You can limit access to users within your organization or specific email addresses.

To adjust these settings:

1. Open the **Share** settings.

2. Click **"Change"** under "Who has access."

3. Select:

   o **Public** (anyone with the link can view).

   o **Restricted** (only invited users can view).

   o **Domain-restricted** (only users in your organization can view).

4. Click **"Save"** to apply changes.

Publishing and Managing Site Visibility

After configuring permissions, you need to decide whether to publish the site immediately or keep it as a draft.

Steps to Publish Your Site

1. Click the **"Publish"** button in the upper-right corner.

2. Choose a site address (URL).

3. Set visibility preferences based on your chosen permissions.

4. Click **"Publish"** to make the site live.

Managing Published vs. Unpublished Versions

- Editors can preview changes before publishing updates.

- Viewers will only see the last published version, not the draft version.

- If you need to **unpublish** the site, go to **Settings > Unpublish Site**.

Best Practices for Configuring Access Permissions

To maintain control over your site while ensuring accessibility, follow these best practices:

1. Assign Roles Carefully

- Avoid giving edit permissions to too many users to prevent accidental changes.

- Restrict publishing rights to key individuals.

2. Regularly Review Permissions

- Check the access settings periodically to ensure only authorized users have editing rights.

- Remove access for users who no longer need it.

3. Use Google Groups for Large Teams

- Instead of adding individual users, use Google Groups for easier permission management.

4. Protect Sensitive Information

- Avoid making confidential content publicly accessible.

- Use **restricted access** for internal or private sites.

5. Test Access Before Going Live

- Use a test account to verify visibility and permissions before officially launching the site.

Troubleshooting Common Permission Issues

Issue 1: Users Can't Access the Site

✓ **Solution**: Check the sharing settings and ensure they have been invited with the correct permissions.

Issue 2: Viewers Can't See Updates

✓ **Solution**: Ensure you have published the latest version of the site.

Issue 3: Collaborators Can't Edit

✓ **Solution**: Confirm they have **Editor** access, not just Viewer access.

Issue 4: Public Site Isn't Visible

✓ **Solution**: Make sure the site is set to **public** and not restricted.

Conclusion

Configuring access permissions in Google Sites is an essential step in managing your website effectively. Whether you're working on a personal site, an educational resource, or a business portal, proper permission settings ensure security and collaboration. By understanding the different roles, sharing options, and best practices, you can control who can view, edit, and manage your site efficiently.

By following the steps outlined in this chapter, you can confidently configure access permissions for your Google Site, ensuring a smooth and secure experience for both you and your users.

7.2.3 Managing Site Versions and Updates

Once you've built your Google Site and published it, managing its versions and updates becomes an essential task. Websites are living documents that often require updates for content accuracy, design improvements, and security enhancements. Google Sites provides several built-in features to help you track, restore, and update different versions of your website effectively.

In this section, we'll explore:

- Understanding version history in Google Sites

- Updating content without disrupting the live site

- Restoring previous versions if mistakes occur

- Managing updates collaboratively with a team

Understanding Version History in Google Sites

Google Sites, like other Google Workspace applications (Docs, Sheets, and Slides), maintains a history of changes made to the site. This version history allows users to:

- Track modifications over time

- Restore previous versions if errors occur

- Identify who made specific changes (in collaborative environments)

How to Access Version History in Google Sites

To view and manage your site's version history:

1. Open your Google Site.

2. Click on the **More (:) Menu** in the upper right corner.

3. Select **Version History**.

4. A panel will appear on the right side, showing different saved versions.

5. Click on any version to preview what the site looked like at that point.

What Version History Tracks

Google Sites automatically saves changes as you edit. While this auto-save feature prevents data loss, it can also create numerous versions. The history tracks:

- Page edits (text, images, layouts)

- Added or removed elements

- Changes to navigation and structure

- Embedded content modifications

Limitations of Version History

Unlike Google Docs, Google Sites does not allow manual naming of saved versions. You can only view and restore automatically created versions. Additionally, version history is only available **before republishing**—once a new version is published, previous versions become unavailable unless manually backed up.

Updating Content Without Disrupting the Live Site

When making updates to a live Google Site, you want to ensure a smooth transition for visitors. Here are best practices for managing updates efficiently:

Using Draft Mode for Edits

Google Sites automatically saves changes in draft mode, allowing you to edit without affecting the published version.

1. Make the necessary edits in **draft mode**.

2. Review all changes carefully.

3. Click **Publish** only when you're ready to make changes live.

Preview Before Publishing

Before finalizing updates, use the preview tool to ensure everything looks and functions correctly:

1. Click on **Preview (eye icon)** in the top right.

2. Test links, buttons, embedded content, and navigation.

3. View the site in different screen sizes (desktop, tablet, mobile).

Creating a Duplicate for Major Updates

If you need to make significant structural changes, consider duplicating the site first:

1. Click the **More (:) Menu**.

2. Select **Duplicate site**.

3. Use the copied site to experiment before updating the original.

Communicating Changes to Users

If your Google Site serves a business, team, or educational purpose, notify users about updates via:

- **A "What's New" section** on the homepage

- **Email or announcements** for major updates

- **A version log** listing key modifications

Restoring Previous Versions of Your Site

Mistakes happen—accidental deletions, formatting errors, or unintended changes can disrupt your site. Fortunately, Google Sites allows you to revert to previous versions under certain conditions.

How to Restore a Previous Version

If you need to go back to an earlier version:

1. Open **Version History** as outlined in *7.2.3.1*.

2. Browse the available versions.

3. Click on the version you want to restore.

4. Manually copy content from that version and reapply it to the current site.

Best Practices for Avoiding Data Loss

- **Manually copy important content** before making major changes.

- **Save external backups** of crucial text, images, and embedded files.
- **Use Google Drive** to store separate drafts of essential site pages.

Managing Updates Collaboratively

If you're working with a team, updating a Google Site requires coordination. Google Sites allows multiple editors, so ensuring smooth collaboration is crucial.

Assigning Editing Roles

To prevent accidental edits, assign appropriate permissions:

- **Full Editor** – Can modify all content and settings
- **Restricted Editor** – Can edit specific pages
- **Viewer** – Can only see the published site

To manage permissions:

1. Click **Share** in the top-right.
2. Enter the email addresses of collaborators.
3. Assign appropriate roles.
4. Click **Done** to apply changes.

Using Google Drive for Team Updates

Since Google Sites integrates with Google Drive, use shared folders to store:

- Draft versions of new content
- Updated images and multimedia files
- Meeting notes and task lists for site maintenance

Tracking Team Changes

Encourage team members to:

- Add update notes in shared Google Docs

- Use comments in Google Drive files for feedback

- Review version history regularly to monitor changes

Maintaining a Consistent Update Schedule

Keeping your site up to date improves user experience and credibility. Consider setting a regular update schedule based on your website's purpose:

Website Type	Recommended Update Frequency
Business Website	Monthly (for services, pricing)
Educational Site	Semesterly or yearly
Personal Portfolio	Every 6 months
Event Page	As needed before/after events

Tips for Managing a Schedule:

- **Set reminders in Google Calendar** for periodic updates.

- **Create a checklist** of pages and content that need frequent updates.

- **Monitor site traffic** to identify areas that may need refreshing.

Conclusion

Managing site versions and updates in Google Sites is essential for maintaining accuracy, consistency, and functionality. By leveraging version history, updating strategically, restoring previous versions when needed, and collaborating efficiently, you can keep your site dynamic and engaging.

Key Takeaways:

✓ Use **version history** to track and restore changes.

✓ Edit in **draft mode** before publishing to prevent disruptions.

✓ Preview and test changes to ensure site quality.

✓ Work collaboratively using **Google Drive and shared permissions**.

✓ Establish a **regular update schedule** to keep content fresh.

With these practices, your Google Site will remain relevant, professional, and easy to manage over time. Now, let's move on to **Chapter 8: Managing and Updating Your Site Over Time**, where we'll explore further strategies for long-term site maintenance.

7.3 Controlling Who Can View or Edit Your Site

When creating a website with Google Sites, one of the most important aspects to consider is controlling who can view or edit your content. Depending on the purpose of your site, you may want it to be accessible to the public, limited to a specific group, or even restricted to just yourself and selected collaborators. In this section, we will explore the different sharing settings available in Google Sites, with a focus on **public vs. private sharing**.

7.3.1 Public vs. Private Sharing

Understanding Google Sites Sharing Settings

Google Sites provides flexible sharing options that allow you to determine who can access your website. You can choose to make your site:

- **Public** – Accessible to anyone on the internet.

- **Private** – Restricted to specific individuals or groups.

- **Internal (Google Workspace users only)** – Available to people within your organization (if using Google Workspace).

These settings can be modified at any time, depending on your needs. Whether you are creating a website for personal use, business, education, or team collaboration, understanding the difference between public and private sharing is essential for security and accessibility.

Public Sharing: When and How to Use It

A publicly shared Google Site means that anyone with the link can access it. This is ideal for websites intended for broad audiences, such as:

- Personal blogs or portfolios

- Business or company websites

- Public event pages

- Educational resources available to all

- Community projects

How to Make Your Site Public

To make your Google Site publicly accessible, follow these steps:

1. **Open your site in Google Sites Editor.**

2. Click on the **"Share"** button in the top-right corner.

3. In the **"Share with people and groups"** window, locate the **"Published Site"** section.

4. Click **"Change"** next to the visibility settings.

5. Select **"Anyone can view"** or **"Anyone can find and view"** (if you want your site to be indexed by search engines).

6. Click **"Done"** to save your changes.

Once the site is public, anyone with the URL can access it. If you want your site to be searchable on Google, ensure that **"Allow search engines to index my site"** is enabled in the site settings.

Advantages of Public Sharing

- Allows your content to reach a wider audience.

- Enables easy sharing via social media, email, or direct links.

- Provides visibility for businesses, portfolios, and projects.

Disadvantages of Public Sharing

- Your content is accessible to anyone, which could lead to unauthorized use.

- If not properly managed, personal or sensitive information could be exposed.

- May attract spam or unwanted visitors.

Private Sharing: Keeping Your Site Restricted

A private Google Site is only accessible to selected users. This is useful for:

- Internal business documentation

- Classroom or student projects

- Personal journals or work-in-progress sites

- Team collaboration where information should be restricted

How to Make Your Site Private

To restrict access to your site, follow these steps:

1. **Open your site in Google Sites Editor.**

2. Click on the **"Share"** button.

3. Under **"Published Site"**, click **"Change"** and select **"Restricted"** or **"Specific people"**.

4. Enter the email addresses of the people you want to grant access to.

5. Click **"Send"** to notify them.

Once the site is private, only the invited users can access it.

Advantages of Private Sharing

- Keeps sensitive information secure.

- Ensures that only authorized users can view or edit content.

- Ideal for teams, organizations, or internal documentation.

Disadvantages of Private Sharing

- Requires manual access management.

- Users must sign in with their Google accounts to access the site.

- Cannot be used for publicly available content.

Comparison: Public vs. Private Sharing

Feature	Public Sharing	Private Sharing
Accessibility	Available to anyone on the internet	Only accessible to selected users
Ideal Use Cases	Blogs, business sites, educational resources, event pages	Internal company pages, private projects, student work
Search Engine Visibility	Can be indexed by Google (optional)	Cannot be indexed
Security Risk	Higher risk of unauthorized access	More secure, access is controlled
Collaboration	Limited to commenting or embedded forms	Full control over who can view and edit

Choosing the Right Sharing Option for Your Needs

Before deciding whether to make your Google Site public or private, ask yourself the following questions:

✅ Do you want your site to be **accessible to everyone**, or only to a specific group?

✅ Is there **sensitive or confidential information** that should remain private?

✅ Will your site require **collaboration from team members**?

✅ Do you need your site to be **searchable on Google**?

If your site contains general information meant for a wide audience, public sharing is the best option. However, if your content is sensitive, private sharing is the safest choice.

Best Practices for Managing Site Visibility

Regardless of whether your site is public or private, follow these best practices:

1. **Regularly Review Sharing Settings** – Periodically check who has access to your site and update permissions if needed.

2. **Use Google Workspace Groups for Easy Management** – If sharing with a team, create a Google Group instead of adding users individually.

3. **Restrict Editing Access** – Only grant editing permissions to trusted collaborators to prevent unwanted changes.

4. **Enable Site Backups** – Keep copies of important content in Google Drive or another backup service.

5. **Check Permissions on Embedded Content** – Ensure that any embedded Google Docs, Sheets, or Forms have appropriate sharing settings.

Conclusion

Controlling who can view or edit your Google Site is a crucial step in managing your website effectively. Public sharing is best for content intended for broad audiences, while private sharing keeps information secure within a restricted group. By carefully configuring your site's permissions, you can ensure that your content reaches the right people while maintaining the necessary level of security.

Now that we have explored public vs. private sharing, the next section (7.3.2) will focus on **inviting collaborators for editing**, where we will learn how to add team members and manage their editing privileges effectively.

7.3.2 Inviting Collaborators for Editing

Google Sites is designed to be a collaborative platform, allowing multiple users to work on the same site simultaneously. This feature is especially useful for teams, businesses, educators, and project groups who need to create and manage content together. In this section, we will explore how to invite collaborators to edit your Google Site, set different permission levels, manage collaboration effectively, and troubleshoot common issues that may arise.

Understanding Collaboration in Google Sites

Unlike traditional website builders that may require separate user accounts and permissions, Google Sites integrates seamlessly with Google Workspace, making it easy to invite users to edit content. When you add collaborators, they can contribute to the design, structure, and content of your site in real time.

Google Sites offers two primary permission levels for collaborators:

- **Editor**: Can edit the site, add or delete pages, modify content, and make structural changes.

- **Viewer**: Can only view the site if it is shared privately and restricted from public access.

For collaboration purposes, you will primarily be working with the **Editor** role, which allows multiple users to contribute to the website's development.

How to Invite Collaborators to Edit Your Google Site

Step 1: Open the Google Sites Editor

To invite collaborators, you must first access your site's editor:

1. Open Google Sites in your browser.

2. Select the site you want to collaborate on or create a new one.

3. Click on the **"Share"** button in the top-right corner of the editor.

Step 2: Add Collaborators

1. In the "Share with people and groups" window, enter the email addresses of the people you want to invite.

2. Google Sites allows you to invite individuals or entire groups (such as Google Workspace groups).

3. After entering the email addresses, select **Editor** as the permission level for each user.

Step 3: Set Editing Permissions

Before sending the invitation, you can modify permissions to control access:

- **Editors can publish changes (default setting)** – If enabled, editors can modify and publish updates to the site. If disabled, they can edit but need approval from the site owner before publishing.

- **Notify people** – Checking this box sends an email notification to collaborators with a link to the site.

Step 4: Send the Invitation

Click **"Send"** to invite collaborators. The invited users will receive an email with a link to access the Google Site and start editing.

Managing Collaboration and Permissions

Once collaborators have been invited, you may need to manage their access, adjust permissions, or remove them from the project.

Viewing and Modifying Collaborators

1. Click the **"Share"** button again to view the list of current collaborators.

2. Next to each person's name, you will see a dropdown menu where you can change their role from **Editor** to **Viewer** (if necessary).

3. If you need to remove someone from the project, click the **"Remove"** option next to their name.

Restricting Editing and Publishing Permissions

If you want to limit who can publish updates:

1. Click **"Settings"** in the Google Sites editor.

2. Under **Permissions**, toggle the option **"Editors can publish"** to off.

3. This ensures that only the site owner can publish changes while others can contribute but not make them public.

Best Practices for Collaborative Editing

1. Establish Clear Roles and Responsibilities

- Assign specific tasks to each collaborator to avoid confusion.

- Use an internal document (such as Google Docs) to track who is responsible for different sections of the site.

2. Use Version History for Tracking Changes

- Google Sites automatically saves edits, allowing you to revert to previous versions if needed.

- Click **More (⋮) > Version History** to see past versions of the site and restore older ones.

3. Communicate Effectively

- Use Google Chat or comments in Google Docs to discuss changes before implementing them in Google Sites.

- Regularly update team members on progress and pending tasks.

4. Limit the Number of Editors

- Too many editors can lead to accidental overwrites or conflicting edits. Keep the core editing team small and organized.

Troubleshooting Common Collaboration Issues

Problem 1: Collaborator Cannot Access the Site

Solution:

- Ensure you have entered the correct email address.

- Check if the site is restricted to a specific Google Workspace domain.

Problem 2: Collaborator Can't Edit the Site

Solution:

- Verify that they have **Editor** access, not **Viewer** access.

- If "Editors can publish" is disabled, inform them they can edit but not publish.

Problem 3: Changes Are Not Saving

Solution:

- Refresh the page and check the internet connection.

- Ensure the collaborator is using a supported browser (Google Chrome, Firefox, Edge).

Conclusion

Inviting collaborators to edit your Google Site is a straightforward process that enhances teamwork and productivity. By setting clear permissions, managing user access, and following best practices, you can ensure a smooth collaboration experience. Whether you're working with a small team or a large group, Google Sites provides the tools needed for seamless content creation and management.

Would you like to explore advanced collaboration techniques, such as embedding Google Drive shared folders or using third-party project management tools? Let's continue building an efficient and engaging website together!

7.3.3 Restricting Access to Specific Users

When creating a website with Google Sites, you may want to control who can access your content. Whether you are building an internal company site, a private portfolio, or a classroom resource, restricting access to specific users ensures that only authorized individuals can view or edit your site. Google Sites provides robust permission settings that allow you to define user access levels and tailor visibility based on your needs.

This section will guide you through the different methods for restricting access to specific users, including setting permissions, understanding user roles, configuring access for groups, and troubleshooting access issues.

1. Understanding User Access Levels in Google Sites

Before diving into restriction settings, it is essential to understand the different levels of user access that Google Sites provides:

Viewers vs. Editors

Google Sites distinguishes between two primary roles:

- **Viewers** – These users can only see the published version of your site. They cannot edit or modify content.

- **Editors** – These users can modify the site, add or remove content, and adjust settings. However, they cannot publish changes unless they have explicit permission.

Owners and Their Special Privileges

The person who creates a Google Site is automatically designated as the **owner**. The owner has the highest level of control and can:

- Add or remove editors and viewers

- Change site visibility settings

- Delete or transfer site ownership

- Publish or unpublish the site

If multiple people need full administrative control, the owner can grant additional **full editing rights** to specific users.

2. Restricting Access to Specific Users

Google Sites allows you to control access on two levels:

1. **Site-Level Restrictions** – Limit access to the entire site.

2. **Page-Level Restrictions** – Restrict access to individual pages within a site.

Let's go through both approaches in detail.

2.1 Restricting Access to the Entire Site

By default, Google Sites provides three visibility options:

- **Public (Anyone on the web)** – Anyone can view your site without restrictions.

- **Restricted (Specific people only)** – Only invited users can access the site.

- **Domain-Specific (Anyone in [your company/school domain])** – Only people within your Google Workspace organization can view the site.

To **restrict access to specific users**, follow these steps:

Step 1: Open Site Sharing Settings

1. In the Google Sites editor, click the **"Share"** button in the top-right corner.

2. A sharing settings window will appear, listing the current access permissions.

Step 2: Change Site Visibility

1. Click **"Restricted"** to ensure that only invited users can access the site.

2. If the site is currently public, you will need to confirm the change to **restrict access**.

Step 3: Add Specific Users

1. Under **"Add people and groups"**, enter the email addresses of the users who should have access.

2. Click the dropdown menu next to each user's name to assign either **Viewer** or **Editor** permissions.

3. Click **"Send"** to notify users about their access.

◆ *Tip:* If you are using Google Workspace, you can also add entire Google Groups instead of individual users, making access management easier.

2.2 Restricting Access to Specific Pages

In some cases, you may want to keep most of your site public but limit access to certain **private pages**. Unfortunately, Google Sites does not currently support **page-level permissions** natively. However, there are workarounds:

Option 1: Use Embedded Google Docs with Restricted Access

1. Instead of placing sensitive content directly on a page, create a **Google Doc, Sheet, or Slide**.

2. Set document sharing permissions to **specific users only**.

3. Embed the restricted document on your Google Site.

4. Only authorized users will be able to see the embedded content.

Option 2: Create Multiple Google Sites with Different Permissions

1. Build a **main public site** and a **private site** for restricted content.

2. Link the two sites with navigation buttons.

3. Set different access permissions for each site.

While this method requires extra effort, it provides a functional way to control access to different sections of your content.

3. Configuring Access for Groups and Organizations

If you are managing a business, school, or nonprofit organization, controlling access for groups can be more efficient than managing individual permissions.

Using Google Groups for Access Management

Instead of adding individual users one by one, you can:

1. **Create a Google Group** in Google Workspace.

2. Add members to the group.

3. Share your Google Site with the group's email address.

4. As new members join or leave the group, access updates automatically.

◈ *Example:* If you are creating a **company intranet**, you can create groups like:

- **Marketing Team** → Can edit the site.

- **Sales Team** → Can view the site only.

- **Executive Team** → Has full admin access.

4. Testing and Troubleshooting Access Permissions

Once you have restricted access, you should test permissions to ensure everything is working correctly.

Testing User Access

1. Open an **incognito window** (Ctrl + Shift + N) to simulate a non-logged-in user.

2. Try accessing the site with different accounts to verify restrictions.

3. If you are using Google Groups, ensure new members receive the correct permissions.

Common Issues and Fixes

◈ **Problem:** A restricted user cannot access the site.
✓ **Solution:** Verify that their email address is spelled correctly and they have accepted the access invitation.

◈ **Problem:** Users see a **"You need permission"** error.
✓ **Solution:** Ensure the site is set to **"Restricted"** and that they are on the access list.

◈ **Problem:** Embedded Google Drive files show a **"You don't have permission"** message.

✓ **Solution:** Go to the **Google Drive file settings** and grant viewing permissions to the correct users.

5. Best Practices for Restricting Access

To ensure smooth site management, consider the following best practices:

✓ **Use Google Groups for Easier Access Control** – Instead of adding users one by one, use Google Groups.

✓ **Regularly Review Permissions** – Periodically check and update site access, especially for employees or students who may leave.

✓ **Limit Editor Permissions** – Only grant editing access to trusted users to prevent accidental changes.

✓ **Use External Storage for Highly Confidential Content** – For sensitive information, consider using **Google Drive with stricter access controls** instead of embedding the content directly in Google Sites.

✓ **Test Permissions Before Launching** – Always test access settings with different accounts before making the site live.

Conclusion

Restricting access to specific users in Google Sites is an essential feature for managing private content securely. Whether you are building an **internal company portal**, a **classroom resource**, or a **private knowledge base**, Google Sites provides flexible access control options to suit your needs.

By understanding **user roles, site-level permissions, and Google Workspace integrations**, you can effectively manage who can view and edit your content. Additionally, testing your access settings and following best practices will ensure a smooth user experience for your audience.

Now that you have secured your site, let's move on to **Chapter 8: Managing and Updating Your Site Over Time**, where we explore how to keep your Google Site fresh and optimized!

CHAPTER VIII
Managing and Updating Your Site Over Time

8.1 Editing and Updating Content

8.1.1 Making Quick Edits and Revisions

Keeping your website up to date is essential for ensuring that visitors receive accurate and relevant information. Google Sites makes it easy to make quick edits and revisions, whether you need to correct a typo, update an image, or add new content. In this section, we will explore the step-by-step process for editing content efficiently, ensuring consistency across pages, and leveraging Google Sites' built-in tools to streamline the revision process.

Why Regular Updates Matter

Before diving into the process of making edits, it is important to understand why keeping your Google Site updated is crucial:

- **Improves Accuracy:** Ensures that outdated information does not mislead visitors.

- **Enhances Engagement:** Fresh content keeps users interested and returning to your site.

- **Boosts Credibility:** A well-maintained site reflects professionalism and trustworthiness.

- **Optimizes SEO:** Search engines favor sites that are regularly updated with fresh content.

With these benefits in mind, let's explore how to efficiently make quick edits and revisions on your Google Site.

Accessing the Google Sites Editor

To make any changes to your site, you must first access the Google Sites editor. Follow these steps:

1. **Open Google Sites:** Go to Google Sites and log in with your Google account.

2. **Select Your Site:** Find the website you want to edit from the list of created sites.

3. **Enter Edit Mode:** Click on the site's thumbnail to open it in the editor mode.

Once inside the editor, you can start making updates to text, images, layouts, and other elements.

Editing Text Content

One of the most common updates involves modifying text content. This can include correcting typos, rewording sentences, or adding new information.

Steps to Edit Text on a Page:

1. **Click on the Text Box:** Navigate to the section you want to edit and click inside the text box.

2. **Make Your Edits:** Type the new content, delete unwanted text, or reformat the text as needed.

3. **Use Formatting Options:**
   - **Bold (B)** and **Italic (I)** for emphasis.
   - **Headings** for structuring content (Title, Heading, Subheading, Normal text).
   - **Lists** (bulleted or numbered) for organizing information.

4. **Undo or Redo Changes:** If you make a mistake, use the **Undo** (Ctrl + Z) or **Redo** (Ctrl + Y) options.

5. **Click Outside the Text Box:** This will save the changes automatically.

Tip: If you need to move text to a different section, you can simply **drag and drop** the text box to a new location.

Updating Images and Multimedia

Visual elements such as images, videos, and embedded files play a crucial role in making your site more engaging. If you need to update an image or replace multimedia content, follow these steps:

Replacing an Image:

1. Click on the Image You Want to Replace.

2. Select the "Replace Image" Option.

3. Choose a New Image: You can upload an image from your computer, select from Google Drive, or search the web.

4. Resize and Adjust the Image: Drag the corners to resize or use the crop tool to adjust the focus.

Updating an Embedded Video:

1. Click on the Embedded Video.

2. Select the "Replace" Option.

3. Insert a New Video URL (from YouTube or Google Drive).

Updating Google Drive Files:

- If you have embedded Google Docs, Sheets, or Slides, they **update automatically** whenever you edit the original file.

- If you need to replace an embedded document, delete the existing one and insert the new version.

Rearranging Content on the Page

Sometimes, you may need to reorganize sections of your page for better readability. Google Sites allows you to quickly move elements around.

How to Rearrange Content:

1. Hover Over the Section You Want to Move.

2. Click and Hold the "Drag" Icon (six small dots).

3. Drag the Section to a New Location on the Page.

4. Release the Mouse Button to Drop the Section.

This feature is especially useful when restructuring content to improve navigation and readability.

Managing Links and Buttons

Updating links is another common revision task. If a linked page has changed or if you want to add a new call-to-action, follow these steps:

Editing a Link:

1. Click on the Linked Text or Button.

2. Select "Edit Link."

3. Enter the New URL or Select a Page from Your Site.

4. Click "Apply" to Save Changes.

If you want to remove a link, simply click on the linked text and select **"Remove Link."**

Saving and Publishing Updates

Google Sites **automatically saves** changes as you make them, but these updates won't be visible to visitors until you publish them.

How to Publish Changes:

1. Click the "Publish" Button (Top Right Corner).

2. Review Changes (if necessary).

3. Click "Confirm" to Make Updates Live.

If you made a mistake, you can revert to a previous version before publishing.

Reverting to Previous Versions

Google Sites keeps track of all past versions of your website, allowing you to restore an earlier version if needed.

How to Restore a Previous Version:

1. Click on the "More" Menu (Three Dots in the Top Right Corner).

2. Select "Version History."

3. Browse Past Versions and Select the One You Want to Restore.

4. Click "Restore This Version" to Revert Back.

This feature is particularly useful if accidental changes were made or if you want to return to a previous design.

Best Practices for Making Quick Edits

To ensure your updates are efficient and effective, follow these best practices:

- **Plan Before Editing:** List all changes needed before opening the editor.

- **Use Consistent Formatting:** Ensure fonts, colors, and layouts match the rest of the site.

- **Preview Changes Before Publishing:** Always check how edits appear on different devices.

- **Keep a Backup:** Maintain a backup of important content in Google Drive.

- **Check for Broken Links:** Ensure all internal and external links function properly.

Conclusion

Making quick edits and revisions on Google Sites is a straightforward process that allows you to keep your website fresh, accurate, and engaging. Whether you're updating text, replacing images, rearranging content, or modifying links, Google Sites provides an intuitive and user-friendly interface that simplifies website management.

By following the steps outlined in this section, you can ensure your website remains well-maintained, professional, and relevant to your audience. In the next section, we will explore how to track your site's performance using Google Analytics and other tools.

8.1.2 Managing Drafts vs. Published Versions

One of the key aspects of managing a Google Site is understanding how to handle drafts and published versions effectively. Whether you're updating information, making design changes, or revising content for accuracy, Google Sites offers tools that allow you to work on a draft version before making changes visible to your audience. This section will explore the differences between drafts and published versions, best practices for managing updates, and strategies for ensuring a smooth publishing workflow.

Understanding Drafts vs. Published Versions

In Google Sites, there are two main states of a website:

1. **Draft Version** – This is the version of your site that is only visible to editors and collaborators with editing permissions. It allows you to make changes privately before publishing them.

2. **Published Version** – This is the version of your site that is visible to the audience based on the permissions you've set. Once you publish changes, your visitors will see the updated content.

Unlike traditional website builders, Google Sites does not have a built-in "preview mode" for drafts, but you can always edit and refine your site without affecting the published version until you're ready.

Key Differences Between Drafts and Published Versions

Feature	Draft Version	Published Version
Visibility	Only visible to editors	Visible to the audience

Editing Access	Can be modified freely	Cannot be edited directly
Changes	Not applied until published	Reflects the last published update
Undo/Restore	Changes can be reverted before publishing	Requires restoring from version history

Making Changes in Draft Mode

Editing Content Without Affecting the Live Site

One of the biggest advantages of Google Sites is that any changes you make remain in draft mode until you actively publish them. This means you can experiment with layouts, update information, or test new features without disrupting the live site experience for your visitors.

Saving Your Draft Automatically

Google Sites automatically saves all changes in real time. You don't need to manually save your work as it's continuously backed up. However, it's important to note that these saved changes remain in draft form until you explicitly publish them.

Best Practices for Working in Draft Mode

- **Plan Major Updates in Draft Mode** – If you're making significant structural changes, keep them in draft mode until you're sure everything looks right.

- **Use a Staging Process** – If you're working with a team, review drafts together before publishing.

- **Double-Check Formatting** – Since Google Sites saves automatically, ensure you don't accidentally make unintended edits before publishing.

Publishing Changes from Draft to Live Version

Once you're satisfied with your changes, you need to publish them for the audience to see.

Steps to Publish Your Updates

1. **Click the "Publish" Button** – In the upper-right corner of the Google Sites editor, you'll see a "Publish" button. Clicking this will open the publishing settings.

2. **Review Changes** – Google Sites provides a comparison between the current published version and the draft version. This helps you confirm what changes are being applied.

3. **Confirm and Publish** – Click "Publish" to apply the changes to your live website.

Managing Updates Efficiently

- **Review Before Publishing** – Always check the "Review Changes" preview to ensure that all edits are correct.

- **Check Permissions** – Make sure visibility settings are correct before publishing sensitive content.

- **Inform Your Team** – If you're working with collaborators, ensure they are aware of the changes before publishing.

Restoring Previous Versions

Even after publishing changes, you may realize that something was incorrect or unnecessary. Google Sites allows you to revert to a previous version using **Version History**.

Accessing and Restoring Previous Versions

1. Click on the three-dot menu in the top-right corner of Google Sites.

2. Select **Version History**.

3. Browse through past versions by selecting timestamps.

4. Click **Restore This Version** if you want to revert.

This is especially useful if you accidentally delete important content or make unwanted changes.

Collaborating on Drafts Before Publishing

If multiple people are working on the same Google Site, drafts play an essential role in maintaining content integrity before publishing.

Using Collaboration Tools Effectively

- **Assigning Roles** – Ensure only necessary team members have editing access to avoid accidental changes.

- **Commenting on Drafts** – While Google Sites does not have built-in commenting like Google Docs, you can communicate changes through emails or Google Chat.

- **Setting Review Processes** – Before publishing, set an approval process within your team to ensure quality control.

Common Issues and Troubleshooting

Even though managing drafts and published versions is straightforward, some common issues may arise. Here are solutions to potential problems:

Issue	Solution
Changes not appearing after publishing	Clear your browser cache and refresh the site.
Draft changes lost	Check **Version History** to restore previous edits.
Site published with mistakes	Use the **Revert to Previous Version** option.
Editor can't see draft changes	Ensure they have **Editor Access**, not just Viewer Access.
Published version showing outdated content	Wait a few minutes or check for caching issues.

Summary and Best Practices

Managing drafts and published versions efficiently ensures that your Google Site remains up-to-date, accurate, and professional. Here are key takeaways:

✅ **Work in Draft Mode** to make changes safely before publishing.
✅ **Review Updates Before Publishing** to avoid mistakes.
✅ **Use Version History** to restore previous versions if needed.

☑ **Collaborate Effectively** to ensure team members contribute without disrupting live content.

☑ **Troubleshoot Common Issues** to maintain a smooth workflow.

By mastering the draft and publishing process, you can confidently manage your Google Site while ensuring a seamless experience for your visitors.

8.1.3 Keeping Content Fresh and Relevant

Keeping your website's content fresh and relevant is crucial for maintaining visitor engagement, improving user experience, and ensuring that your information remains accurate. A well-maintained Google Site can serve as a reliable resource, whether it is for a business, educational purpose, portfolio, or internal communication. In this section, we will explore why content freshness matters, strategies for keeping your site up to date, tools to help streamline content updates, and best practices for long-term content management.

Why Keeping Content Fresh and Relevant Matters

A website that remains static for too long can quickly become outdated, making it less useful to visitors. Here are a few reasons why regular content updates are essential:

1. Improves User Engagement

- Visitors are more likely to return to your site if they see new and updated content.
- Fresh content encourages users to explore more pages, increasing the time they spend on your site.
- Updated resources keep your audience engaged and satisfied.

2. Enhances Credibility and Trust

- Inaccurate or outdated information can lead to confusion and mistrust.
- Keeping your site current ensures that visitors perceive your content as reliable and professional.

3. Boosts SEO and Discoverability

- While Google Sites itself does not offer advanced SEO tools, search engines favor websites that are regularly updated.

- Frequent updates signal that your site is active, which may improve search engine ranking.

4. Supports Business and Organizational Goals

- For businesses, keeping content updated ensures that marketing messages, promotions, and product information remain relevant.

- Educational or internal sites benefit from updated policies, guidelines, and learning materials.

Strategies for Keeping Content Updated

1. Set a Content Review Schedule

Establish a regular schedule to review and update your site. Depending on the type of content, the frequency may vary:

- **Weekly:** Blogs, news updates, promotions, events.

- **Monthly:** Product or service pages, internal announcements, educational resources.

- **Quarterly:** About Us page, company policies, long-term project updates.

- **Annually:** Contact information, team pages, mission statements, FAQs.

2. Use Google Calendar for Content Planning

Since Google Sites integrates well with Google Workspace, you can use **Google Calendar** to schedule reminders for content updates. Assign tasks to team members responsible for different sections of the website.

3. Enable Collaboration for Continuous Updates

If multiple people contribute to your site, make sure they have the correct **editing permissions** (covered in *Chapter 7*). Assign roles such as:

- **Content Managers:** Regularly update and verify information.

- **Design Editors:** Improve layouts and enhance visuals.

- **SEO and Analytics Specialists:** Track site performance and suggest content improvements.

4. Monitor and Remove Outdated Content

Some content naturally becomes obsolete over time. Regularly audit your site to:

- **Remove old announcements and promotions.**

- **Update outdated references and broken links.**

- **Ensure images and multimedia are still relevant.**

5. Repurpose and Refresh Old Content

Instead of creating entirely new pages, consider repurposing existing content:

- Convert **old blog posts into infographics**.

- Update **case studies with new data**.

- Merge similar pages for better organization.

Tools to Help Keep Content Fresh

Google Sites offers several built-in and external tools to make content updates easier:

1. Google Drive for Dynamic Content

Embedding Google Docs, Sheets, or Slides ensures that information updates automatically without manually editing your site. This is useful for:

- **Live reports from Google Sheets.**

- **Presentation updates via Google Slides.**

- **Shared policy documents in Google Docs.**

2. Google Forms for User Feedback

Gather feedback from your audience by embedding Google Forms. Regularly reviewing responses helps you understand what content needs improvement.

3. Google Analytics for Performance Insights

Tracking which pages receive the most traffic can guide your content update priorities. If certain pages have high bounce rates, consider refreshing the content with new visuals or information.

4. Google Alerts for Industry Trends

Setting up **Google Alerts** for relevant topics can help you stay updated on industry trends, allowing you to keep your site aligned with current events and best practices.

Best Practices for Long-Term Content Management

1. Prioritize High-Impact Updates

Not every piece of content needs constant changes. Focus on updates that add the most value to your visitors.

2. Maintain a Consistent Style and Branding

Ensure that new content follows the same format, tone, and design style as the rest of your site.

3. Archive Old Content Instead of Deleting It

If content is no longer relevant but may be useful for historical reference, move it to an "Archive" section instead of deleting it completely.

4. Train Your Team on Content Management

If multiple people manage the site, provide guidelines on when and how to update content.

5. Perform a Full Site Audit Annually

At least once a year, go through your entire site and:

- Check for broken links.
- Update outdated information.
- Improve navigation and user experience.

Conclusion

Keeping your Google Site's content fresh and relevant is essential for maintaining engagement, credibility, and functionality. By setting a structured update schedule, using Google's suite of tools, and implementing best practices, you can ensure that your site remains a valuable resource over time. Whether you're managing a business website, educational portal, or personal project, regular content updates will help maximize its effectiveness.

By following these guidelines, you can maintain a professional and up-to-date Google Site with minimal effort. Now, let's move on to **Section 8.2: Tracking Site Performance and User Engagement** to learn how to measure the impact of your updates!

8.2 Tracking Site Performance and User Engagement

8.2.1 Using Google Analytics with Google Sites

Once you have published your Google Site, understanding how visitors interact with it is crucial for improving its effectiveness. Google Analytics is a powerful tool that allows you to track your site's performance, analyze visitor behavior, and make data-driven decisions to enhance the user experience. In this section, we will explore how to integrate Google Analytics with Google Sites, interpret key metrics, and use insights to optimize your website.

1. What is Google Analytics?

Google Analytics is a web analytics service provided by Google that helps website owners track and report website traffic. It provides detailed insights into visitor demographics, behavior, and engagement, allowing you to measure the effectiveness of your site. Some of the key benefits of using Google Analytics include:

- **Tracking visitor numbers** – See how many people visit your site.

- **Understanding visitor demographics** – Learn where your visitors are coming from and what devices they are using.

- **Analyzing user behavior** – Identify which pages are the most popular and how long users stay on your site.

- **Measuring engagement** – Determine if visitors are interacting with your content.

- **Optimizing your site** – Use data-driven insights to make improvements.

For Google Sites users, integrating Google Analytics ensures that you have access to valuable data that can help you refine your website strategy.

2. Setting Up Google Analytics for Google Sites

Before you can start tracking your Google Site's performance, you need to set up Google Analytics and connect it to your site. Follow these steps:

Step 1: Create a Google Analytics Account

If you don't already have a Google Analytics account, follow these steps:

1. Go to Google Analytics. https://analytics.google.com/

2. Sign in with your Google account.

3. Click **Admin** (gear icon in the bottom left corner).

4. Under the **Account** column, click **Create Account**.

5. Enter an account name and configure your data-sharing settings.

6. Click **Next** to proceed to the property setup.

Step 2: Set Up a New Property for Your Google Site

1. Under the **Property** section, click **Create Property**.

2. Enter a **Property Name** (e.g., "My Google Site Analytics").

3. Select your reporting time zone and currency.

4. Click **Next**, then choose your business category and objectives.

5. Click **Create** to generate your analytics property.

Step 3: Get the Measurement ID

Google Analytics uses a **Measurement ID** to track data. To find it:

1. In Google Analytics, go to **Admin > Data Streams**.

2. Click **Web** and enter your Google Site URL.

3. Click **Create Stream** to generate the Measurement ID.

4. Copy the **Measurement ID** (it looks like "G-XXXXXXXXXX").

Step 4: Add Google Analytics to Google Sites

1. Open your Google Site.

2. Click **Settings** (gear icon in the top-right corner).

3. Scroll down to **Analytics**.

4. Paste the **Measurement ID** into the field provided.

5. Click **Save** to apply the changes.

Your Google Site is now connected to Google Analytics, and data collection will begin.

3. Understanding Google Analytics Metrics

Once Google Analytics is set up, you can start analyzing your site's performance. Here are some key metrics to track:

Audience Overview

This section provides general insights into your visitors, including:

- **Total Visitors** – The number of people who have visited your site.

- **New vs. Returning Visitors** – Tracks whether visitors are new or returning users.

- **Device Usage** – Shows how many visitors access your site via desktop, tablet, or mobile.

- **Geographical Data** – Displays visitor locations based on country or region.

Acquisition Reports

These reports help you understand how users find your site:

- **Direct Traffic** – Visitors who type your website URL directly.

- **Organic Search** – Visitors who find your site through search engines.

- **Referral Traffic** – Visitors who arrive from links on other websites.

- **Social Media Traffic** – Visitors who land on your site via social media platforms.

Behavior Reports

These reports help you analyze how users interact with your content:

- **Pageviews** – The total number of times a page has been viewed.

- **Bounce Rate** – The percentage of visitors who leave after viewing only one page.

- **Average Session Duration** – The average time a visitor spends on your site.

- **Top Performing Pages** – A list of your most visited pages.

Engagement Reports

This section shows how visitors interact with different elements of your site:

- **Click-through Rate (CTR)** – Measures how many visitors click on buttons or links.

- **Form Submission Rate** – If you have a Google Form embedded, tracks how many people submit responses.

- **Video Play Rate** – If you have embedded videos, tracks how many visitors watch them.

4. Optimizing Your Site Based on Analytics Data

Once you have collected enough data, you can use insights from Google Analytics to improve your site.

Improving User Experience

- Reduce **bounce rate** by making navigation intuitive and improving content quality.

- Optimize for **mobile users** by ensuring your site is mobile-friendly.

- Increase **session duration** by adding engaging content like videos, quizzes, and interactive elements.

Enhancing SEO Performance

- Improve **organic search rankings** by incorporating relevant keywords.

- Increase **site speed** by optimizing images and reducing unnecessary elements.

- Encourage **external links** by promoting your site on social media or other websites.

Boosting Engagement

- If a page has **low engagement**, consider adding calls-to-action (CTAs) or updating content.

- Use **Google Forms and Surveys** to gather visitor feedback.

- Track **button clicks** to understand which sections attract the most attention.

5. Advanced Google Analytics Features for Google Sites

For those who want deeper insights, consider using these advanced features:

Event Tracking

Set up **custom events** in Google Analytics to track specific actions, such as:

- Clicking a specific button

- Downloading a file

- Playing an embedded video

Goal Tracking

Define **conversion goals** in Google Analytics, such as:

- Form submissions

- Newsletter sign-ups

- Time spent on a page

Google Tag Manager Integration

Google Tag Manager allows for **more detailed tracking** without editing your site's code. It enables:

- Adding tracking pixels for marketing campaigns

- Monitoring user actions beyond basic Google Analytics

6. Conclusion

Integrating Google Analytics with Google Sites is a powerful way to monitor and improve your website's performance. By tracking key metrics, analyzing visitor behavior, and making data-driven adjustments, you can enhance user engagement and achieve your site's objectives. Whether you're managing a business website, an educational portal, or a personal project, Google Analytics provides the insights needed to grow and optimize your site effectively.

Now that you've learned how to set up and use Google Analytics, you can move forward with **analyzing your data** and making strategic improvements to your Google Site!

8.2.2 Analyzing Visitor Behavior and Traffic

Once your Google Site is published, understanding how visitors interact with your content is essential for optimizing the user experience and ensuring your site meets its intended goals. Analyzing visitor behavior and traffic helps you gain insights into how users navigate your site, which pages attract the most attention, and where improvements are needed.

Why Analyzing Visitor Behavior Matters

Monitoring user behavior and site traffic provides valuable data for decision-making. Here are some reasons why this analysis is crucial:

- **Understanding Audience Interests**: Identifying the most popular pages and topics allows you to tailor content to user preferences.

- **Improving User Experience (UX)**: By analyzing bounce rates, session durations, and navigation patterns, you can enhance site usability.

- **Optimizing Content Strategy**: Knowing which pages perform well helps you refine your content and improve engagement.

- **Identifying Technical Issues**: High exit rates or broken navigation links may indicate problems that need to be addressed.

Using Google Analytics to Track Traffic and Behavior

Google Sites does not have built-in analytics tools, but you can integrate Google Analytics to collect and analyze visitor data. Google Analytics provides detailed insights into:

- **Total visitors and page views**

- **Traffic sources (search engines, direct visits, referral links, etc.)**

- **User demographics (location, device type, etc.)**

- **Time spent on pages and bounce rates**

- **Navigation flow and user interactions**

How to Set Up Google Analytics for Google Sites

1. **Create a Google Analytics Account**

   o   Go to Google Analytics, https://analytics.google.com/ and sign in with your Google account.

   o   Click on **"Admin"** and select **"Create Property."**

o   Choose **"Web"** as your platform and enter your site's details.

2. **Get Your Tracking ID**

    o   After setting up your property, Google Analytics will generate a **Tracking ID** (UA-XXXXXXX or GA4 measurement ID).

    o   Copy this ID for use in Google Sites.

3. **Link Google Analytics to Google Sites**

    o   Open your **Google Site** and click on the **Settings (⚙☐) menu.**

    o   Select **"Analytics"** and paste the **Tracking ID** into the designated field.

    o   Click **"Save"** to apply changes.

4. **Verify the Connection**

    o   Wait a few hours for data to appear in Google Analytics.

    o   Open the **"Realtime"** report in Analytics to see if your visits are being tracked.

Key Metrics to Monitor in Google Analytics

Once your Google Site is linked to Google Analytics, you can track essential metrics to analyze visitor behavior effectively.

1. Traffic Sources: Where Are Visitors Coming From?

Understanding traffic sources helps you determine how users discover your website. Google Analytics categorizes traffic into:

- **Organic Search**: Users who found your site through search engines like Google.

- **Direct Traffic**: Visitors who typed your site URL directly.

- **Referral Traffic**: Users who arrived from links on other websites.

- **Social Media Traffic**: Visitors who clicked on links shared on social platforms like Facebook, LinkedIn, or Twitter.

- **Paid Search or Ads**: Users who reached your site through Google Ads campaigns.

📌 *Tip:* If you want to increase organic traffic, focus on search engine optimization (SEO) techniques such as using relevant keywords and meta descriptions.

2. Page Views and User Engagement

Monitoring **page views, unique visitors, and session duration** provides insights into content performance.

- **High page views** indicate popular content.

- **Low time spent on pages** may mean content is not engaging enough.

- **High bounce rates** (when visitors leave after viewing only one page) suggest that users didn't find what they were looking for.

📌 *Tip:* Improve engagement by adding **interactive content**, clear call-to-action (CTA) buttons, and internal links to guide visitors through your site.

3. Behavior Flow: How Do Users Navigate Your Site?

Google Analytics provides a **Behavior Flow Report**, which visualizes how users move from one page to another.

- Identify **drop-off points** where users leave the site.

- Discover the **most common paths** visitors take.

- Optimize **internal linking** to guide users toward important pages.

📌 *Tip:* If users frequently exit from a specific page, consider adding more engaging content, links to related pages, or a compelling CTA.

4. Device and Browser Data: Are Visitors Using Mobile or Desktop?

Google Analytics tracks **device type and browser usage**, which is crucial for optimizing your site's design.

- A high percentage of **mobile users** means you should prioritize mobile-friendly layouts.

- If users from a specific browser (e.g., Safari, Chrome) experience issues, check for compatibility problems.

📌 *Tip:* Always preview and test your Google Site on different devices to ensure a seamless experience.

5. User Demographics: Who Are Your Visitors?

Google Analytics provides insights into **user location, age, language, and interests.**

- If most visitors are from a specific country, consider **localizing your content** to match their needs.

- Understanding audience interests helps you tailor content for better engagement.

📌 *Tip:* Use **Google Translate integration** if your site attracts an international audience.

Using Google Search Console for SEO Insights

In addition to Google Analytics, **Google Search Console** is a valuable tool for analyzing search performance and indexing issues.

How to Set Up Google Search Console for Your Site

1. Visit Google Search Console. https://search.google.com/search-console/welcome

2. Click **"Add Property"** and enter your Google Sites URL.

3. Choose **"URL Prefix"** and verify ownership via Google Analytics or a verification tag.

4. Once verified, Google will start collecting data about search traffic.

Key Insights from Google Search Console

- **Search Queries**: What keywords bring visitors to your site?

- **Click-Through Rate (CTR)**: How often do people click on your site in search results?

- **Indexing Issues**: Are there pages that Google has trouble indexing?

- **Mobile Usability**: Are there any errors affecting mobile visitors?

✦ *Tip:* Improve your **SEO strategy** by using relevant keywords in page titles, descriptions, and content.

Making Data-Driven Improvements

Once you've gathered insights from Google Analytics and Search Console, take action to improve your site.

- **If bounce rates are high**: Add better navigation and engaging content.

- **If organic traffic is low**: Optimize for SEO with relevant keywords.

- **If mobile users struggle with site layout**: Adjust fonts, buttons, and spacing for better mobile usability.

✦ *Final Tip:* Regularly review your analytics data and make small adjustments over time for continuous improvement.

By analyzing visitor behavior and traffic, you gain a deeper understanding of how people interact with your Google Site. Using tools like **Google Analytics** and **Google Search Console**, you can make data-driven improvements that enhance user experience, increase engagement, and drive more traffic to your site.

8.2.3 Optimizing Content Based on Data Insights

Once you have collected data on your site's performance and user engagement, the next step is to optimize your content to enhance user experience, increase engagement, and achieve your goals. Data-driven content optimization allows you to refine your site's structure, improve readability, and boost the effectiveness of your pages. This section will guide you through the process of interpreting analytics data and making informed improvements to your Google Site.

Understanding the Role of Data in Content Optimization

Optimizing content based on data insights means using real-world user behavior and performance metrics to make decisions rather than relying on intuition. This approach ensures that you are making improvements that directly impact user experience, engagement, and conversions.

Key benefits of data-driven content optimization:

- Enhances user experience by addressing pain points.

- Increases engagement through better content delivery.

- Boosts visibility by optimizing for search engines.

- Encourages visitors to take desired actions, such as signing up or contacting you.

To effectively optimize your content, you must first analyze the data collected from tools like Google Analytics, heatmaps, and user feedback.

Step 1: Analyzing User Behavior with Google Analytics

Google Analytics provides valuable data about how visitors interact with your Google Site. Here are key metrics you should analyze to optimize your content:

1. Page Views and Popular Content

- Identify which pages receive the most and least traffic.

- Focus on enhancing high-traffic pages with updated information and better visuals.

- Improve low-performing pages by refining content or restructuring navigation.

2. Bounce Rate and Session Duration

- A high bounce rate (users leaving after viewing just one page) indicates that the content may not be engaging or relevant.

- Improve session duration by making your pages more interactive with images, videos, and internal links.

3. User Flow and Navigation Patterns

- Analyze how users move through your site.

- If users exit quickly from a particular page, consider restructuring its content or making calls-to-action more prominent.

4. Traffic Sources and Audience Demographics

- Understand where your visitors come from (search engines, social media, direct links).

- Adjust your content strategy based on user demographics and interests.

Step 2: Improving Content Based on User Engagement

Once you have analyzed user behavior, it's time to make data-driven improvements to your content.

1. Refining Page Layout and Design

- Ensure a clean, readable layout with proper headings, bullet points, and whitespace.

- Use shorter paragraphs and highlight key points to improve readability.

- Ensure mobile responsiveness by testing your site on different devices.

2. Updating and Expanding Content

- Regularly update outdated information to keep content relevant.

- Expand on topics that users spend more time reading.

- Add FAQs, case studies, or examples to make content more comprehensive.

3. Improving Call-to-Action (CTA) Effectiveness

- Review CTA placement to ensure they are visible and compelling.

- Use action-oriented language, such as "Get Started Now" instead of "Click Here."

- Experiment with different button colors and sizes to increase conversions.

4. Enhancing Internal Linking

- Guide users to relevant pages within your site to increase engagement.

- Use descriptive anchor text rather than generic phrases like "click here."

- Link to related content, such as blog posts, case studies, or resource pages.

Step 3: Using Heatmaps and User Feedback for Deeper Insights

Heatmaps and direct user feedback provide additional insights into user behavior beyond analytics data.

1. Implementing Heatmaps

- Heatmaps track where users click, scroll, and spend the most time on a page.

- Identify areas where users drop off or ignore content.

- Adjust placement of key elements like CTAs and images based on user activity.

2. Collecting User Feedback

- Use Google Forms or embedded surveys to ask visitors about their experience.

- Pay attention to common complaints or suggestions.

- Implement changes based on feedback, such as simplifying navigation or improving content clarity.

Step 4: SEO Optimization for Better Visibility

Optimizing content for search engines (SEO) helps attract more visitors to your Google Site.

1. Using Keywords Strategically

- Identify keywords that your audience searches for and naturally incorporate them into your content.

- Avoid keyword stuffing; focus on readability and relevance.

2. Optimizing Page Titles and Meta Descriptions

- Write clear, compelling page titles with relevant keywords.

- Use concise meta descriptions (150-160 characters) to summarize page content.

3. Enhancing Image SEO

- Use descriptive file names and alt text for images.

- Optimize image size to improve page load speed.

4. Improving Mobile-Friendliness

- Test how your site appears on different devices.

- Adjust fonts, spacing, and interactive elements for better mobile usability.

Step 5: Measuring the Impact of Your Optimizations

After implementing changes, it's important to measure their effectiveness.

1. Monitoring Key Metrics

- Track improvements in page views, bounce rates, and engagement.

- Look for increases in session duration and CTA clicks.

2. A/B Testing Changes

- Compare different versions of content, layouts, or CTAs to see what performs best.

- Gradually implement successful changes across the site.

3. Continuous Improvement Strategy

- Regularly review analytics and make adjustments as needed.

- Keep content fresh by updating information, adding new resources, and improving design elements.

Conclusion: Turning Insights into Action

Optimizing content based on data insights ensures that your Google Site remains engaging, relevant, and effective. By analyzing visitor behavior, refining content structure, improving SEO, and continuously testing enhancements, you can create a website that meets user needs and achieves its objectives.

Key takeaways from this section:

✓ Use analytics data to understand how users interact with your site.

✓ Improve content readability, navigation, and engagement.

✓ Optimize pages for SEO to increase visibility.

✓ Continuously track performance and refine content based on insights.

By applying these strategies, you will be able to maintain a high-quality, user-friendly Google Site that continues to grow and improve over time.

8.3 Maintaining Site Security and Backups

8.3.1 Protecting Sensitive Information

Google Sites provides an easy-to-use platform for creating websites, but ensuring the security of your content is just as important as building the site itself. Whether you're using Google Sites for personal projects, business purposes, or educational materials, protecting sensitive information from unauthorized access is crucial. This section explores various strategies and best practices to keep your Google Site secure.

Understanding the Risks of Exposing Sensitive Information

Before diving into security measures, it's important to understand the risks associated with unprotected information on your Google Site:

1. **Unauthorized Access** – If site permissions are not properly set, anyone with the link may be able to view or edit your content.

2. **Data Breaches** – Sensitive business documents, private client data, or personal information could be accessed or leaked if security settings are too permissive.

3. **Phishing and Cyber Threats** – If confidential links or embedded content are exposed, hackers may exploit them to target users.

4. **Accidental Sharing** – Google Sites allows for easy collaboration, but mistakenly granting access to the wrong people can lead to unintended information exposure.

5. **Search Engine Indexing** – If your site is public, search engines can index it, making information accessible to anyone on the internet.

By recognizing these risks, you can take proactive steps to safeguard your Google Site.

Configuring Access Permissions for Maximum Security

Google Sites offers flexible permission settings that allow you to control who can view and edit your site. Properly configuring these permissions is essential to prevent unauthorized access.

1. Setting Site-Level Permissions

When publishing your Google Site, you have three main visibility options:

- **Public on the web** – Anyone on the internet can view your site.
- **Anyone with the link** – Only those who have the direct link can access the site.
- **Restricted** – Only specific users you invite can view or edit the site.

To configure site visibility:

1. Click the **Share** button in the top-right corner of Google Sites.
2. Under **Get Link**, choose from the three visibility options.
3. If setting to "Restricted," enter the emails of specific people who should have access.

Best Practice: If your site contains confidential information, always set it to **Restricted** and invite only necessary users.

2. Controlling Editing Permissions

Google Sites allows you to define user roles with different levels of control:

- **Viewer** – Can only view the site but cannot make changes.
- **Editor** – Can modify site content but cannot change sharing settings.
- **Owner** – Has full control over the site, including deleting it or modifying access permissions.

To assign roles:

1. Open the **Share** settings.
2. Enter the email addresses of the users you want to grant access.

3. Select their role: **Viewer**, **Editor**, or **Owner**.

4. Click **Send** to notify them.

Best Practice: Only grant **Editor** access to trusted individuals. Avoid giving **Owner** access unless absolutely necessary.

3. Managing Page-Specific Permissions

In some cases, you may want to limit access to certain pages while keeping the rest of the site accessible. Google Sites allows you to set permissions on individual pages.

To do this:

1. Click on the three-dot menu **(More options)** next to a page in the site editor.

2. Select **Restrict access** and specify who can view or edit that page.

Example Use Case: If you have an internal website for employees, you might restrict certain HR or financial documents so only specific departments can access them.

Preventing Unauthorized Sharing

Even if you configure permissions correctly, there is always a risk that authorized users might share links with others who should not have access.

1. Disabling Link Sharing

By default, users with **Editor** access can share the site with others. You can disable this by:

1. Opening **Share settings**.

2. Clicking **Settings (gear icon)**.

3. Unchecking **Editors can change permissions and share**.

This prevents editors from inviting new people without approval.

2. Using Google Groups for Access Control

Instead of granting access to individuals, you can assign permissions to a Google Group. This makes it easier to manage large teams and prevents unauthorized individuals from being added manually.

3. Monitoring Site Access Logs

To keep track of who is viewing or editing your site, consider integrating Google Analytics. This helps detect unauthorized access or unusual activity.

Protecting Embedded Content and External Integrations

Many Google Sites include embedded documents, forms, or third-party content. If not managed properly, these elements can create security vulnerabilities.

1. Securing Embedded Google Drive Files

When embedding Google Docs, Sheets, or Slides, check their individual **sharing settings** to ensure they are not publicly accessible.

Best Practice:

- Set embedded documents to **"Anyone with the link can view"** only if necessary.
- For sensitive content, restrict access to specific users.

2. Controlling Google Forms Data Access

If your site includes a Google Form for collecting responses:

- Limit form access to specific domains (e.g., only your company or school).
- Disable **"Allow users to edit responses"** to prevent data tampering.
- Ensure that response sheets are stored in a **secure** Google Drive folder with limited access.

3. Handling Third-Party Integrations

Some users add widgets or embed content from external sources like YouTube, social media, or third-party analytics tools. Ensure that:

- The sources are **trusted and secure**.

- They do not require **excessive permissions** (e.g., tracking scripts).
- They comply with **privacy regulations** if collecting user data.

Preventing Accidental Deletion or Data Loss

Even with proper security settings, accidental deletion or unauthorized edits can still happen. Implement these strategies to safeguard your content.

1. Enabling Site Version History

Google Sites automatically saves previous versions of your site, allowing you to restore earlier versions if needed.

To access version history:

1. Click **More (three-dot menu)** in the top-right corner.
2. Select **Version History**.
3. Choose a previous version to restore.

2. Making Regular Backups

Since Google Sites does not offer a built-in backup tool, you can manually back up your content by:

- **Exporting site pages as PDFs** for offline reference.
- **Copying text and images** to a Google Docs file.
- **Duplicating your site** by creating a copy in Google Drive.

3. Using Google Vault for Enterprise Users

If you're using Google Workspace (formerly G Suite), **Google Vault** allows admins to archive and retrieve site data in case of loss or legal requirements.

Conclusion

Securing your Google Site is just as important as designing it. By properly configuring permissions, preventing unauthorized sharing, securing embedded content, and maintaining backups, you can protect your site's data and ensure its integrity over time. Whether you're managing a personal portfolio, a business website, or an internal company portal, implementing these best practices will help you safeguard your content from potential security threats.

Now that you understand how to protect sensitive information, the next section will explore how to restore previous versions of your Google Site in case of accidental edits or data loss.

8.3.2 Restoring Previous Versions of Your Site

One of the advantages of Google Sites is its ability to track changes and allow users to restore previous versions of a website. Whether you've made an accidental edit, deleted important content, or want to revert to an earlier layout, Google Sites provides a simple and effective way to recover past versions. In this section, we'll explore the importance of version control, the steps to restore previous versions, and best practices for maintaining backups of your site.

Why Version Control Matters in Google Sites

Version control is an essential feature in any website or document management system. Here's why it is crucial for managing your Google Site:

- **Prevents Accidental Data Loss** – If you mistakenly delete a page, section, or content, version control allows you to retrieve the lost data.

- **Allows for Experimentation** – You can try different design changes and content updates without fear of permanently losing previous iterations.

- **Enables Collaboration with Confidence** – When multiple people edit a site, version control ensures that no important changes are overwritten without the ability to restore.

- **Provides a Safety Net** – In case of unintended formatting issues or broken layouts, you can always go back to a stable version of your site.

Now, let's go step by step on how to restore an earlier version of your Google Site.

How to Restore a Previous Version of Your Google Site

Google Sites does not have a traditional "version history" feature like Google Docs or Google Sheets, but it does provide a way to revert changes. You can restore previous versions of pages and content using the **undo** function, manually restoring content from backups, or reusing previous drafts. Below are the methods you can use to restore your site:

Method 1: Using the Undo and Redo Functions for Immediate Changes

If you made a mistake while editing and haven't published your site yet, you can use the **Undo (Ctrl + Z or Command + Z)** and **Redo (Ctrl + Y or Command + Shift + Z)** options to revert recent edits. However, this only works within the current editing session and does not help if the changes were made days ago.

Method 2: Restoring a Page from Google Drive Version History (Classic Google Sites Only)

If you are using the older version of Google Sites (Classic Google Sites), you can access a **revision history** from Google Drive. However, in the new Google Sites, this feature is no longer available.

To check for older versions in Classic Google Sites:

1. Open your Google Site.

2. Click on **More Actions (⋮) > Revision History**.

3. Select a previous version and click **Restore**.

Method 3: Manually Restoring Content Using a Previously Published Version

Since the new Google Sites does not have a built-in version history, one effective way to restore older content is by using the **published version of your site** as a reference:

1. **Check the live (published) version of your site**

   o   If you made changes but haven't published them yet, the previous version of your site is still accessible.

- ○ Open your **Published Site** in a separate tab.

- ○ Compare it to your current editing version.

2. **Copy and paste content from the published version**

- ○ If you need to retrieve text or images, manually copy them from the published site and reinsert them into the editor.

3. **Recreate deleted pages manually**

- ○ If a page was deleted, you may need to create a new one and manually reconstruct its content using references from cached or saved versions.

Method 4: Using Google Takeout to Recover a Backup Copy

If you have regularly backed up your Google Site using **Google Takeout**, you can restore previous content by importing an older backup:

1. **Go to** Google Takeout, https://takeout.google.com/?pli=1 and log in with your Google account.

2. Look for **Google Sites** in the list of exportable data.

3. Download the backup file from a previous date.

4. Manually extract the content and reinsert it into your current site.

Method 5: Checking Google Cache for Previous Versions

If your site was indexed by Google, you might be able to retrieve older content through cached versions.

1. **Go to Google Search** and type: cache:yourwebsite.google.com.

2. If a cached version exists, it will display a snapshot of your site from the last time Google indexed it.

3. Copy any necessary content and restore it manually.

Best Practices for Maintaining Backup Copies of Your Google Site

Because Google Sites does not have a built-in automatic version history, you should take proactive measures to keep track of your changes. Here are some best practices:

1. Save Drafts Before Publishing

- Before making significant changes, **duplicate pages** or copy content into a Google Doc.

- Keep a backup version in Google Drive to reference later.

2. Use Google Takeout for Periodic Backups

- Schedule a **monthly or weekly backup** of your Google Sites content using Google Takeout.

- Save backups in an organized folder with timestamps.

3. Maintain a Manual Change Log

- If multiple people edit the site, create a **Google Sheets document** to log major changes.

- Include details like **date, editor name, and description of changes**.

4. Use a Google Docs Backup for Important Content

- Before deleting or replacing large sections of content, paste them into a **Google Docs file** for safekeeping.

5. Keep Screenshots of Important Pages

- If your site layout is critical, take **screenshots** before making design changes.

- This is helpful when needing to visually recreate a previous look.

What to Do If You Cannot Restore Your Site?

If you cannot restore a previous version and have lost important content, consider the following steps:

1. **Check all available backups** – Look through Google Drive, Takeout backups, and any stored Google Docs that might contain old content.

2. **Contact Google Support** – If your site is critical and you need assistance, visit Google Support and check for recovery options.

3. **Recreate from memory or external sources** – If no backup exists, use any old emails, documents, or external resources where content might have been copied.

Final Thoughts

While Google Sites offers a simple and effective way to create websites, its lack of built-in version history means you need to be proactive in maintaining backups and tracking changes. By following best practices such as using Google Takeout, keeping draft copies, and maintaining a manual change log, you can safeguard your content and avoid irreversible losses.

The ability to restore previous versions is essential for website maintenance, whether you're making simple edits or managing a large collaborative project. By implementing a structured approach to backups and revisions, you can ensure that your Google Site remains secure, up-to-date, and easily recoverable in case of accidental edits or deletions.

8.3.3 Handling Unauthorized Access or Edits

Ensuring the security of your Google Site is crucial, especially when managing sensitive or professional content. Unauthorized access or edits can compromise your website's integrity, damage your reputation, and potentially expose confidential information. In this section, we will explore how to prevent unauthorized access, detect suspicious activities, and restore your site in case of unauthorized changes.

Understanding Unauthorized Access in Google Sites

Unauthorized access can occur when someone gains control over your site without permission. This can happen due to:

- **Accidental permission misconfiguration** – Granting editing rights to the wrong person.

- **Shared accounts or weak passwords** – If your Google account is compromised, so is your Google Site.

- **Phishing attacks or malware** – Cybercriminals may attempt to steal your credentials.

- **Internal misuse** – A team member with editing privileges may make unintended or malicious changes.

Types of Unauthorized Edits

Unauthorized edits can take different forms, such as:

- **Content Deletion** – Important text, images, or embedded files may be removed.

- **Unwanted Modifications** – Someone may alter the layout, design, or information.

- **Malicious Content Insertion** – Unauthorized users could add misleading links, offensive content, or harmful scripts.

- **Site Takeover** – A user with owner access may remove other contributors and take control of the site.

To prevent and mitigate these issues, it's essential to follow security best practices.

Preventing Unauthorized Access

1. Configuring Site Permissions Properly

One of the most effective ways to prevent unauthorized access is by carefully managing permissions. Google Sites provides different access levels:

- **Owner** – Full control over the site, including the ability to delete it.

- **Editor** – Can modify content but cannot change permissions or delete the site.

- **Viewer** – Can only view the site but cannot edit it.

To configure permissions properly:

1. **Navigate to the "Share" settings**

   o   Open your Google Site.

   o   Click on the **Share** button in the top-right corner.

2. **Set appropriate roles**

   o   **Grant editing rights only to trusted users.** Avoid giving edit access to large groups.

   o   **Restrict ownership transfer.** Only assign ownership to yourself or trusted administrators.

3. **Use domain restrictions (for Google Workspace users)**

   o   If using Google Sites within a business or educational institution, limit access to your domain.

   o   Prevent public access unless necessary.

2. Using Google Account Security Features

Securing your Google account is essential for protecting your Google Site. Follow these best practices:

- **Enable two-factor authentication (2FA)**

  - Go to your **Google Account Settings** → **Security** → Enable **2-Step Verification**.

  - This adds an extra layer of security by requiring a verification code in addition to your password.

- **Use strong, unique passwords**

  - Avoid using easily guessed passwords (e.g., "password123").

  - Use a **password manager** to generate and store complex passwords.

- **Monitor account activity**

  - Regularly check your **Google Account's Security Checkup** for any unusual activity.

3. Restricting Access to Specific Users

To prevent unauthorized edits, you can:

- **Disable public editing** – Ensure only trusted users have editing rights.

- **Limit sharing links** – Set access to "Restricted" instead of "Anyone with the link."

- **Remove inactive users** – Periodically review and revoke access from users who no longer need it.

Detecting Unauthorized Changes

Despite preventive measures, unauthorized changes may still occur. To quickly identify such changes:

1. Reviewing Version History

Google Sites automatically saves a version history, allowing you to track changes.

To check version history:

1. Open your site and click **More Options (⬚)** in the top-right corner.

2. Select **Version history**.

3. Browse through past versions and identify unauthorized edits.

If you notice an unwanted change, you can restore a previous version of your site.

2. Monitoring Email Notifications

Google sends email alerts for certain changes, especially when permissions are modified. If you receive an unexpected notification, investigate immediately.

3. Using Google Workspace Audit Logs (for Business Users)

For Google Workspace administrators, audit logs provide detailed records of site activity.

To access logs:

1. Go to **Google Admin Console**.

2. Navigate to **Reports → Audit log → Google Sites**.

3. Review who made changes and what actions were performed.

Restoring Your Site After Unauthorized Edits

If you discover unauthorized modifications, follow these steps to restore your site:

1. Revert to a Previous Version

1. Open your site.

2. Click **More Options (□) → Version History**.

3. Select a previous version and click **Restore This Version**.

This will undo unwanted changes and revert your site to its earlier state.

2. Remove Unauthorized Users

If an unauthorized person has editing access:

1. Click **Share** → Locate the user.

2. Click **Remove Access** or change their role to **Viewer**.

3. Reset Permissions and Strengthen Security

- Change site sharing settings to "Restricted."

- Enable two-factor authentication on your Google account.

- Notify other collaborators about the incident and reinforce security protocols.

4. Contact Google Support (if necessary)

If your site has been significantly compromised or taken over, reach out to Google Support:

1. Visit **Google Support → Report a Security Issue**.

2. Provide details of the unauthorized changes.

3. Request assistance in recovering your site.

Best Practices for Long-Term Site Security

To prevent future security incidents:

✓ **Regularly review permissions** – Remove unnecessary access.
✓ **Keep track of version history** – Restore previous versions if needed.
✓ **Educate collaborators on security best practices** – Encourage strong passwords and 2FA.
✓ **Use Google Workspace security tools** – Enable additional protections for business users.

By following these guidelines, you can ensure that your Google Site remains secure, well-managed, and protected from unauthorized edits or access.

Conclusion and Next Steps

10.1 Recap of Key Lessons

As we reach the conclusion of this guide, it is essential to reflect on the key lessons covered throughout the book. By now, you should have a strong understanding of Google Sites and how to leverage its features to create an effective, well-structured website. This chapter will summarize the critical takeaways from each chapter, reinforcing the most valuable concepts and ensuring that you are fully equipped to build, manage, and optimize your Google Site successfully.

Understanding Google Sites (Chapter 1 & 2 Recap)

At the beginning of this book, we explored the **fundamentals of Google Sites** and why it is an excellent tool for individuals, businesses, and organizations. Some of the essential points we covered include:

- **What Google Sites is**: A free, user-friendly website builder that allows you to create and manage websites without coding.

- **Why use Google Sites?** It integrates seamlessly with Google Workspace, offers real-time collaboration, and simplifies website creation.

- **Google Sites' key features**:
  - Drag-and-drop editing
  - Pre-designed templates for easy customization
  - Integration with Google Drive, Docs, Sheets, Slides, and Forms
  - Automatic mobile responsiveness
  - Built-in collaboration tools for multiple editors

- **Limitations of Google Sites**: While powerful for basic and internal sites, it lacks advanced customization options like HTML/CSS editing, plugins, or e-commerce features.

We then covered **how to get started** with Google Sites, including:

- How to **create a new site**, either from a blank template or using pre-designed layouts.

- The **Google Sites interface**, including the **toolbar, sidebar menu, and editor layout**.

- Configuring **basic settings**, such as site title, navigation menus, and permissions.

By mastering these fundamentals, you gained the confidence to start building your own site and structuring it effectively.

Designing and Structuring Your Website (Chapter 3 & 4 Recap)

Once you created your site, we focused on the **design and organization** of your content. Key takeaways include:

Themes and Customization

- Choosing a theme to establish a professional look and feel.

- Adjusting colors, fonts, and layout to match your branding or project needs.

- Using sections and page layouts for better readability.

Adding and Formatting Content

- Inserting text boxes, headings, and paragraphs for clear communication.

- Formatting options such as bold, italics, lists, and tables.

- Adding images and videos to make content visually appealing.

- Embedding Google Drive files, Google Maps, and YouTube videos for rich media integration.

Managing Pages and Navigation

- Creating and organizing multiple pages for a structured site.

- Setting up automatic or manual navigation menus for ease of use.

- Implementing anchor links to improve navigation within long pages.

A well-structured site ensures visitors can find information easily and stay engaged with your content.

Enhancing Your Site with Google Workspace (Chapter 5 Recap)

One of the most powerful aspects of Google Sites is its ability to integrate with **Google Workspace tools**, allowing you to create a **dynamic and interactive website**. Key lessons from this section include:

- **Embedding Google Docs, Sheets, and Slides**

  - How to display Google Docs for policy documents, guides, or wikis.

  - Using Google Sheets to showcase real-time data updates.

  - Embedding Google Slides for presentations, tutorials, or portfolios.

- **Using Google Forms for Data Collection**

  - Creating and embedding contact forms, surveys, and feedback forms.

  - Automatically collecting and analyzing responses.

- **Adding Google Calendar and Google Maps**

  - Embedding a Google Calendar for scheduling events or meetings.

  - Displaying Google Maps to showcase business locations or directions.

By incorporating Google Workspace tools, your website becomes more interactive and functional.

Customizing, Optimizing, and Publishing Your Website (Chapters 6 & 7 Recap)

A well-designed website is only effective if it is accessible, properly optimized, and easy to navigate. Some of the key lessons from these chapters include:

Customizing Your Site Further

- Setting up a custom domain to give your site a professional identity.

- Adding buttons, hyperlinks, and call-to-action sections to guide visitors.

- Embedding third-party content, social media feeds, and HTML code to enhance functionality.

Publishing and Sharing Your Website

- Previewing your site to check its appearance on different devices.

- Publishing your site and managing visibility settings (public vs. private).

- Controlling who can edit or view the content using permission settings.

Publishing your site is the final step in making your website accessible to others, whether for personal, educational, or business purposes.

Managing and Updating Your Site (Chapter 8 Recap)

Once your site is live, **maintenance is essential** to ensure it remains up to date and relevant. Some key takeaways include:

- **Editing and updating content regularly**
  - Keeping information fresh and removing outdated material.
  - Maintaining visual consistency as new content is added.

- **Tracking site performance with Google Analytics**
  - Understanding visitor behavior and engagement.
  - Identifying which pages are most popular and improving navigation.

- **Ensuring site security and managing backups**
  - Using Google's version history to restore previous site versions.

     o   Keeping sensitive information private with access restrictions.

Regular site management ensures a professional and effective online presence over time.

Final Thoughts

Throughout this book, we have covered everything from basic setup to advanced customization, giving you all the tools necessary to build and manage an effective website with Google Sites. Whether you're creating a personal website, business page, educational resource, or team collaboration hub, Google Sites provides a simple yet powerful platform to achieve your goals.

Acknowledgments

First and foremost, thank you for choosing ***Google Sites Made Simple: Create and Manage Your Website with Ease.*** I truly appreciate your time and trust in this book as a guide on your journey to mastering Google Sites.

Writing this book has been a rewarding experience, and knowing that it might help you build your website with confidence and ease is incredibly fulfilling. Whether you're using Google Sites for personal projects, business, education, or nonprofit work, I hope this book has provided you with the knowledge and tools to create a website that meets your needs.

I would also like to express my gratitude to the countless individuals who have contributed to the knowledge shared in this book—from Google's developers and documentation writers to educators, business professionals, and content creators who continue to explore and expand the possibilities of Google Sites. The online community of users who share insights, tutorials, and creative website ideas has been an inspiration.

To my readers—thank you for your support. Your curiosity, creativity, and willingness to learn are what drive books like this to be written. If this book has helped you in any way, I would love to hear about your experience. Feel free to share your feedback, ideas, or even your Google Sites projects.

Finally, learning is a continuous journey. Keep exploring, keep creating, and never stop improving your skills. I wish you great success in building and managing your websites!

With gratitude,

www.ingramcontent.com/pod-product-compliance
Lightning Source LLC
LaVergne TN
LVHW081331050326
832903LV00024B/1108